KLEE MUTATIONS

KLEE MUTATIONS

III

Published by Tempo Haus
tempohaus.com

Designed by Duncan Blachford

ISBN: 978-0-6480466-3-9

This book was made as part of a studio in the
Master of Communication Design at RMIT University
in the second semester of 2017, led by Stuart Geddes.

The starting point for this book was the essay
'Journey to the Centre of Google Earth' by Simon Sellars.
The essay was originally commissioned for NyMusikk's
Only Connect Festival of Sound 2014: J.G. Ballard.

It was published in the Only Connect catalogue,
May 2014, edited by Anne Hilde Neset and Audun Vinger.
The original essay can be found at simonsellars.com/
journey-to-the-centre-of-google-earth

CONTENTS

For the undone things

"The machine teaches us how to remember."
    – Simon Sellars, *Journey to the Centre of Google Earth*[1]

METHODOLOGY

WARPED ILLUMINATED REFLECTIVE GLASS

I invest my faith in an unnamable search engine (SE) as the generative God of Pedagogy. I commit to follow this SE on its human initiated trails: to chase the logic of algorithmic tangents; to use unholy translation tools; to traverse the possibilities of a non-linear post-digital self-education.

I do not propose to approach this process as a blank slate: I will investigate my ability (or inability) to relinquish personal interests and research biases; to participate in a collaborative editorial exercise with the machine.

The SE becomes my mirror, albeit a transient reflection within a digital funhouse of expansive architecture. The results provide warped self-image in the confines of a fixed environment as pages takes shape.

I chase the light of a warped illuminated reflective glass, deep into the ether, as the SE becomes the SE.

MEMORIES OF THE WORLD

The "Memory of the World Programme" is an international initiative
launched by the United Nations Educational, Scientific and Cultural
Organization (UNESCO) to safeguard the documentary heritage of
humanity against collective amnesia, neglect, the ravages of time and
climatic conditions, and willful and deliberate destruction. It calls for the
preservation of valuable archival holdings, library collections and private
individual compendia all over the world for posterity, the reconstitution
of dispersed or displaced documentary heritage, and the increased
accessibility to and dissemination of these items.[2]

"Public Library" is a recognized art project that inherits objectives of
UNESCO's "Memory of the World" programme and builds its infrastructure
at memoryoftheworld.org following the dream of Henry La Fontain who
coined the phrase at the beginning of 20th century and who together with
Paul Otlet envisoned "the city of knowledge" which would serve as a central
repository for the world's information.[3]

Monoskop is a repository aggregating, documenting and mapping works, artists and intiatives related to the avant-gardes, media arts and theory and activism. Initially it focused on Eastern and Central Europe. Built on a Wiki that everyone can contribute to and scrupulously curated by its *spiritus movens* Dušan Barok, it provides both an exhaustive, indexical overview of those fields and provides digital access to rare historic finds.[4]
—Public Library, Memory of the World

Unofficial Channels [Name Redacted[5]]:

[Redacted] is a multilingual, free-content encyclopedia project supported by the [Redacted] Foundation and based on a model of openly editable content.

The fundamental principles by which [Redacted] operates are the five pillars.

- [Redacted] is an encyclopedia
- [Redacted] is written from a neutral point of view
- [Redacted] is free content that anyone can use, edit, and distribute
- [Redacted]'s editors should treat each other with respect and civility
- [Redacted] has no firm rules

The [Redacted] community has developed many policies and guidelines to improve the encyclopedia; however, it is not a formal requirement to be familiar with them before contributing.

[Redacted] is a live collaboration differing from paper-based reference sources in important ways. Unlike printed encyclopedias, [Redacted] is continually created and updated, with articles on historic events appearing within minutes, rather than months or years. Because everybody can help improve it, [Redacted] has become more comprehensive than any other encyclopedia. In addition to quantity, its contributors work on improving quality as well. [Redacted] is a work-in-progress, with articles in various stages of completion. As articles develop, they tend to become more comprehensive and balanced. Quality also improves over time as misinformation and other errors are removed or repaired. However, because anyone can edit at any time and add stuff in, any article may contain undetected misinformation, errors, or vandalism. Awareness of this helps the reader to obtain valid information, avoid recently added misinformation, and fix the article.

PÄDAGOGISCHES SKIZZENBUCH

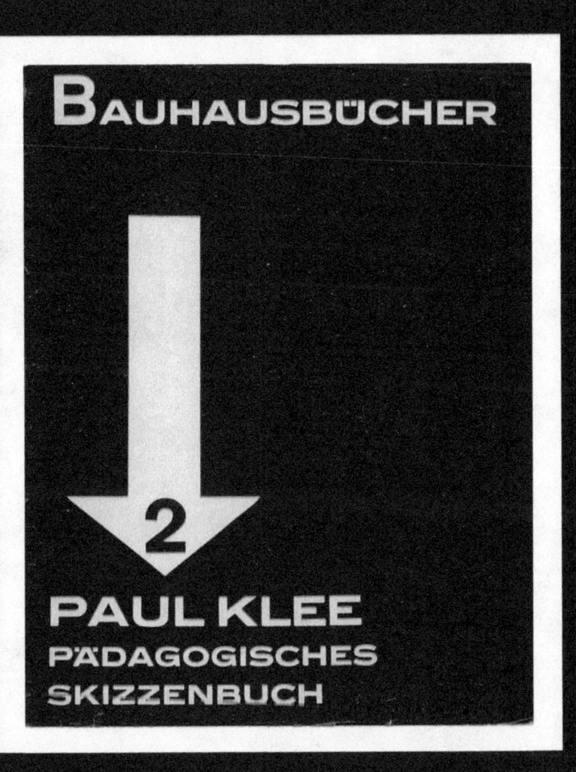

The fount of mutant pedagogy

What follows is a post-digital reading of Klee's seminal text:

Paul Klee's *Pädagogisches Skizzenbuch (Pedagogical Sketchbook)* was based on extensive lectures on visual form at Bauhaus Staatliche Art School where Klee was a teacher in between 1921-1931.

Originally handwritten – as a pile of working notes he used in his lectures – it was eventually edited by Walter Gropius, designed by László Moholy-Nagy and published in 1925 as a Bauhaus student manual (Bauhausbucher No.2, the second in the series of the fourteen Bauhaus books).[1]

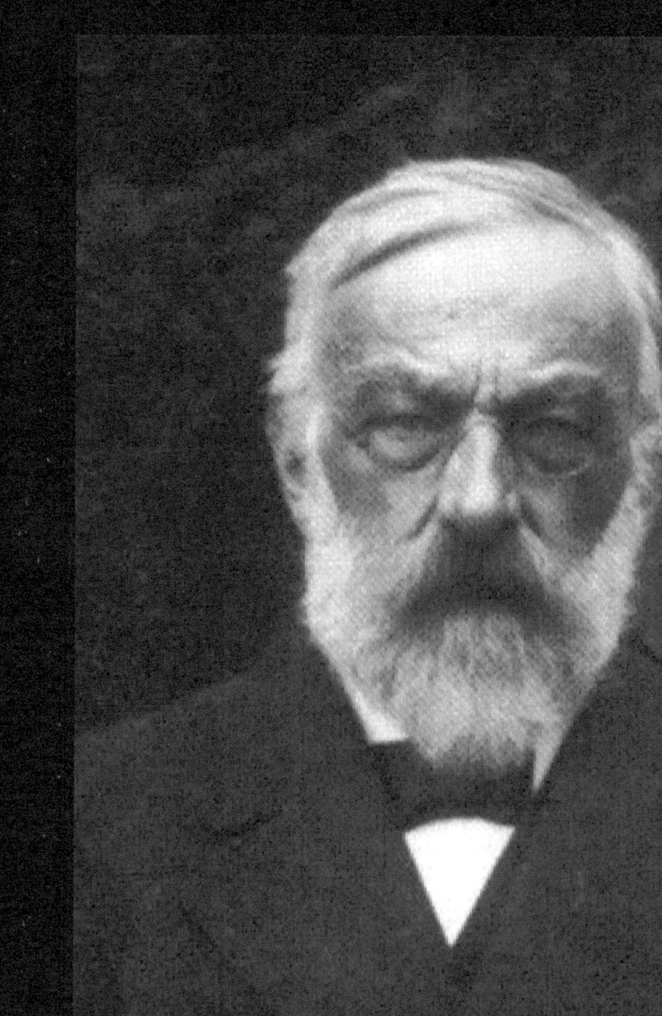

BÜCHER

Research mutation*: Bücher

Karl Wilhelm Bücher
Born: 16 February 1847, Hesse, Germany
Died: 12 November 1930, Leipzig, Germany

Karl Wilhelm Bücher was a German economist, one of the
founders of non-market economics, and the founder of
journalism as an academic discipline.[2]

Industrial Evolution is Karl Bucher's most important book,
and the foundational study of non-market (exchange and gift)
economics. The book deals with the historical evolution of
economic and industrial organization, with the transition from
handicrafts to manufacturing, the rise of trade unionism and
urban migration.[3]

*   Research that is not directly
related to content in the
Pädagogisches Skizzenbuch;
generated through attempts to
translate/mistranslate particular
words, or the curiosity to delve
into wayward SE results that
generate interest in the SE.

CHAPTER I.

PRIMITIVE ECONOMIC CONDITIONS.

ALL scientific investigation of industry starts with the assumption that man has a peculiar " economic nature " belonging to no other living creature. From this economic nature a principle is supposed to spring, which controls all his actions that are directed to the satisfaction of his wants. This is the economic principle, the fundamental principle of economic activity. This principle reveals itself in man's endeavour always and everywhere to attain the highest possible satisfaction with the least possible sacrifice (labour)—the " principle of least sacrifice."

According to this view all man's economic actions are actions directed toward an end and guided by considerations of profit. Whether or not the final impulse to economic labour is to be sought in the instincts of man (the instinct of self-preservation and of self-interest), the satisfaction of these instincts is always the result of a series of successive mental operations. Man estimates the extent of the discomfort that would arise from the non-satisfaction of a want felt by him; he measures the discomfort that the labour necessary to meet the want can cause him; he compares the discomforts with each other, and resolves to undertake the labour only when the accompanying sacrifice is less than the sacrifice of remaining unsatisfied.   Moreover, upon undertaking the labour he again chooses the least burdensome among the various possible methods of procedure, and thus has a further series of considerations, estimations, comparisons, and judgments to enter upon.

In fact the whole science of political economy proceeds on the assumption that economic actions have behind them a rational motive and call into play the higher mental faculties; and it has evolved a kind of psychology of labour, by means of which it seeks to explain those actions in their typical progress.   Economic activity is, therefore, something especially human; indeed the question whether the lower animals display similar activity, seems never to have been broached.   The economic nature of man is something absolute, inseparable from the very character of man.[1]

Yet even among civilized mankind, from whose manifold activity the principle of economy has been deduced, indications are not wanting to show that the economic nature must be characteristic of different individuals in different degree.   Between the industrious and the indolent, the provident and the improvident, the sparing and the spendthrift, there are innumerable gradations;   and if we only observe the conduct of the child towards his possessions, we are easily convinced that the " economic nature " must be acquired anew by each human being, and that it is a result of education and custom, in which individuals differ no less than in their whole physical and mental development.

Having once reached this point, we shall scarcely be

---

[1] " The elements of economic character are firmly rooted in the physical and intellectual organization of man, and change just as little as his outward character does, at least in the periods which come within the scope of the history of mankind."—Wagner, *Grundlegung d. polit. Oekonomie* (3. Aufl.), I, p. 82. [As for animal sociology, it can hardly be said to have advanced as yet beyond animal psychology.—ED.]

Research mutation: Wagner

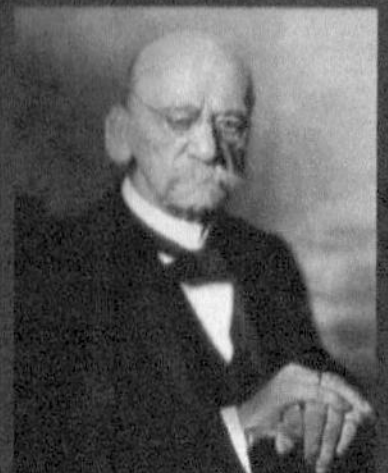

A. Wagner circa 1910

Adolph Wagner (1835 – 1917) was a German economist and politician, a leading *Kathedersozialist* (academic socialist), a public finance scholar and advocate of agrarianism, and the author of *Grundlegung der politischen Oekonomie* (*Foundation of Political Economy*) a work cited in the footnote of Karl Wilhelm Bücher's *Industrial Evolution* on the previous spread.

Wagner is the main protagonist of a specific school of economics and social policy, called "State Socialism" ("Staatssozialismus"), which is a specific form of *Kathedersozialismus*. He was a member of the Historical School, as his general review essay on Alfred Marshall's *Principles of Economics* so clearly demonstrates. However, he did fundamentally differentiate himself from what he called the 'younger' and more 'extreme' members of the German historical school such as Gustav von Schmoller who, according to Wagner, tended to dismiss too hastily what the latter terms the more deductive work of English writers (in short, those in the tradition of classical economics).

Wagner had a very combative and harsh personality. He did not take insults lightly and never phrased things diplomatically. He had difficulties with Schmoller and was an enemy of Lujo Brentano – and these two were about his closest colleagues.

In the 1890s, Wagner would so enrage an industrial-conservative member of the Reichstag . . . with a defense of the *Kathedersozialist* influence within the University, that the deputy challenged him to a duel. (Wagner did not categorically refuse, but it was never fought.)

An even more famous case was Wagner's altercation with Eugen Dühring (against whom Friedrich Engels' *Anti-Dühring* is directed), and which in the very end resulted in Dühring's remotion and dismissal from the University of Berlin.

Together with Schmoller, Wagner belongs to the most important economists of the Bismarck period. He was a member of the *Verein für Socialpolitik* (Society for Social Policy).

Wagner formulated the Law of Increasing State Spending, also known as "Wagner's Law."

His works set the stage for the development of the monetary and credit systems in Germany and substantially influenced the central bank policy and financial practice before World War I. [5]

Wagner was also a nasty anti-semite fucker – a trait found among a number of German economists of his era. [*]

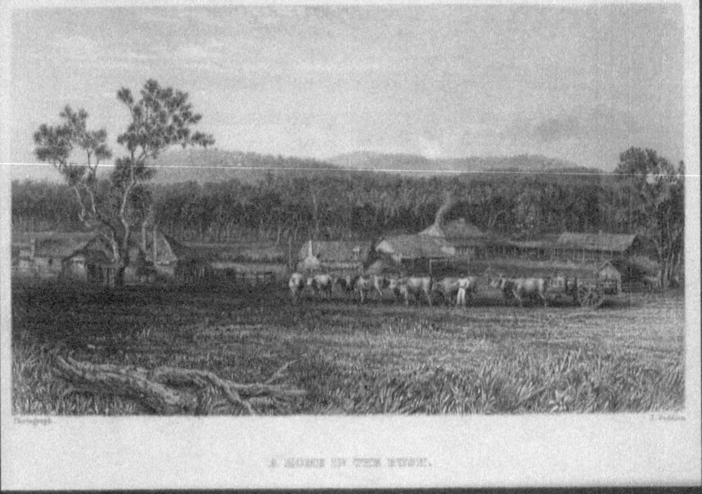

A Home in the Bush engraving by J. Saddler (1874-1876; slv.vic.gov.au)

Research mutation: Agrarianism

Agrarianism is a social philosophy or political philosophy which values rural society as superior to urban society, the independent farmer as superior to the paid worker, and sees farming as a way of life that can shape the ideal social values.

The Australian historian F.K. Crowley found:

> Australian farmers and their spokesman have always considered that life on the land is inherently more virtuous, as well as more healthy, more important and more productive, than life in the towns and cities. The farmers complained that something was wrong with an electoral system which produced parliamentarians who spent money beautifying vampire-cities instead of developing the interior.[6]

---

*   As detailed in Matthew Lange's *Antisemitic Elements in the Critique of Capitalism in German Culture, 1850-1933* and *Behemoth: The Structure and Practice of National Socialism, 1933-1944* by Franze Neumann.

Research mutation: Kathedersozialismus

Kathedersozialismus is primarily associated with three German economists: Adolph Wagner, Gustav Schmoller and Lujo Brentano.

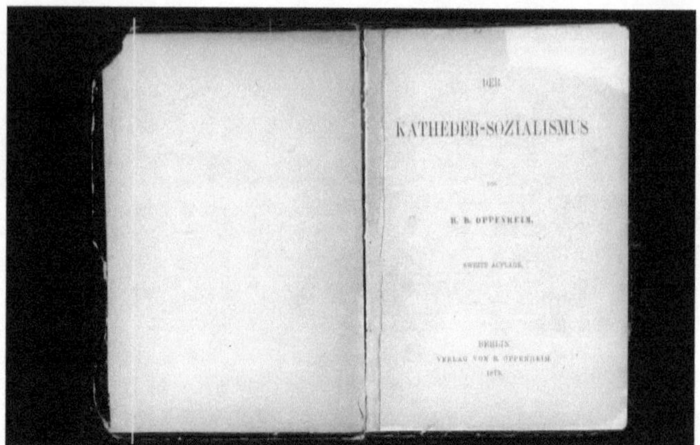

Kathedersozialismus by H.B Oppenheim (1873)

Kathedersozialismus means 'Socialism of the Lectern': it is an originally pejorative term that was intended to delegitimise the movement both by calling it socialist and by pointing to the fact the its protagonists were mostly university professors (and thus, presumably, more armchair intellectuals). Coined by the journalist Heinrich Bernhard Oppenheim, the term stuck, and like many a term meant critically before, it was soon taken up by those who were criticised, although slowly and at first in quotation marks.

> – Wolfgang Dreschsler, *Handbook of Alternative Theories of Economic Development*

Heinrich Bernhard Oppenheim

Heinrich Bernhard Oppenheim obtained a law degree from the University of Heidelberg in 1839 at the age of nineteen. He taught law for a time but was denied a position as a professor of law because he was Jewish. His legal training enabled him to become a well-known journalist for liberal and radical-left causes for nearly 40 years.

As a young man, Heinrich was a member of the intellectual and literary circle around Countess Bettina von Arnim in Berlin. He was known as a great conversationalist and a man of "uncommon wit" (Carl Schurz). In the von Arnim salon he befriended some of the leading European thinkers and progressive political figures of the day. For a time he shared rooms with Abraham Geiger, the German rabbi and scholar considered the founding father of Reform Judaism, and he was good friends with the young Karl Marx.

Generative Mistranslation as Pedagogical Design Strategy

In March 1848, Heinrich participated in the political uprising in Berlin in a failed attempt to wrest a more democratic form of government from King Friedrich Wilhelm IV of Prussia. He addressed several of the mass demonstrations in the Tiergarten park in the Prussian capitol. Later in 1848, Heinrich fled to the southern Duchy of Baden where he continued his revolutionary activities with a left extremist wing led by Gustav Struve in Karlsruhe and Lörrach.

In July 1849, the Baden revolution collapsed and Heinrich was driven into an eleven year exile in Switzerland, France, Belgium and England. He was unable to return to Germany until 1861. During his political exile, he continued to publish pro-democracy commentary, much of it in French.

When he was finally able to return to Germany, Heinrich continued his liberal political writing. Oppenheim's articles targeted the attacks as a political strategy of conservatives to discredit governmental reforms being pressed by liberal activists, many of whom were Jews.

On March 29, 1880, a few weeks after publishing his rebuke to the Berlin antisemites, Heinrich died of a chronic lung ailment. His funeral was attended by many representatives of the Berlin news corps as well as liberal political activists from all over Germany. Shortly thereafter, his colleagues published a long pamphlet collecting numerous speeches about him and the obituaries published in the many newspapers in Germany. The pamphlet contains the only known portrait of Heinrich Bernhard Oppenheim.[7]

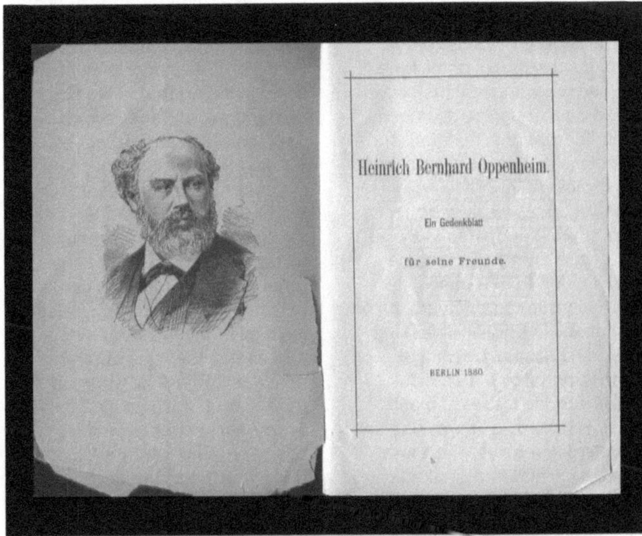

Ein Gedenkblatt fur seine Freunde (_A memorial sheet for his friends_) containing the only known portrait of Oppenheim.

Research mutation: Alfred Marshall

Alfred Marshall (26 July 1842 – 13 July 1924) was one of the most influential economists of his time. His book, *Principles of Economics* (1890), was the dominant economic textbook in England for many years. It brings the ideas of supply and demand, marginal utility, and costs of production into a coherent whole. He is known as one of the founders of neoclassical economics. Although Marshall took economics to a more mathematically rigorous level, he did not want mathematics to overshadow economics and thus make economics irrelevant to the layman.

Principles of Economics (1890)

Marshall began his economic work, the *Principles of Economics*, in 1881, and spent much of the next decade at work on the treatise. His plan for the work gradually extended to a two-volume compilation on the whole of economic thought. The first volume was published in 1890 to worldwide acclaim, establishing him as one of the leading economists of his time. The second volume, which was to address foreign trade, money, trade fluctuations, taxation, and collectivism, was never published.

Principles of Economics established his worldwide reputation. It appeared in 8 editions, starting at 750 pages and growing to 870 pages. It decisively shaped the teaching of economics in English-speaking countries. Its main technical contribution was a masterful analysis of the issues of elasticity, consumer surplus, increasing and diminishing returns, short and long terms, and marginal utility. Many of the ideas were original with Marshall; others were improved versions of the ideas by W. S. Jevons and others.

In a broader sense Marshall hoped to reconcile the classical and modern theories of value. John Stuart Mill had examined the relationship between the value of commodities and their production costs, on the theory that value depends on the effort expended in manufacture. Jevons and the Marginal Utility theorists had elaborated a theory of value based on the idea of maximising utility, holding that value depends on demand. Marshall's work used both these approaches, but he focused more on costs. He noted that, in the short run, supply cannot be changed and market value depends mainly on demand. In an intermediate time period, production can be expanded by existing facilities, such as buildings and machinery, but, since these do not require renewal within this intermediate period, their costs (called fixed, overhead, or supplementary costs) have little influence on the sale price of the product. Marshall pointed out that it is the prime or variable costs, which constantly recur, that influence the sale price most in this period. In a still longer period, machines and buildings wear out and have to be replaced, so that the sale price of the product must be high enough to cover such replacement costs. This classification of costs into fixed and variable and the emphasis given to the element of time probably represent one of Marshall's chief contributions to economic theory. He was committed to partial equilibrium models over general equilibrium on the grounds that the inherently dynamical nature of economics made the former more practically useful.

Much of the success of Marshall's teaching and Principles book derived from his effective use of diagrams, which were soon emulated by other teachers worldwide.

Alfrod Marshall was the first to develop the standard supply and demand graph demonstrating a number of fundamentals regarding supply and demand including the supply and demand curves, market equilibrium, the relationship between quantity and price in regards to supply and demand, the law of marginal utility, the law of diminishing returns, and the ideas of consumer and producer surpluses. This model is now used by economists in various forms using different variables to demonstrate several other economic principles. Marshall's model allowed a visual representation of complex economic fundamentals where before all the ideas and theories were only capable of being explained through words. These models are now critical throughout the study of economics because they allow a clear and concise representation of the fundamentals or theories being explained.[8]

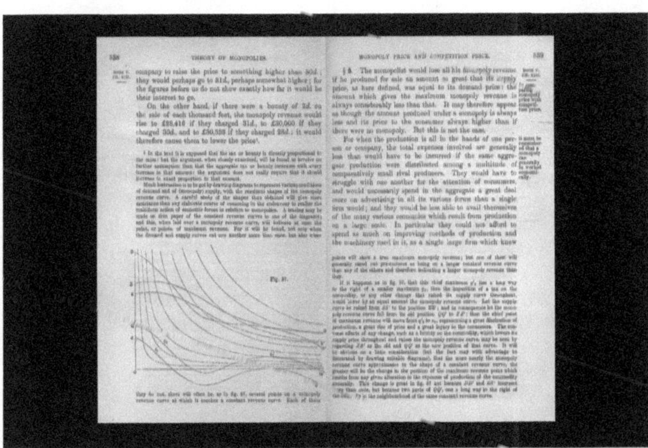

Principles of Economics (1890) replete with extensive diagrams

Research mutation: Gustav von Schmoller

Gustav von Schmoller (24 June 1838 – 27 June 1917) was the leader of the "younger" German historical school of economics.

Schmoller was born in Heilbronn. His father was a Württemberg civil servant. Young Schmoller studied *Staatswissenschaften* (a combination of economics, law, history, and civil administration) at the University of Tübingen (1857–61). In 1861, he obtained an appointment at the Württemberg Statistical Department. During his academic career, he held appointments as a professor at the universities of Halle (1864–72), Strasbourg (1872–82), and Berlin (1882–1913). After 1899, he represented the University of Berlin in the Prussian House of Lords. He was a leading *Sozialpolitiker* (more derisively, *Kathedersozialist*, "Socialist of the Chair"), and a founder and long-time chairman of the *Verein für Socialpolitik*, the German Economic Association, which continues to exist. Schmoller's influence on academic policy, economic, social and fiscal reform, and economics as an academic discipline for the time between 1875 and 1910 can hardly be overrated. He was also an outspoken proponent of the assertion of German naval power and the expansion of the German overseas empire.

As an outspoken leader of the "younger" historical school, Schmoller opposed what he saw as the axiomatic-deductive approach of classical economics and, later, the Austrian school – indeed, Schmoller coined the term to suggest provincialism in an unfavorable review of the 1883 book *Investigations into the Method of the Social Sciences with Special Reference to Economics* (*Untersuchungen über die Methode der Socialwissenschaften und der politischen Oekonomie insbesondere*) by Carl Menger, which attacked the methods of the historical school. This led to the controversy known as the *Methodenstreit*, which today often appears as a waste of energies and one of the main reasons for the later demise of the whole historical school, although – as Joseph Schumpeter once pointed out – this was really a quarrel within that school. Schmoller's primarily inductive approach, requesting careful study, comparative in time and space, of economic performance and phenomena generally, his focus on the evolution of economic processes and institutions, and his insistence on the cultural specificity of economics and the centrality of values in shaping economic exchanges stand in stark contrast to some classical and most neoclassical economists,

Gustav von Schmoller (1917)

so that he and his school fell out of the mainstream of economics by the 1930s, being replaced in Germany by the successor Freiburg school.

However, it is often overlooked that Schmoller's primary preoccupation in his lifetime was not with economic *method* but with economic and social *policy* to address the challenges posed by rapid industrialization and urbanization. That is, Schmoller was first and foremost a social reformer. As such, Schmoller's influence extended throughout Europe, to the Progressive movement in the United States, and to social reformers in Meiji Japan. His most prominent non-German students and followers included William J. Ashley, W.E.B. Du Bois, Richard T. Ely, Noburu Kanai, Albion W. Small, and E.R.A. Seligman.

Since the 1980s, Schmoller's work has been re-evaluated and found relevant to some branches of heterodox economics, especially development economics, behavioral economics, evolutionary economics, and neo-institutional economics. He has long had an influence within the subfield of economic history and the discipline of sociology.[9]

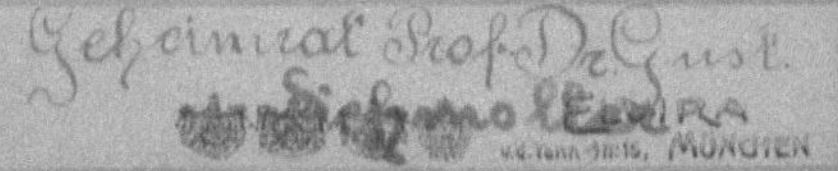

Research mutation: Lujo Brentano

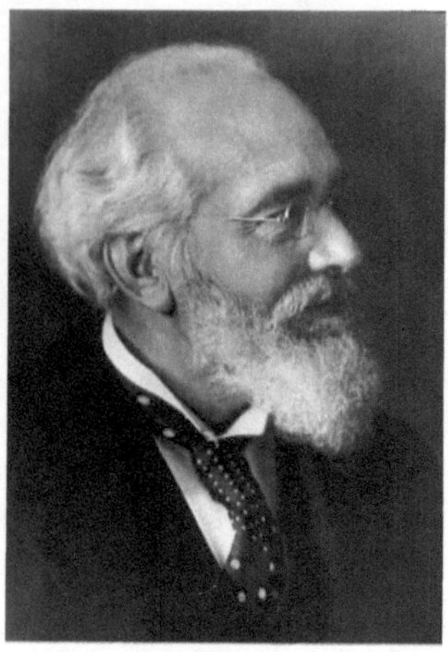

Lujo Brentano, 1927

Lujo Brentano (1844–1931) was an eminent German economist and social reformer.[10]

Born in Aschaffenburg into a distinguished German Roman Catholic intellectual families (originally of Italian descent). He became a professor of economics and state sciences at the universities of Breslau, Strasbourg, Vienna, Leipzig, and most importantly, Munich (1891–1914). With Ernst Engel, the statistician, he made an investigation of the English trade unions. In 1914, he signed the *Manifesto of the Ninety-Three* "an astounding document which denied any German wrongdoing in Belgium and bewilderingly accused the Allies of 'inciting Mongolians and negroes against the white race.'"[11] After the revolution of November 1918,

he served in minister-president Kurt Eisner's government of the People's State of Bavaria as People's Commissar (Minister) for Trade, but only for some days in December 1918.

Brentano was a *Kathedersozialist* (reform-minded) and a founding member of the *Verein für Socialpolitik*. His influence on the social market economy, and on many Germans who would be leaders just after the end of World War II, can hardly be overrated. He also influenced later economists, such as his doctoral student Arthur Salz.

Manifesto of the Ninety-Three

The *Manifesto of the Ninety-Three* is the name commonly given to a 4 October 1914, proclamation endorsed by 93 prominent German scientists, scholars and artists, declaring their unequivocal support of German military actions in the early period of World War I. These actions were elsewhere called the *Rape of Belgium*. The *Manifesto* galvanized support for the war throughout German schools and universities, but many foreign intellectuals were outraged.

Wilhelm Foerster soon repented having signed the document and soon with Georg Friedrich Nicolai they drew up the *Manifesto to the Europeans*. They argued "it seems not just a good thing, but a dire necessity, that educated men of all nations direct their influence in such a way that the terms of the peace not become the wellspring of future wars – uncertain though the outcome of the war may now still seem. The fact that this war has plunged all European relations into an equally unstable and plastic state should rather be put to use to create out of Europe an organic whole." Whilst various people expressed sympathy with these sentiments, only Otto Buek and Albert Einstein agreed to sign it and it remained unpublished at the time. It was subsequently brought to light by Einstein.

A report in 1921 in *The New York Times* found that of 76 surviving signatories, 60 expressed varying degrees of regret. Some claimed not to have seen what they had signed.[12]

Atrocities in Belgium

What is widely known as the *Rape of Belgium* was the German mistreatment of civilians during the invasion and subsequent occupation of Belgium during World War I. The term initially had a propaganda use but recent historiography confirms its reality. One modern author uses it more narrowly to describe a series of German war crimes in the opening months of the war (August- September 1914).

The neutrality of Belgium had been guaranteed by the Treaty of London (1839), which had been signed by Prussia. However, the *German Schlieffen Plan* required that German

armed forces violate Belgium's neutrality in order to outflank the French Army, concentrated in eastern France. The German Chancellor Theobald von Bethmann Hollweg dismissed the treaty of 1839 as a "scrap of paper". Throughout the beginning of the war, the German army engaged in numerous atrocities against the civilian population of Belgium, including the destruction of civilian property; 6,000 Belgians were killed, and 17,700 died during expulsion, deportation, imprisonment, or a death sentence by court. 25,000 homes and other buildings in 837 communities were destroyed in 1914 alone, and 1.5 million Belgians (20% of the entire population) fled from the invading German army.[13]

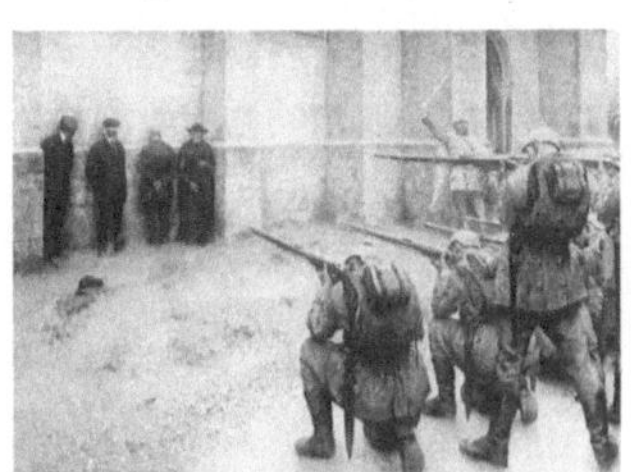

Évariste Carpentier's depiction of the execution of civilians in Blégny in 1914, during the early months of the WWI German occupation of Belgium.

Research mutation: Verein für Socialpolitik

The *Verein für Socialpolitik* (Social Policy Association) is an important society of economists in the German-speaking area.

The *Verein* was founded in Eisenach in 1872 as a response to the "social question". Among its founders were eminent economists like Gustav von Schmoller, Lujo Brentano and Adolph Wagner, who sought a middle path between socialist and laissez-faire economic policies. On the contrary, the liberal publicist Heinrich Bernhard Oppenheim, critical of their "fanciful positions", dubbed them the *Kathedersozialisten* (socialists of the chair), meant as pejorative term.

Among its later members were prominent sociologists like Max Weber and Werner Sombart. They took part in the famous *Werturteilsstreit* with the older generation of the Verein just before the First World War. The *Verein* was dissolved in 1936 under the Nazis, but was re-created in 1948 at a conference in Marburg.[14]

Research mutation: *Werturteilsstreit*

The *Werturteilsstreit* (German for "value judgment dispute") is a *Methodenstreit*, a quarrel in German sociology and economics around the question whether the social sciences are a normative obligatory statement in politics and its measures applied in political actions, and whether their measures can be justified scientifically.

The quarrel took place in the years before World War I, between the members of the *Verein für Socialpolitik*. Main opponents were Max Weber, Werner Sombart and Gustav Schmoller.[15]

Research mutation: Max Weber

Maximilian Karl Emil "Max" Weber (1864–1920) was a German sociologist, philosopher, jurist, political economist and the husband of women's rights activist, Marianne Schnitger. His ideas profoundly influenced social theory and social research. Weber is often cited, with Émile Durkheim and Karl Marx, as among the three founders of sociology.[16]

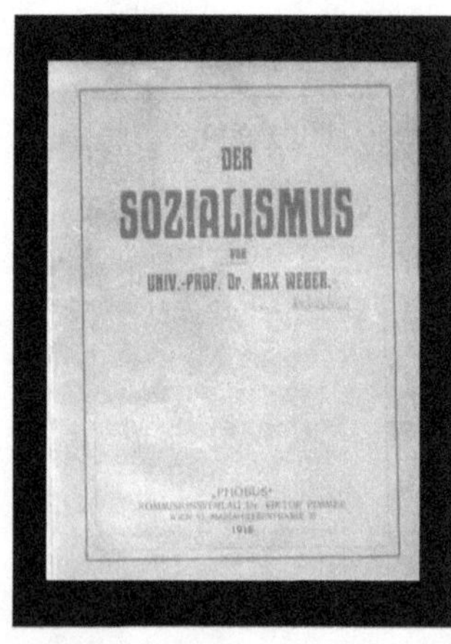

Max Weber, *Der Sozialismus* (1918)

Research mutation: Right-wing socialism in Germany

Bismarckian state socialism and *Kathedersozialismus*

19th-century German Chancellor Otto von Bismarck adopted policies of state-organized compulsory insurance for workers against sickness, accident, incapacity, and old age in what has been nicknamed "Bismarckian socialism". Bismarck himself was not a socialist and enacted the Anti-Socialist Laws, his actions were designed to offset the growth of the Social Democratic Party of Germany. Bismarck's policies have been viewed as a form of state socialism. The state socialism of Bismarck was based upon Romantic political thought in which the state was supreme and carried out Bismarck's agenda of supporting "the protest of collectivism against individualism" and of "nationality against cosmopolitanism" and stated that "the duty of the State is to maintain and promote the interests, the well-being of the nation as such."

The academic equivalent of Bismarck's state socialism at the time was *Kathedersozialismus* of Gustav Schmoller and Adolf Wagner. Schmoller was an opponent of both liberalism and Marxian proletarian socialism. Wagner had originally been a Manchester liberal but had developed into a far-right conservative and antisemite. *Kathedersozialists* held in common three tenets: that "economic freedom cannot be absolute, the economy must obey ethical as well as practical demands, and that the state must intervene to provide a degree of social justice". Schmoller denied that free trade and laissez faire economics were suitable for Germany, instead advocating state intervention in the economy to foster industrialism and improving conditions for labourers. Schmoller endorsed the Prussian monarchy as historically being a "benevolent and socially mediating institution". Schmoller stated "A firm monarchy is a great blessing when it is bound up with traditions like those of the Prussian monarchy, which recognizes its duties." [17]

Research mutation: The Social Question

As a consequence of the Industrial Revolution, pauperism increased within the working class. Therefore, the so-called Social Question came up dealing with possible solutions for this socio-economic effect.

—Iris Fassbender [18]

Research mutation: The Bismarck Period

Otto von Bismarck
Born: 1 April 1815, Schönhausen, Prussia
Died: 30 July 1898, Friedrichsruh, German Empire

Otto Eduard Leopold, Prince of Bismarck, Duke of Lauenburg, known as Otto von Bismarck, was a conservative Prussian statesman who dominated German and European affairs from the 1860s until 1890.

In the 1860s, he engineered a series of wars that unified the German states, deliberately excluding Austria, into a powerful German Empire under Prussian leadership. With that accomplished by 1871, he skillfully used balance of power diplomacy to maintain Germany's position in a Europe which, despite many disputes and war scares, remained at peace. For historian Eric Hobsbawm, it was Bismarck who "remained undisputed world champion at the game of multilateral diplomatic chess for almost twenty years after 1871, [and] devoted himself exclusively, and successfully, to maintaining peace between the powers". However, his annexation of Alsace-Lorraine gave new fuel to French nationalism and promoted Germanophobia in France. This helped set the stage for the First World War.

In 1862, King Wilhelm I appointed Bismarck as Minister President of Prussia, a position he would hold until 1890 (except for a short break in 1873). He provoked three short, decisive wars against Denmark, Austria, and France, aligning the smaller German states behind Prussia in its defeat of France. In 1871, he formed the German Empire with himself as Chancellor, while retaining control of Prussia. His diplomacy of realpolitik and powerful rule at home gained him the nickname the "Iron Chancellor".

He disliked colonialism but reluctantly built an overseas empire when it was demanded by both elite and mass opinion. Juggling a very complex interlocking series of conferences, negotiations and alliances, he used his diplomatic skills to maintain Germany's position and used the balance of power to keep Europe at peace in the 1870s and 1880s.

A master of complex politics at home, Bismarck created the first welfare state in the modern world, with the goal of gaining working class support that might otherwise go to his Socialist enemies. In the 1870s, he allied himself with the Liberals (who were low-tariff and anti-Catholic) and fought the Catholic Church in what was called the *Kulturkampf* ("culture struggle"). He lost that battle as the Catholics responded by forming a powerful Centre party and using universal male suffrage to gain a bloc of seats.

Bismarck then reversed himself, ended the *Kulturkampf*, broke with the Liberals, imposed protective tariffs, and formed a political alliance with the Centre Party to fight the Socialists.

Bismarck distrusted democracy and ruled through a strong, well-trained bureaucracy with power in the hands of a traditional Junker elite that consisted of the landed nobility in eastern Prussia. Under Wilhelm I, Bismarck largely controlled domestic and foreign affairs, until he was removed by the young Kaiser Wilhelm II in 1890, at the age of seventy-five.

Bismarck – a Junker himself – was strong-willed, outspoken and sometimes judged overbearing, but he could also be polite, charming and witty. Occasionally he displayed a violent temper, and he kept his power by melodramatically threatening resignation time and again, which cowed Wilhelm I. He possessed not only a long-term national and international vision but also the short-term ability to juggle complex developments.

As the leader of what historians call "revolutionary conservatism", Bismarck became a hero to German nationalists; they built many monuments honoring the founder of the new Reich.

Many historians praise him as a visionary who was instrumental in uniting Germany and, once that had been accomplished, kept the peace in Europe through adroit diplomacy.

According to the historian Jonathan Steinberg, Bismarck's achievements in 1862–71 were "the greatest diplomatic and political achievement by any leader in the last two centuries."[19]

Research mutation: Eugen Dühring

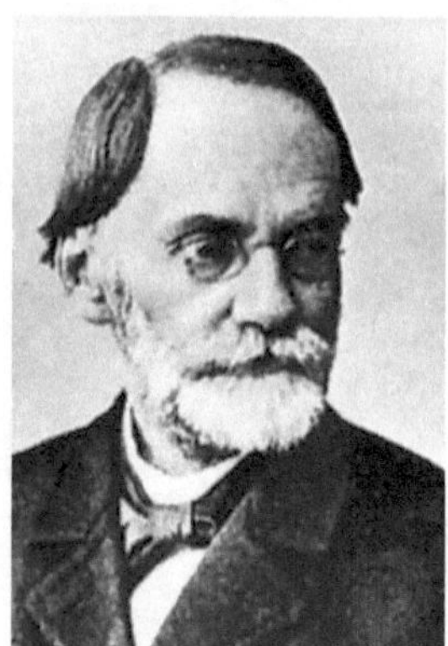

Eugen Dühring circa. 1900

Eugen Karl Dühring (1833–1921) was a German ex-socialist, philosopher, and economist, who was a strong critic of Marxism and an infamous antisemitic extremist:

> Perhaps the most influential writers shaping Hitler's formulation of race theory were philosopher Eugen Dühring and journalist Wilhelm Marr. Basing their shrill message on pseudoscientific arguments, they expounded a biologically based antisemitism ... they urged the adoption of special laws against Jews, and – hauntingly – called for their deportation.[20]

Well-known prophet of anti-Semitism. From 1864 to 1877 Duhring was lecturer in philosophy and national economy at Berlin was lecturer in philosophy at Berlin University. His ideas were the object of a celebrated critique by Frederich Eagles. In his *Die Judenfrage also Racen-, Sitten und Culturfrage* of November 1880, he preached a radical racial anti-Semitism, accusing the Jews of exploiting and damaging the peoples among whom they lived, and tracing this back to an unalterable "race character." Düring called for the revocation of the emancipation of the Jews. He also discussed social isolation, internment, and even deportation as possible "solutions" for the "Jewish question," which he claimed was a "life-or-death matter for modern peoples."

> —Michael Schabitz (trans. Cyprian Blamires), *World Fascism: A Historical Encyclopedia, Volume 1*

Düring's proposed solutions to the Jewish Question were more radical than those of his antisemetic contemporaries. *The Jewish Question as a Racial, Moral, and Cultural Problem* (1881, 6th ed. 1930) and *The Replacement of Religion by Something More Perfect and the Elimination of Jewry by Means of the Modern Wolk-Spirit* (1883, 4th ed. 1929) can be read as anticipating the Final Solution.

> — Richard S. Levy, *Antisemitism: A Historical Encyclopedia of Prejudice and Persecution, Volume 1*

Research mutation: *Anti-Dühring*

Anti-Dühring is a book by Friedrich Engels, first published in German in 1878. This work was Engels's major contribution to the exposition and development of Marxist theory. Its full title translates as *Herr Eugen Dühring's Revolution in Science*: this is meant ironically and polemically.

Eugen Dühring had produced his own version of socialism, intended as a replacement for Marxism. Since Karl Marx was busy at the time with writing *Das Kapital*, it was left to Engels to write a general defence. The sections are Philosophy, Political Economy and Socialism.

Among Communists, it is a popular and enduring work which, as Engels wrote to Marx, was an attempt "to produce an encyclopaedic survey of our conception of the philosophical, natural-science and historical problems."

In this book, Engels articulated one of the classic definitions of the term Political economy: "Political economy, in the widest sense, is the science of the laws governing the production and exchange of the material means of subsistence in human society . . . Political economy is therefore essentially a historical science. It deals with material which is historical, that is, constantly changing."

This work is also the source of a widely quoted aphorism:

"The state is not abolished, it withers away." [21]

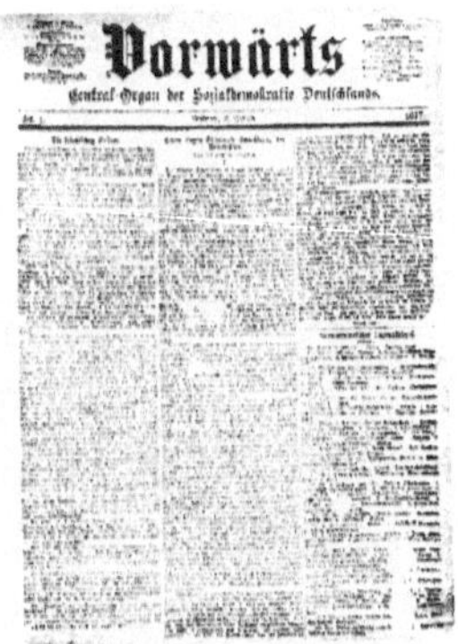

Part one of *Anti-Dühring* was first published as a series of articles entitled 'Herrn Eugen Dühring's Umwälzung der Philosophie' in *Vorwärts*, 1877.

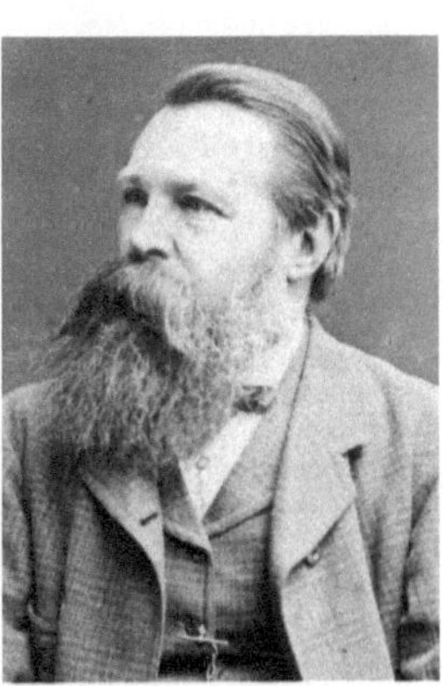

Engels in 1877 by William Hall, Brighton

Research mutation: Friedrich Engels

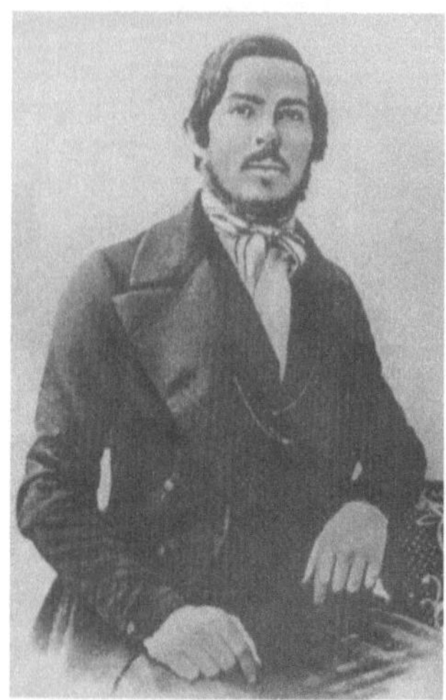

Friedrich Engels aged 25 (1845) while living and working in England

Friedrich Engels (28 November 1820 – 5 August 1895) was a German philosopher, social scientist, journalist, and businessman. He founded Marxist theory together with Karl Marx. In 1845, he published *The Condition of the Working Class in England*, based on personal observations and research into the slums in Manchester, of their horrors, notably child labour, the despoiled environment, and overworked and impoverished labourers.

In 1848, he co-authored *The Communist Manifesto* with Marx, and he also authored and co-authored (primarily with Marx) many other works. Later he supported Marx financially to do research and write *Das Kapital*. After Marx's death, Engels edited the second and third volumes. Additionally, Engels organised Marx's notes on the *Theories of Surplus Value*, which he later published as the "fourth volume" of Capital.

After Marx's death, Engels devoted much of his remaining years to editing Marx's unfinished volumes of *Capital*. However, he also contributed significantly in other areas. Engels made an argument using anthropological evidence of the time to show that family structures changed over history, and that the concept of monogamous marriage came from the necessity within class society for men to control women to ensure their own children would inherit their property. He argued a future communist society would allow people to make decisions about their relationships free of economic constraints. One of the best examples of Engels's thoughts on these issues are in his work *The Origin of the Family, Private Property and the State*.

Vladimir Lenin wrote: "After his friend Karl Marx (who died in 1883), Engels was the finest scholar and teacher of the modern proletariat in the whole civilised world . . . In their scientific works, Marx and Engels were the first to explain that socialism is not the invention of dreamers, but the final aim and necessary result of the development of the productive forces in modern society. All recorded history hitherto has been a history of class struggle,

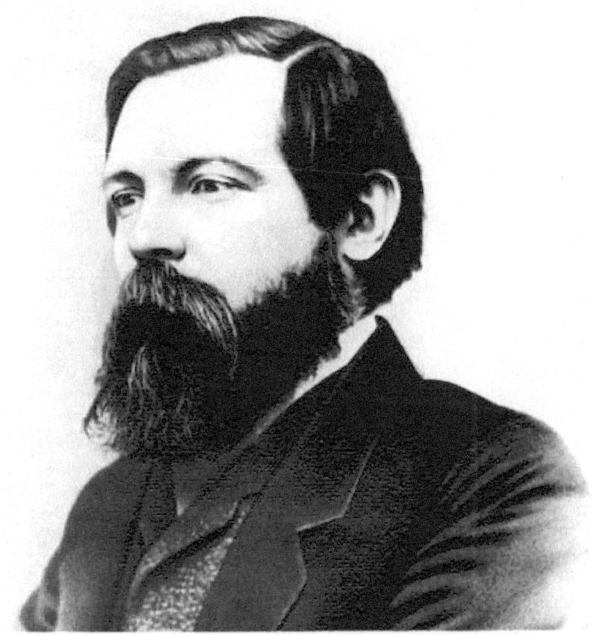

Engels in 1856

of the succession of the rule and victory of certain social classes over others."

But Labour Party politician Tristram Hunt argues that Engels has become a convenient scapegoat, too easily blamed for the state crimes of the Soviet Union, Communist Southeast Asia and China. "Engels is left holding the bag of 20th century ideological extremism," Hunt writes, "while Marx is rebranded as the acceptable, postpolitical seer of global capitalism." Hunt largely exonerates Engels stating that "in no intelligible sense can Engels or Marx bear culpability for the crimes of historical actors carried out generations later, even if the policies were offered up in their honor."

Other writers, while admitting the distance between Marx and Engels and Stalin, are less charitable, noting for example that the anarchist Bakunin predicted the oppressive potential of their ideas. "It is a fallacy that Marxism's flaws were exposed only after it was tried out in power . . . [Marx and Engels] were centralisers. While talking about 'free associations of producers', they advocated discipline and hierarchy."[22]

Research mutation: Karl Marx

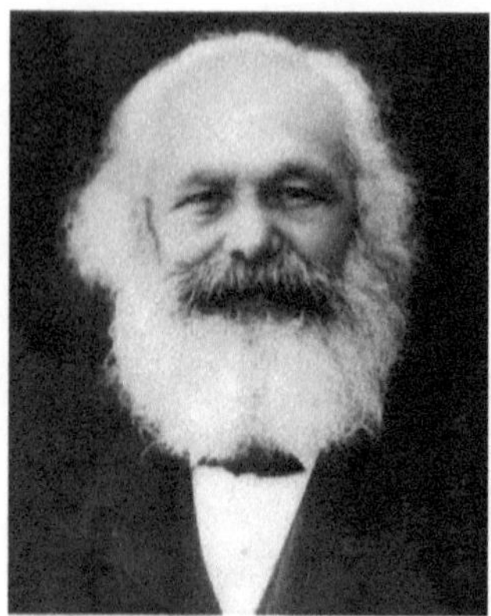

Marx in 1882

Karl Marx (5 May 1818 – 14 March 1883) was a Prussian-born philosopher, economist, political theorist, sociologist, journalist, and revolutionary socialist. Born in Trier to a middle-class family, he later studied political economy and Hegelian philosophy. As an adult, Marx became stateless and spent much of his life in London, England, where he continued to develop his thought in collaboration with German thinker Friedrich Engels and published various works, the most well-known being the 1848 pamphlet *The Communist Manifesto*. His work has since influenced subsequent intellectual, economic, and political history.

Marx's theories about society, economics, and politics – collectively understood as Marxism – hold that human societies develop through class struggle; in capitalism, this manifests itself in the conflict between the ruling classes (known as the bourgeoisie) that control the means of production and working classes (known as the proletariat) that enable these means by selling their labour for wages. Employing a critical approach known as historical materialism, Marx predicted that, like previous socioeconomic systems, capitalism produced internal tensions which would lead to its self-destruction and replacement by a new system: socialism. For Marx, class antagonisms under capitalism, owing in part to its instability and crisis-prone nature, would eventuate the working class' development of class consciousness, leading to their conquest of political power and eventually the establishment of a classless, communist society constituted by a free association of producers. Marx actively fought for its implementation, arguing that the working class should carry out organised revolutionary action to topple capitalism and bring about socio-economic emancipation.

Marx has been described as one of the most influential figures in human history, and his work has been both lauded and criticised. His work in economics laid the basis for much of the current understanding of labour and its relation to capital, and subsequent economic thought. Many intellectuals, labour unions, artists and political parties worldwide have been influenced by Marx's work, with many modifying or adapting his ideas. Marx is typically cited as one of the principal architects of modern social science.

Marx's view of history, which came to be called historical materialism (controversially adapted as the philosophy of dialectical materialism by Engels and Lenin) certainly shows the influence of Hegel's claim that one should view reality (and history) dialectically. However, Hegel had thought in idealist terms, putting ideas in the forefront, whereas Marx sought to rewrite dialectics in materialist terms, arguing for the primacy of matter over idea. Where Hegel saw the "spirit" as driving history, Marx saw this as an unnecessary mystification, obscuring the reality of humanity and its physical actions shaping the world. He wrote that Hegelianism stood the movement of reality on its head, and that one needed to set it upon its feet. Despite his dislike of mystical terms Marx used Gothic language in several of his works. In Das Kapital he refers to capital as "necromancy that surrounds the products of labour".

Though inspired by French socialist and sociological thought, Marx criticised utopian socialists, arguing that their favoured small-scale socialistic communities would be bound to marginalisation and poverty, and that only a large-scale change in the economic system can bring about real change.

The other important contribution to Marx's revision of Hegelianism came from Engels's book, The Condition of the Working Class in England in 1844, which led Marx to conceive of the historical dialectic in terms of class conflict and to see the modern working class as the most progressive force for revolution.

Marx believed that he could study history and society scientifically and discern tendencies of history and the resulting outcome of social conflicts. Some followers of Marx concluded, therefore, that a communist revolution would inevitably occur. However, Marx famously asserted in the eleventh of his "Theses on Feuerbach" that "philosophers have only interpreted the world, in various ways; the point however is to change it", and he clearly dedicated himself to trying to alter the world.[23]

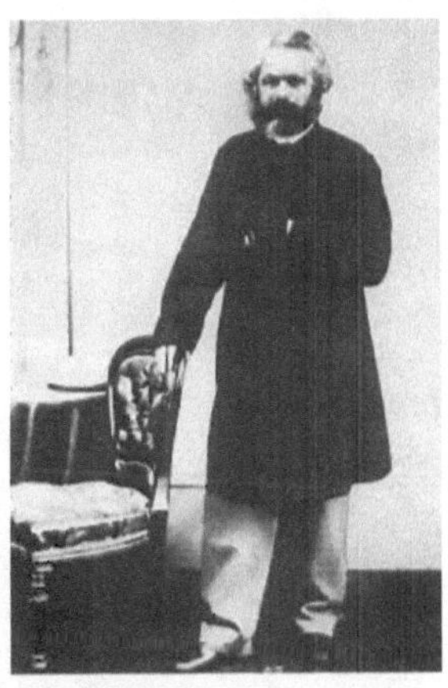

Marx in 1866

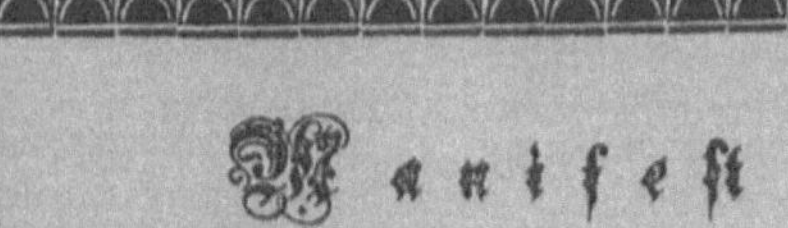

Manifest

der

Kommunistischen Partei.

Veröffentlicht im Februar 1848.

Proletarier aller Länder vereinigt Euch!

London.

Gedruckt in der Office der „Bildungs-Gesellschaft für Arbeiter"
von J. E. Burghard.

46, Liverpool Street, Bishopsgate.

The first edition of *The Manifesto of the Communist Party*,
published in German in 1848

Das Kapital.

Kritik der politischen Oekonomie.

Von

Karl Marx.

Erster Band.

Buch I: Der Produktionsprocess des Kapitals.

Hamburg

Verlag von Otto Meissner.

1867.

New-York: L. W. Schmidt, 24 Barclay-Street.

Research mutation: Marxism

Marxism is a form of socioeconomic analysis that analyses class relations and societal conflict using a materialist interpretation of historical development and a dialectical view of social transformation. It originates from the mid-to-late 19th century works of German philosophers Karl Marx and Friedrich Engels.

Marxist methodology originally used a method of economic and sociopolitical inquiry known as historical materialism to analyze and critique the development of capitalism and the role of class struggle in systemic economic change. According to Marxist perspective, class conflict within capitalism arises due to intensifying contradictions between the highly productive mechanized and socialized production performed by the proletariat, and the private ownership and appropriation of the surplus product (profit) by a small minority of the population who are private owners called the bourgeoisie. The contradiction, between the forces and relations of production intensifies leading to crisis. The haute bourgeoisie and its managerial proxies are unable to manage the intensifying alienation of labor which the proletariat experiences, albeit with varying degrees of class consciousness, until social revolution ultimately results. The eventual long-term outcome of this revolution would be the establishment of socialism – a socioeconomic system based on social ownership of the means of production, distribution based on one's contribution, and production organized directly for use. As the productive forces and technology continued to advance, Marx hypothesized that socialism would eventually give way to a communist stage of social development, which would be a classless, stateless, humane society erected on common ownership and the principle of "From each according to his ability, to each according to his (sic) needs".

Marxism has since developed into different branches and schools of thought, and there is now no single definitive Marxist theory. Different Marxian schools place a greater emphasis on certain aspects of classical Marxism while de-emphasizing or rejecting other aspects, and sometimes combine Marxist analysis with non-Marxian concepts; as a result, they might reach contradictory conclusions from each other. Lately, however, there is movement toward the recognition that the main aspect of Marxism is philosophy of dialectical materialism and historicism, which should result in more agreement between different schools.

Overview

Marxist analyses and methodologies have influenced multiple political ideologies and social movements, and Marxist understandings of history and society have been adopted by some academics in the disciplines of archaeology, anthropology, media studies, political science, theater, history, sociology, art history and theory, cultural studies, education, economics, geography, literary criticism, aesthetics, critical psychology, and philosophy.

The Marxian analysis begins with an analysis of the material conditions and the economic activities required to satisfy society's material needs. It is assumed that the form of economic organization, or mode of production, gives rise to, or at least directly influences, most other social phenomena – including social relations, political and legal systems, moral codes and ideology. The economic system and these social relations form a base and superstructure. As forces of production, most notably technology, improve, existing forms of social organization become inefficient and stifle further progress. As Karl Marx observed: "At a certain stage of development, the material productive forces of society come into conflict with the existing relations of production or – this merely expresses the same thing in legal terms – with the property relations within the framework of which they have operated hitherto. From forms of development of the productive forces these relations turn into their fetters. Then begins an era of social revolution." These inefficiencies manifest themselves as social contradictions in society in the

form of class struggle. Under the capitalist mode of production, this struggle materializes between the minority (the bourgeoisie) who own the means of production, and the vast majority of the population (the proletariat) who produce goods and services. Starting with the assumption that social change occurs because of the struggle between different classes within society who are under contradiction against each other, a Marxist analyst would summarize by saying that capitalism exploits and oppresses the proletariat, which leads to a proletarian revolution.

Capitalism (according to Marxist theory) can no longer sustain the living standards of the population due to its need to compensate for falling rates of profit by driving down wages, cutting social benefits and pursuing military aggression. The socialist system would succeed capitalism as humanity's mode of production through workers' revolution. According to Marxism, especially arising from crisis theory, socialism is a historical necessity (but not an inevitability).

In a socialist society private property, in the form of the means of production, would be replaced by co-operative ownership. A socialist economy would not base production on the creation of private profits, but on the criteria of satisfying human needs – that is, production would be carried out directly for use. As Engels said: "Then the capitalist mode of appropriation in which the product enslaves first the producer, and then appropriator, is replaced by the mode of appropriation of the product that is based upon the nature of the modern means of production; upon the one hand, direct social appropriation, as means to the maintenance and extension of production on the other, direct individual appropriation, as means of subsistence and of enjoyment."

Historical materialism

The historical materialist theory of history analyses the underlying causes of societal development and change from the perspective of the collective ways that humans make their living. All constituent features of a society (social classes, political pyramid, ideologies) are assumed to stem from economic activity, an idea often portrayed with the metaphor of the base and superstructure.

The base and superstructure metaphor portrays the totality of social relations by which humans produce and re-produce their social existence. According to Marx, "The sum total of the forces of production accessible to men determines the condition of society," and forms a society's economic base. The base includes the material forces of production, that is, the labour and material means of production, and relations of production, i.e. the social and political arrangements that regulate production and distribution. From this base rises a superstructure of legal and political "forms of social consciousness" of political and legal institutions that derive from the economic base which conditions the superstructure and a society's dominant ideology. Conflicts between the development of material productive forces and the relations of production provokes social revolutions, and thus, the resultant changes to the economic base will lead to the transformation of the superstructure. This relationship is reflexive; at first the base gives rise to the superstructure and remains the foundation of a form of social organization. Hence, that formed social organization can act again upon both parts of the base and superstructure, so, that relationship not one-way but a dialogue (a dialectic), expressed and driven by conflicts and contradictions. As Friedrich Engels clarified: "The history of all hitherto existing society is the history of class struggles. Freeman and slave, patrician and plebeian, lord and serf, guild-master and journeyman, in a word, oppressor and oppressed, stood in constant opposition to one another, carried on uninterrupted, now hidden, now open fight, a fight that each time ended, either in a revolutionary reconstitution of society at large, or in the common ruin of the contending classes."'

Marx considered these socio-economic conflicts as the driving force of human history since these recurring conflicts have manifested themselves as distinct transitional stages of development in Western Europe. Accordingly, Marx designated human history as encompassing four stages of development in relations of production.

1. Primitive Communism: as in co-operative tribal societies.
2. Slave Society: a development of tribal to city-state; aristocracy is born.
3. Feudalism: aristocrats are the ruling class; merchants evolve into capitalists.
4. Capitalism: capitalists are the ruling class, who create and employ the proletariat.

Criticism of capitalism

According to the Marxist theoretician and revolutionary Vladimir Lenin, "the principal content of Marxism" was "Marx's economic doctrine". Marx believed that the capitalist bourgeois and their economists were promoting what he saw as the lie that "The interests of the capitalist and of the worker are . . . one and the same"; he believed that they did this by purporting the concept that "the fastest possible growth of productive capital" was best not only for the wealthy capitalists but also for the workers because it provided them with employment.

Exploitation is a matter of surplus labour – the amount of labour one performs beyond what one receives in goods. Exploitation has been a socio-economic feature of every class society, and is one of the principal features distinguishing the social classes. The power of one social class to control the means of production enables its exploitation of the other classes.

In capitalism, the labour theory of value is the operative concern; the value of a commodity equals the socially necessary labour time required to produce it. Under that condition, surplus value (the difference between the value produced and the value received by a labourer) is synonymous with the term "surplus labour"; thus, capitalist exploitation is realised as deriving surplus value from the worker.

In pre-capitalist economies, exploitation of the worker was achieved via physical coercion. In the capitalist mode of production, that result is more subtly achieved; because the worker does not own the means of production, he or she must voluntarily enter into an exploitive work relationship with a capitalist in order to earn the necessities of life. The worker's entry into such employment is voluntary in that he or she chooses which capitalist to work for. However, the worker must work or starve. Thus, exploitation is inevitable, and the "voluntary" nature of a worker participating in a capitalist society is illusory.

Alienation is the estrangement of people from their humanity (German: *Gattungswesen*, "species-essence", "species-being"), which is a systematic result of capitalism. Under capitalism, the fruits of production belong to the employers, who expropriate the surplus created by others, and so generate alienated labourers. In Marx's view, alienation is an objective characterization of the worker's situation in capitalism –

his or her self-awareness of this condition is not prerequisite.

Social classes

The identity of a social class derives from its relationship to the means of production; Marx describes the social classes in capitalist societies:

- Proletariat: "the class of modern wage labourers who, having no means of production of their own, are reduced to selling their labour power in order to live". As Andrei Platonov expressed "The working class is my home country and my future is linked with the proletariat." The capitalist mode of production establishes the conditions enabling the bourgeoisie to exploit the proletariat because the workers' labour generates a surplus value greater than the workers' wages.
- Bourgeoisie: those who "own the means of production" and buy labour power from the proletariat, thus exploiting the proletariat; they subdivide as bourgeoisie and the petite bourgeoisie.
- Petite bourgeoisie are those who work and can afford to buy little labour power i.e. small business owners, peasant landlords, trade workers et al. Marxism predicts that the continual reinvention of the means of production eventually would destroy the petite bourgeoisie, degrading them from the middle class to the proletariat.
- Lumpenproletariat: the outcasts of society such as criminals, vagabonds, beggars, prostitutes, et al., who have no stake in the economy and no mind of their own and so are decoyed by every bidder.
- Landlords: a historically important social class whose members retain some wealth and power.
- Peasantry and farmers: a scattered class incapable of organizing and effecting socio-economic change, most of whom would enter the proletariat while some became landlords.

Class consciousness denotes the awareness – of itself and the social world – that a social class possesses, and its capacity to rationally act in their best interests; hence, class consciousness is required before they can effect a successful revolution.

Without defining ideology, Marx used the term to denote the production of images of social reality; according to Engels, "ideology is a process accomplished by the so-called thinker consciously, it is true, but with a false consciousness. The real motive forces impelling him remain unknown to him; otherwise it simply would not be an ideological process. Hence he imagines false or seeming motive forces". Because the ruling class controls the society's means of production, the superstructure of society (the ruling social ideas), are determined by the best interests of the ruling class. In *The German Ideology*, "the ideas of the ruling class are in every epoch the ruling ideas, i.e. the class which is the ruling material force of society, is, at the same time, its ruling intellectual force".

The term "political economy" originally denoted the study of the conditions under which economic production was organised in the capitalist system. In Marxism, political economy is the study of the means of production, specifically of capital, and how that manifests as economic activity.

Relation with industrial revolution

This new way of thinking was invented because socialists believed that common ownership of the "means of production," (that is the industries, the land, the wealth of nature, the trade apparatus, the wealth of the society, etc.) will abolish the exploitative working conditions experienced under capitalism. Through working class revolution, the State (which Marxists see as a weapon for the subjugation of one class by another) is seized and used to suppress the hitherto ruling class of capitalists, and, by implementing a commonly-owned, democratically controlled workplace, create the society of communism, which Marxists see as true democracy. An economy based on co operation, on human need and social betterment, rather than competition for profit of many independently acting profit seekers, would also be the end of class society, which Marx saw as the fundamental division of all hitherto existing history.

Marx saw work, the effort by humans to transform the environment for their needs, as a fundamental feature of human kind. Capitalism, in which the product of the worker's labor is taken from them and sold at market rather than being part of the worker's life, is therefore alienating to the worker. Additionally, the worker is compelled by various means (some nicer than others) to work harder, faster, for longer hours. While this is happening, the employer is constantly trying to save on labor costs: pay the workers less, figure out how to use cheaper equipment, etc. This allows the employer to extract the largest mount of work (and therefore potential wealth) from their workers. The fundamental nature of capitalist society is no different from that of slave society: one small group of society exploiting the larger group.

Through common ownership of the means of production, the profit motive is eliminated and the motive of furthering human flourishing is introduced. Because the surplus produced by the workers is property of the society as whole, there are no classes of producers and appropriators. Additionally, the State, which has its origins in the bands of retainers hired by the first ruling classes to protect their economic privilege, will disappear, as its conditions of existence have disappeared.[24]

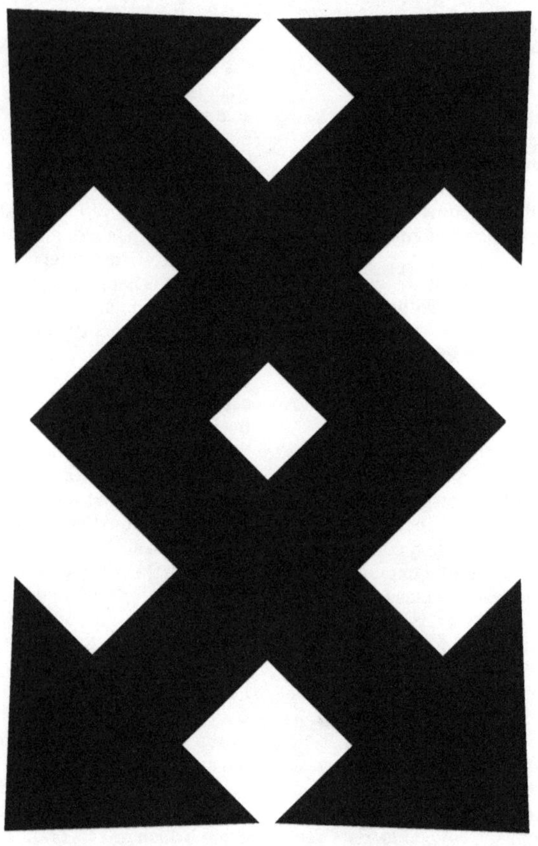

REFLECTION ON

RESEARCH MUTATIONS

A sense of editorial responsibility quickly rears its head.

As with Adolph Wagner (p.8) and Eugen Dühring (p.22), under the surface of [Redacted]'s attempt to provide "a neutral point of view" (p.xix) lies an ugly politik of hateful extremism; the history books are left open for all to scrawl in, provided they say nothing.

A blank ideology.

Such cursory research for the curation of printing seems treacherous: the probability of inaccurately presenting false allegiances to, or casting in a positive light (or even a dimly neutral light) such deeply unsavoury subjects goes unchecked.

Publishing: not something to be treated cavalierly.

Caveat.

A shadow dances on the wall,
fills me with a fear
of past and future haunts

Of course when said aloud, this all
sounds especially obvious: as it is
with the tongue, it is doubly so with
the glyph

From a single page of the source
material; the SE generates a
deep pedagogocial wormhole:
evidence of the deviations in
focus inherent in our post-digital
existence. Such incredible scope
for non-linear investigations,
allows for the publication
of new narratives that are

post-knowledge.

More generously, an
SE enables the SE
to perform an act of
improvised knowledge
acquisition as archival
performance. SE as AI.

A RETURN TO THE FOUNT OF MUTANT PEDAGOGY*

*   *Pädagogisches Skizzenbuch*

BAUHAU[S]

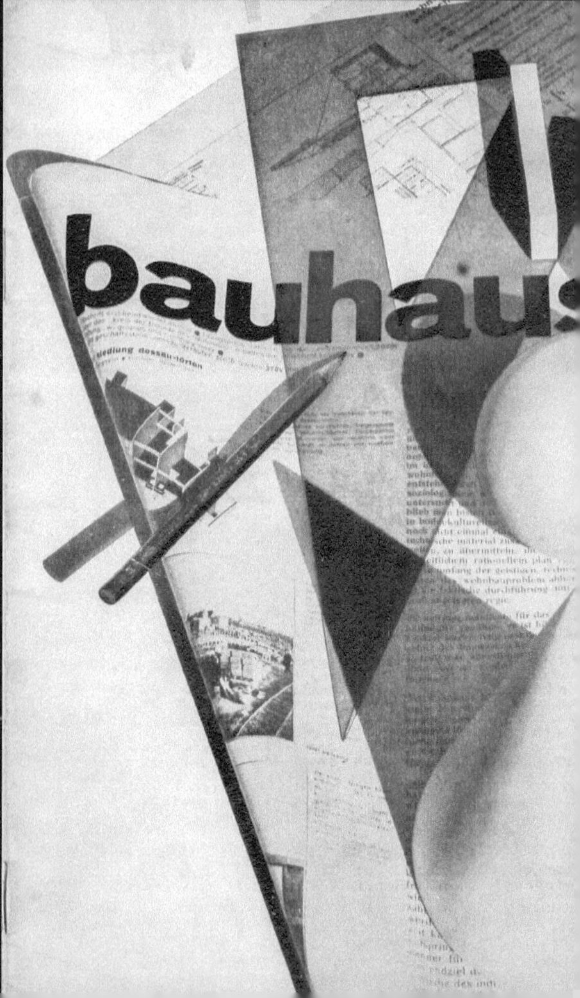

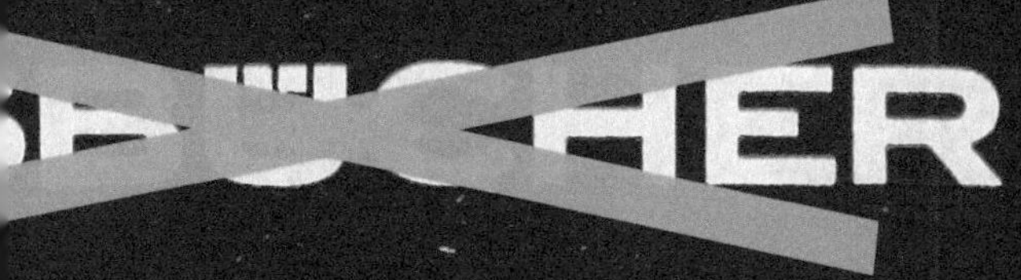

Research mutation: Bauhaus

Staatliches Bauhaus, commonly known as Bauhaus, was a German art school operational from 1919 to 1933 that combined crafts and the fine arts, and was famous for the approach to design that it publicised and taught.

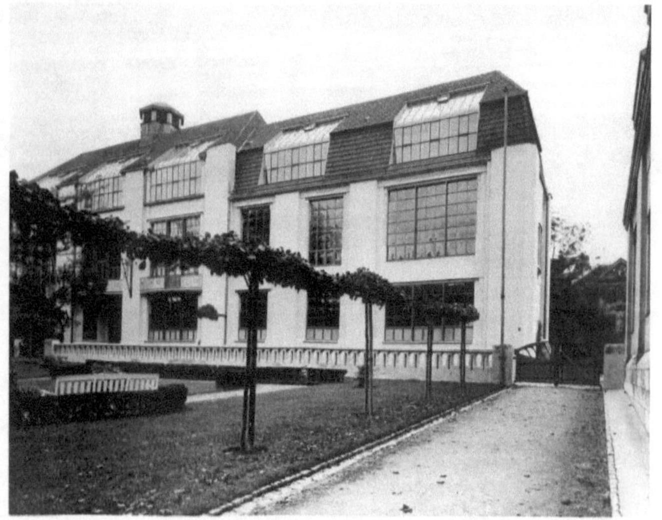

Building of the School of Art in Weimar
Architect: Henry van de Velde
Photo: Louis Held, circa 1911.

Mutation continued: Bauhaus

The Bauhaus was founded by Walter Gropius in Weimar. The German term *Bauhaus* – literally "construction house" – was understood as meaning "School of Building", but in spite of its name and the fact that its founder was an architect, the Bauhaus did not have an architecture department during its first years of existence. Nonetheless, it was founded with the idea of creating a "total" work of art (Gesamtkunstwerk) in which all arts, including architecture, would eventually be brought together. The Bauhaus style later became one of the most influential currents in modern design, Modernist architecture and art, design and architectural education. The Bauhaus had a profound influence upon subsequent developments in art, architecture, graphic design, interior design, industrial design, and typography.

The school existed in three German cities: Weimar from 1919 to 1925, Dessau from 1925 to 1932 and Berlin from 1932 to 1933, under three different architect-directors: Walter Gropius from 1919 to 1928, Hannes Meyer from 1928 to 1930 and Ludwig Mies van der Rohe from 1930 until 1933, when the school was closed by its own leadership under pressure from the Nazi regime, having been painted as a centre of communist intellectualism. Although the school was closed, the staff continued to spread its idealistic precepts as they left Germany and emigrated all over the world.

The changes of venue and leadership resulted in a constant shifting of focus, technique, instructors, and politics. For example, the pottery shop was discontinued when the school moved from Weimar to Dessau, even though it had been an important revenue source; when Mies van der Rohe took over the school in 1930, he transformed it into a private school, and would not allow any supporters of Hannes Meyer to attend it.

Bauhaus and German modernism

Germany's defeat in World War I, the fall of the German monarchy and the abolition of censorship under the new, liberal Weimar Republic allowed an upsurge of radical experimentation in all the arts, which had been suppressed by the old regime. Many Germans of left-wing views were influenced by the cultural experimentation that followed the Russian Revolution, such as constructivism. Such influences can be overstated: Gropius did not share these radical views, and said that Bauhaus was entirely apolitical. Just as important was the influence of the 19th century English designer William Morris, who had argued that art should meet the needs of society and that there should be no distinction between form and function. Thus, the Bauhaus style, also known as the International Style, was marked by the absence of ornamentation and by harmony between the function of an object or a building and its design.

However, the most important influence on Bauhaus was modernism, a cultural movement whose origins lay as early as the 1880s, and which had already made its presence felt in Germany before the World War, despite the prevailing conservatism. The design innovations commonly associated with Gropius and the Bauhaus – the radically simplified forms, the rationality and functionality, and the idea that mass production was reconcilable with the individual artistic spirit – were already partly developed in Germany before the Bauhaus was founded. The German national designers' organization Deutscher Werkbund was formed in 1907 by Hermann Muthesius to harness the new potentials of mass production, with a mind towards preserving Germany's economic competitiveness with England. In its first seven years, the Werkbund came to be regarded as the authoritative body on questions of design in Germany, and was copied in other countries. Many fundamental questions of craftsmanship versus mass production, the relationship of usefulness and beauty, the practical purpose of formal beauty in a commonplace object, and whether or not a single proper form could exist, were argued out among its 1,870 members (by 1914).

The entire movement of German architectural modernism was known as Neues Bauen. Beginning in June 1907, Peter Behrens' pioneering industrial design work for the German electrical company AEG successfully integrated art and mass production on a large scale. He designed consumer products, standardized parts, created clean-lined designs for the company's graphics, developed a consistent corporate identity, built the modernist landmark AEG Turbine Factory, and made full use of newly developed materials such as poured concrete and exposed steel. Behrens was a founding member of the Werkbund, and both Walter Gropius and Adolf Meyer worked for him in this period.

The Bauhaus was founded at a time when the German zeitgeist had turned from emotional Expressionism to the matter-of-fact New Objectivity. An entire group of working architects, including Erich Mendelsohn, Bruno Taut and Hans Poelzig, turned away from fanciful experimentation, and turned toward rational, functional, sometimes standardized building. Beyond the Bauhaus, many other significant German-speaking architects in the 1920s responded to the same aesthetic issues and material possibilities as the school. They also responded to the promise of a "minimal dwelling" written into the new Weimar Constitution. Ernst May, Bruno Taut, and Martin Wagner, among others, built large housing blocks in Frankfurt and Berlin. The acceptance of modernist design into everyday life was the subject of publicity campaigns, well-attended public exhibitions like the Weissenhof Estate, films, and sometimes fierce public debate.

Bauhaus and Vkhutemas

The Vkhutemas, the Russian state art and technical school founded in 1920 in Moscow, has been compared to Bauhaus. Founded a year after the Bauhaus school, Vkhutemas has close parallels to the German Bauhaus in its intent, organization and scope. The two schools were the first to train artist-designers in a modern manner. Both schools were state-sponsored initiatives to merge the craft tradition with modern technology, with a basic course in aesthetic principles, courses in color theory, industrial design, and architecture. Vkhutemas was a larger school than the Bauhaus, but it was less publicised outside the Soviet Union and consequently, is less familiar in the West.

With the internationalism of modern architecture and design, there were many exchanges between the Vkhutemas and the Bauhaus. The second Bauhaus director Hannes Meyer attempted to organise an exchange between the two schools, while Hinnerk Scheper of the Bauhaus collaborated with various Vkhutein members on the use of colour in architecture. In addition, El Lissitzky's book *Russia: an Architecture for World Revolution* published in German in 1930 featured several illustrations of Vkhutemas/ Vkhutein projects there.

History of the Bauhaus
Weimar

The school was founded by Walter Gropius in Weimar in 1919 as a merger of the Grand Ducal School of Arts and Crafts and the Weimar Academy of Fine Art. Its roots lay in the arts and crafts school founded by the Grand Duke of Saxe-Weimar-Eisenach in 1906 and directed by Belgian Art Nouveau architect Henry van de Velde. When van de Velde was forced to resign in 1915 because he was Belgian, he suggested Gropius, Hermann Obrist and August Endell as possible successors. In 1919, after delays caused by the destruction of World War I and a lengthy debate over who should head the institution and the socio-economic meanings of a reconciliation of the fine

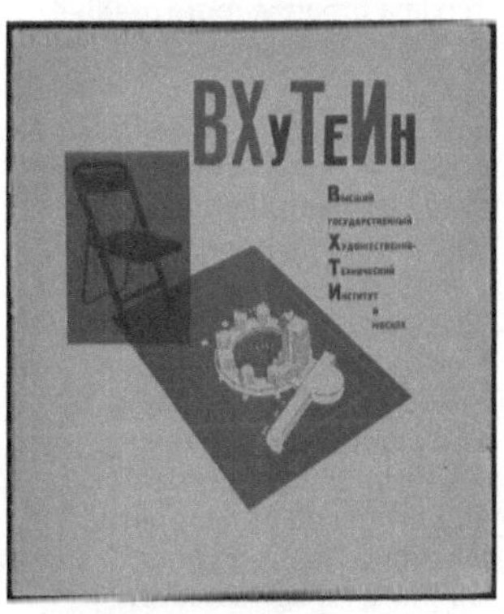

VKHuTein, 1929

arts and the applied arts (an issue which remained a defining one throughout the school's existence), Gropius was made the director of a new institution integrating the two called the Bauhaus. In the pamphlet for an April 1919 exhibition entitled "Exhibition of Unknown Architects", Gropius proclaimed his goal as being "to create a new guild of craftsmen, without the class distinctions which raise an arrogant barrier between craftsman and artist." Gropius' neologism Bauhaus references both building and the Bauhütte, a premodern guild of stonemasons. The early intention was for the Bauhaus to be a combined architecture school, crafts school, and academy of the arts. In 1919 Swiss painter Johannes Itten, German-American painter Lyonel Feininger, and German sculptor Gerhard Marcks, along with Gropius, comprised the faculty of the Bauhaus. By the following year their ranks had grown to include German painter, sculptor and designer Oskar Schlemmer who headed the theater workshop, and Swiss painter Paul Klee, joined in 1922 by Russian painter Wassily Kandinsky. A tumultuous year at the Bauhaus, 1922 also saw the move of Dutch painter Theo van Doesburg to Weimar to promote De Stijl ("The Style"), and a visit to the Bauhaus by Russian Constructivist artist and architect El Lissitzky.

From 1919 to 1922 the school was shaped by the pedagogical and aesthetic ideas of Johannes Itten, who taught the *Vorkurs* or "preliminary course" that was the introduction to the ideas of the Bauhaus. Itten was heavily influenced in his teaching by the ideas of Franz Cižek and Friedrich Wilhelm August Fröbel. He was also influenced in respect to aesthetics by the work of the *Blaue Reiter* group in Munich as well as the work of Austrian Expressionist Oskar Kokoschka. The influence of German Expressionism favoured by Itten was analogous in some ways to the fine arts side of the ongoing debate. This influence culminated with the addition of *Der Blaue Reiter* founding member Wassily Kandinsky to the faculty and ended when Itten resigned in late 1922. Itten was replaced by the Hungarian designer László Moholy-Nagy, who rewrote the *Vorkurs* with a leaning towards the New Objectivity favored by Gropius, which was analogous in some ways to the applied arts side of the debate. Although this shift was an important one, it did not represent a radical break from the past so much as a small step in a broader, more gradual socio-economic movement that had been going on at least since 1907 when van de Velde had argued for a craft basis for design while Hermann Muthesius had begun implementing industrial prototypes.

Gropius was not necessarily against Expressionism, and in fact himself in the same 1919 pamphlet proclaiming this "new guild of craftsmen, without the class snobbery," described "painting and sculpture rising to heaven out of the hands of a million craftsmen, the crystal symbol of the new faith of the future." By 1923 however, Gropius was no longer evoking images of soaring Romanesque cathedrals and the craft-driven aesthetic of the "Völkisch movement", instead declaring "we want an architecture adapted to our world of machines, radios and fast cars." Gropius argued that a new period of history had begun with the end of the war. He wanted to create a new architectural style to reflect this new era. His style in architecture and consumer goods was to be functional, cheap and consistent with mass production. To these ends, Gropius wanted to reunite art and craft to arrive at high-end functional products with artistic merit. The Bauhaus issued a magazine called *Bauhaus* and a series of books called "Bauhausbücher". Since the Weimar Republic lacked the quantity of raw materials available to the United States and Great Britain, it had to rely on the proficiency of a skilled labor force and an ability to export innovative and high quality goods. Therefore, designers were needed and so was a new type of art education. The school's philosophy stated that the artist should be trained to work with the industry.

Weimar was in the German state of Thuringia, and the Bauhaus school received state support from the Social Democrat-controlled Thuringian state government. The school in Weimar experienced political pressure from conservative

circles in Thuringian politics, increasingly so after 1923 as political tension rose.

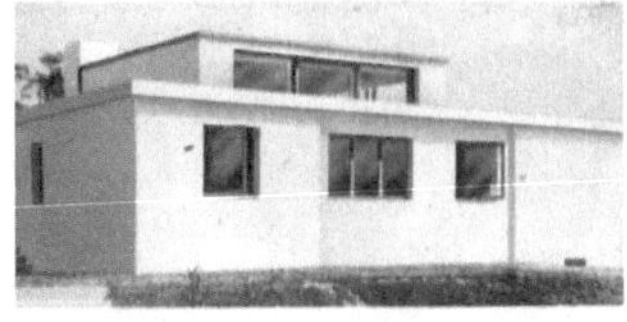

Georg Muche and Adolf Meyer, Haus am Horn, Weimar 1923.

One condition placed on the Bauhaus in this new political environment was the exhibition of work undertaken at the school. This condition was met in 1923 with the Bauhaus' exhibition of the experimental Haus am Horn. In February 1924, the Social Democrats lost control of the state parliament to the Nationalists. The Ministry of Education placed the staff on six-month contracts and cut the school's funding in half. On 26 December 1924 the Bauhaus issued a press release and setting the closure of the school for the end of March 1925. At this point they had already been looking for alternative sources of funding. After the Bauhaus moved to Dessau, a school of industrial design with teachers and staff less antagonistic to the conservative political regime remained in Weimar. This school was eventually known as the Technical University of Architecture and Civil Engineering, and in 1996 changed its name to Bauhaus-University Weimar.

Klee Mutations

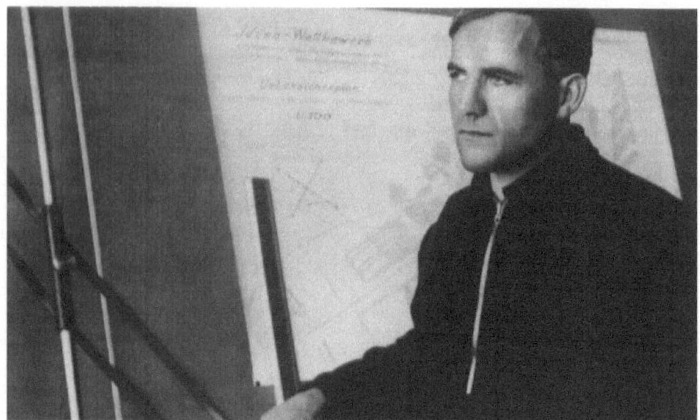

Hannes Meyer became the second Bauhuas director in February 1928

Dessau

Gropius's design for the Dessau facilities was a return to the futuristic Gropius of 1914 that had more in common with the International style lines of the Fagus Factory than the stripped down Neo-classical of the Werkbund pavilion or the Völkisch Sommerfeld House. During the Dessau years, there was a remarkable change in direction for the school. According to Elaine Hoffman, Gropius had approached the Dutch architect Mart Stam to run the newly founded architecture program, and when Stam declined the position, Gropius turned to Stam's friend and colleague in the ABC group, Hannes Meyer.

Meyer became director when Gropius resigned in February 1928, and brought the Bauhaus its two most significant building commissions, both of which still exist: five apartment buildings in the city of Dessau, and the Bundesschule des Allgemeinen Deutschen Gewerkschaftsbundes (ADGB Trade Union School) in Bernau bei Berlin. Meyer favored measurements and calculations in his presentations to clients, along with the use of off-the-shelf architectural components to reduce costs. This approach proved attractive to potential clients. The school turned its first profit under his leadership in 1929.

But Meyer also generated a great deal of conflict. As a radical functionalist, he had no patience with the aesthetic program, and forced the resignations of Herbert Bayer, Marcel Breuer, and other long-time instructors. Even though Meyer shifted the orientation of the school further to the left than it had been under Gropius, he didn't want the school to become a tool of left-wing party politics. He prevented the formation of a student communist cell, and in the increasingly dangerous political atmosphere, this became a threat to the existence of the Dessau school. Dessau mayor Fritz Hesse fired him in the summer of 1930. The Dessau city council attempted to convince Gropius to return as head of the school, but Gropius instead suggested Ludwig Mies van der Rohe. Mies was appointed in 1930, and immediately interviewed each student, dismissing those that he deemed uncommitted. Mies halted the school's manufacture of goods so that the school could focus on teaching. Mies appointed no new faculty other than his close confidant Lilly Reich. By 1931, the National Socialist German Workers' Party (Nazi Party) was becoming more influential in German politics. When they gained control of the Dessau City Council they moved to close the school.

Berlin

In late 1932, Mies rented a derelict factory in Berlin to use as the new Bauhaus with his own money. The students and faculty rehabilitated the building, painting the interior white. The school operated for ten months without further interference from the Nazi Party. In 1933, the Gestapo closed down the Berlin school. Mies protested the decision, eventually speaking to the head of the Gestapo, who agreed to allow the school to re open. However, shortly after receiving a letter permitting the opening of the Bauhaus, Mies

and the other faculty agreed to voluntarily shut down the school.

Although neither the Nazi Party nor Adolf Hitler had a cohesive architectural policy before they came to power in 1933, Nazi writers like Wilhelm Frick and Alfred Rosenberg had already labeled the Bauhaus "un-German" and criticized its modernist styles, deliberately generating public controversy over issues like flat roofs. Increasingly through the early 1930s, they characterized the Bauhaus as a front for communists and social liberals. Indeed, a number of communist students loyal to Meyer moved to the Soviet Union when he was fired in 1930.

Even before the Nazis came to power, political pressure on Bauhaus had increased. The Nazi movement, from nearly the start, denounced the Bauhaus for its "degenerate art", and the Nazi regime was determined to crack down on what it saw as the foreign, probably Jewish influences of "cosmopolitan modernism". Despite Gropius's protestations that as a war veteran and a patriot his work had no subversive political intent, the Berlin Bauhaus was pressured to close in April 1933. Emigrants did succeed, however, in spreading the concepts of the Bauhaus to other countries, including the "New Bauhaus" of Chicago: Mies decided to emigrate to the United States for the directorship of the School of Architecture at the Armour Institute (now Illinois Institute of Technology) in Chicago and to seek building commissions. The simple engineering-oriented functionalism of stripped-down modernism, however, did lead to some Bauhaus influences living on in Nazi Germany. When Hitler's chief engineer, Fritz Todt, began opening the new autobahn (highways) in 1935, many of the bridges and service stations were "bold examples of modernism" – among those submitting designs was Mies van der Rohe.

Architectural output

The paradox of the early Bauhaus was that, although its manifesto proclaimed that the aim of all creative activity was building, the school did not offer classes in architecture until 1927. During the years under Gropius (1919–1927), he and his partner Adolf Meyer observed no real distinction between the output of his architectural office and the school. So the built output of Bauhaus architecture in these years is the output of Gropius: the Sommerfeld house in Berlin,

the Otte house in Berlin, the Auerbach house in Jena, and the competition design for the Chicago Tribune Tower, which brought the school much attention. The definitive 1926 Bauhaus building in Dessau is also attributed to Gropius. Apart from contributions to the 1923 Haus am Horn, student architectural work amounted to un-built projects, interior finishes, and craft work like cabinets, chairs and pottery.

In the next two years under Meyer, the architectural focus shifted away from aesthetics and towards functionality. There were major commissions: one from the city of Dessau for five tightly designed "Laubenganghäuser" (apartment buildings with balcony access), which are still in use today, and another for the Bundesschule des Allgemeinen Deutschen Gewerkschaftsbundes (ADGB Trade Union School) in Bernau bei Berlin. Meyer's approach was to research users' needs and scientifically develop the design solution.

Mies van der Rohe repudiated Meyer's politics, his supporters, and his architectural approach. As opposed to Gropius's "study of essentials", and Meyer's research into user requirements, Mies advocated a "spatial implementation of intellectual decisions", which effectively meant an adoption of his own aesthetics. Neither van der Rohe nor his Bauhaus students saw any projects built during the 1930s.

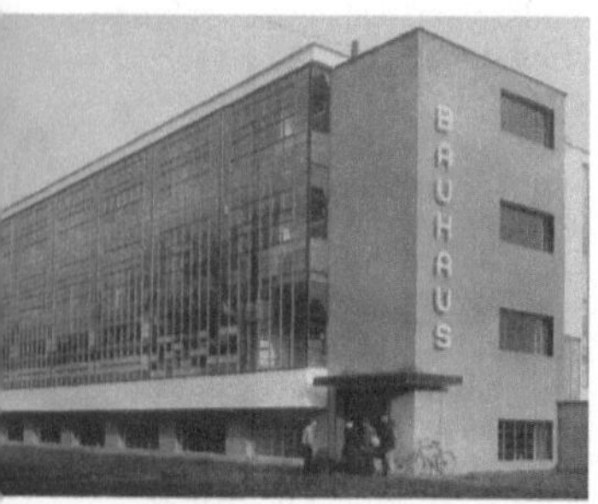

**Bauhaus Building,
Dessau, 1925-1926**

Impact

The Bauhaus had a major impact on art and architecture trends in Western Europe, the United States, Canada and Israel in the decades following its demise, as many of the artists involved fled, or were exiled by, the Nazi regime. Tel Aviv in 2004 was named to the list of world heritage sites by the UN due to its abundance of Bauhaus architecture; it had some 4,000 Bauhaus buildings erected from 1933 onwards.

In 1928, the Hungarian painter Alexander Bortnyik founded a school of design in Budapest called Miihely (also "Muhely" or "Mugely"), which means "the studio". Located on the seventh floor of a house on Nagymezo Street, it was meant to be the Hungarian equivalent to the Bauhaus. The literature sometimes refers to it – in an oversimplified manner – as "the Budapest Bauhaus". Bortnyik was a great admirer of László Moholy-Nagy and had met Walter Gropius in Weimar between 1923 and 1925. Moholy-Nagy himself taught at the Miihely. Victor Vasarely, a pioneer of Op Art, studied at this school before establishing in Paris in 1930.

Walter Gropius, Marcel Breuer, and Moholy-Nagy re-assembled in Britain during the mid 1930s to live and work in the Isokon project before the war caught up with them. Gropius and Breuer went to teach at the Harvard Graduate School of Design and worked together before their professional split.

Their collaboration produced The Aluminum City Terrace in New Kensington, Pennsylvania and the Alan I W Frank House in Pittsburgh, among other projects. The Harvard School was enormously influential in America in the late 1920s and early 1930s, producing such students as Philip Johnson, I.M. Pei, Lawrence Halprin and Paul Rudolph, among many others.

In the late 1930s, Mies van der Rohe re-settled in Chicago, enjoyed the sponsorship of the influential Philip Johnson, and became one of the pre-eminent architects in the world. Moholy-Nagy also went to Chicago and founded the New Bauhaus school under the sponsorship of industrialist and philanthropist Walter Paepcke. This school became the Institute of Design, part of the Illinois Institute of Technology. Printmaker and painter Werner Drewes was also largely responsible for bringing the Bauhaus aesthetic to America and taught at both Columbia University and Washington University in St. Louis. Herbert Bayer, sponsored by Paepcke, moved to Aspen, Colorado in support of Paepcke's Aspen projects at the Aspen Institute. In 1953, Max Bill, together with Inge Aicher-Scholl and Otl Aicher, founded the Ulm School of Design (German: Hochschule für Gestaltung – HfG Ulm) in Ulm, Germany, a design school in the tradition of the Bauhaus. The school is notable for its inclusion of semiotics as a field of study. The school closed in 1968, but the "Ulm Model" concept continues to influence international design education.

The influence of the Bauhaus on design education was significant. One of the main objectives of the Bauhaus was to unify art, craft, and technology, and this approach was incorporated into the curriculum of the Bauhaus. The structure of the Bauhaus *Vorkurs* (preliminary course) reflected a pragmatic approach to integrating theory and application. In their first year, students learnt the basic elements and principles of design and colour theory, and experimented with a range of materials and processes. This approach to design education became a common feature of architectural and design school in many countries. For example, the Shillito Design School in Sydney stands as a unique link between Australia and the Bauhaus. The colour and design syllabus of the Shillito Design School was firmly underpinned by the theories and ideologies of the Bauhaus. Its first year foundational course mimicked the *Vorkurs* and focused on the elements and principles of design plus colour theory and application. The founder of the school, Phyllis Shillito, which opened in 1962 and closed in 1980, firmly believed that "A student who has mastered the basic principles of design, can design anything from a dress to a kitchen stove".

One of the most important contributions of the Bauhaus is in the field of modern furniture design. The ubiquitous Cantilever chair and the Wassily Chair designed by Marcel Breuer are two examples. (Breuer eventually lost a legal battle in Germany with Dutch architect/designer Mart Stam over the rights to the cantilever chair patent. Although Stam had worked on the design of the Bauhaus's 1923 exhibit in Weimar, and guest-lectured at the Bauhaus later in the 1920s, he was not formally associated with the school, and he and Breuer had worked independently on the cantilever concept, thus leading to the patent dispute.) The single most profitable tangible product of the Bauhaus was its wallpaper.[1]

"The single most profitable tangible product of the Bauhaus was its wallpaper."

A scanned version of Klee's original *Pädagogisches Skizzenbuch* was made easily accessible via Monoskop– who reference Bibliothèque Kandinsky's online archive (Centre Pompidou, Paris), which published many Bauhausbücher editions online on an unknown date; an important milestone in the digitisation of essential but hard-to-get art publications for the public use:

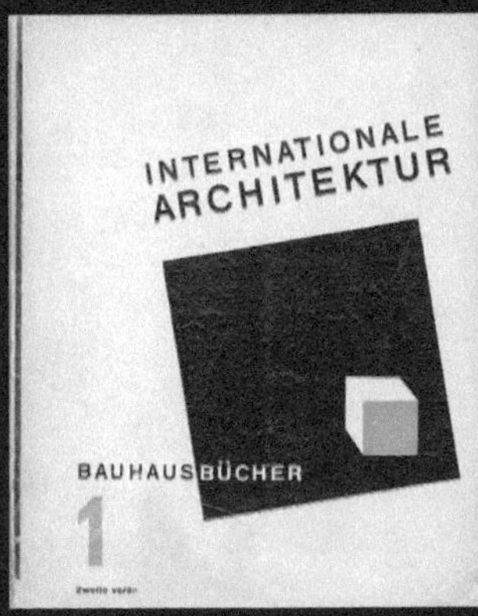

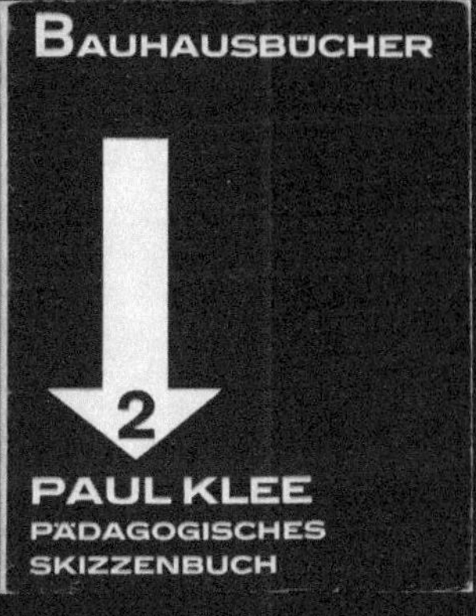

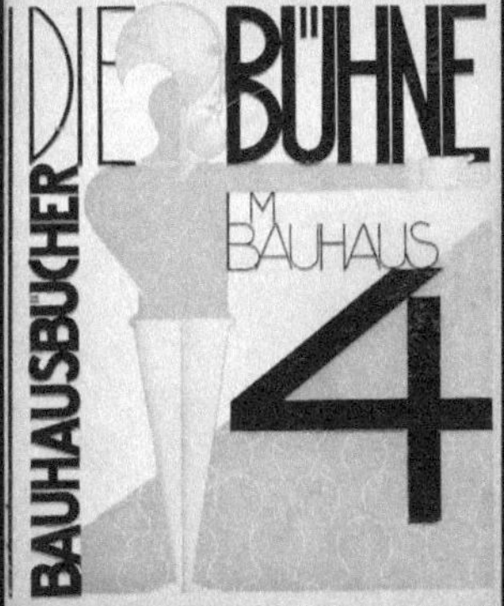

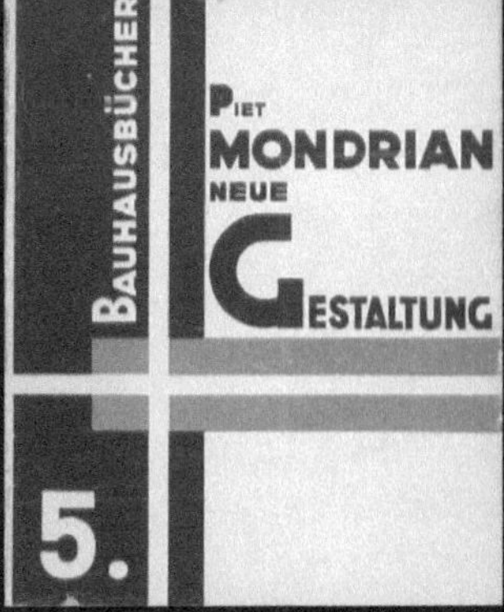

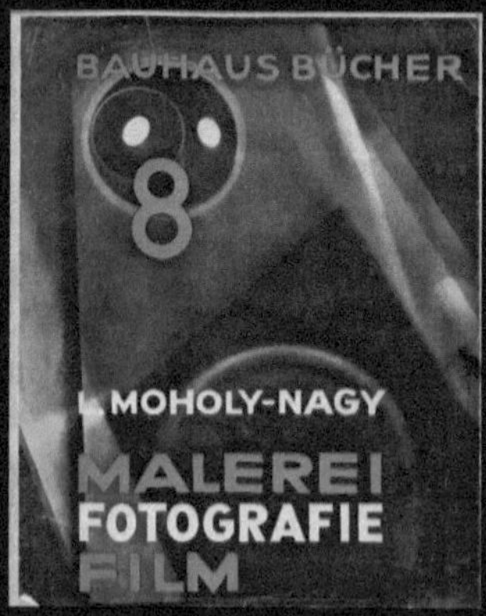

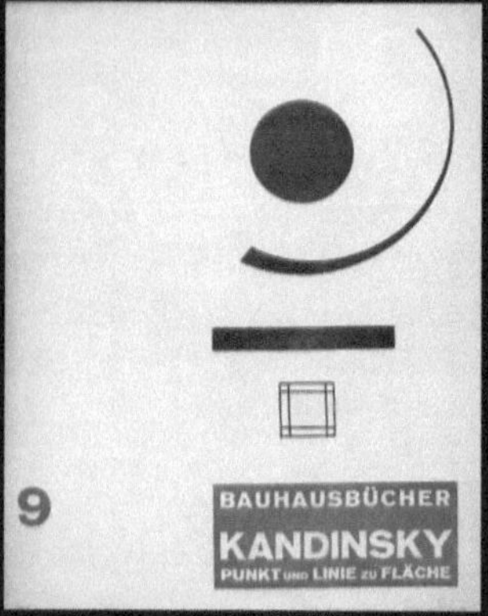

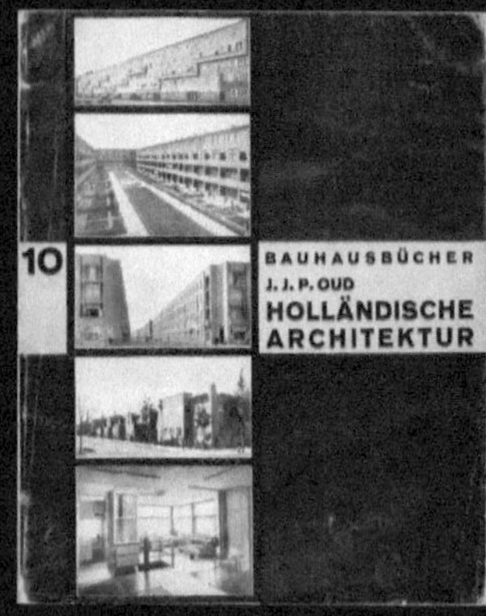

1. Walter Gropius (ed.), *Internationale Architektur*, 1925
2. Paul Klee, *Pädagogisches Skizzenbuch*, 1925
4. *Die Bühne am Bauhaus*, 1925
5. Piet Mondrian, *Neue Gestaltung, Neoplastizimus, Nieuwe Beelding*, 1925
7. Walter Gropius (ed.), *Neue Arbeiten der Bauhauswerkstäffen*, 1925
8. László Moholy-Nagy, *Malerei, Fotografie, Film*, 1925
9. Kandinsky, *Punkt und Linie zu Fläche: Beitrag zur Analyse der malerischen Elemente*, 1926
10. J.J.P. Oud, *Holländische Architektur*, 1929

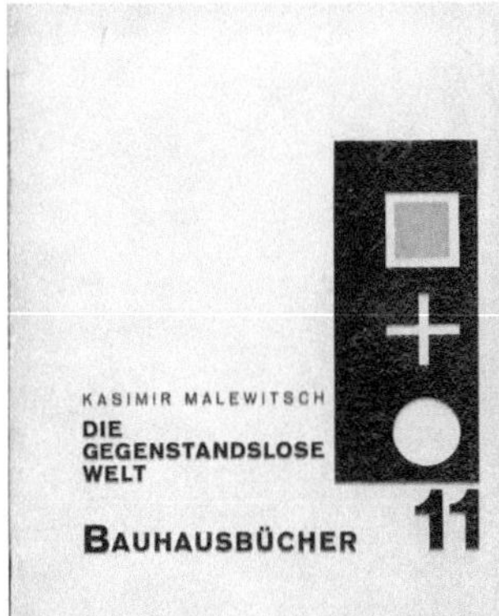

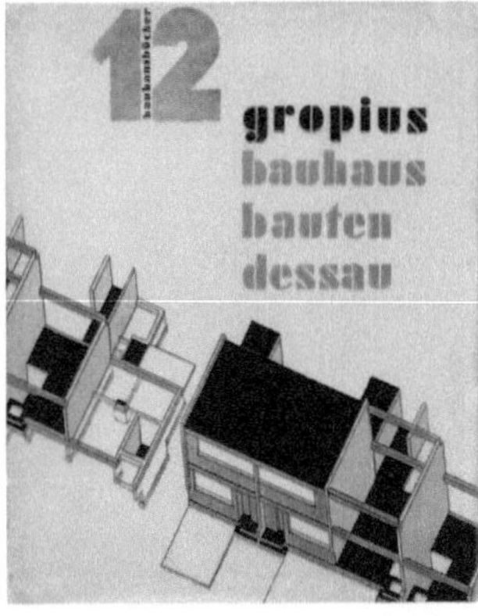

11.   Kasimir Malewitsch, *Die gegenstandslose Welt*, 1927 (Russian original, 1923)
12.   Walter Gropius, *Bauhausbauten Dessau*, 1930

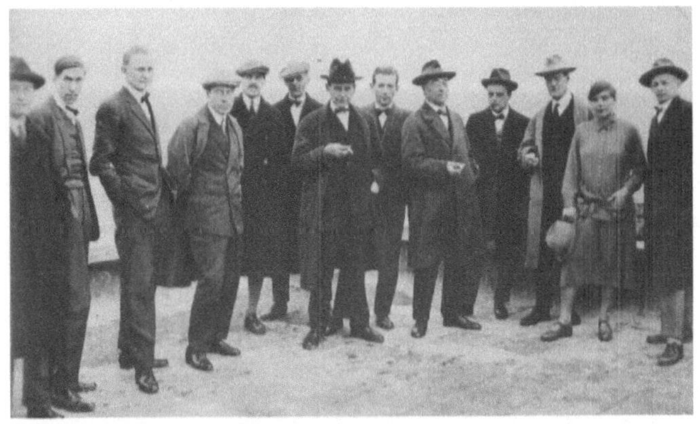

Teachers on the Roof of the Bauhaus Studio Building in Dessau, circa 1926.
L-R: Josef Albers, Hinnerk Scheper, Georg Much, László Moholy-Nagy, Herbert
Bayer, Joost Schmidt, Walter Gropius, Marcel Breuer, Wassily Kandinsky, Paul
Klee, Lyonel Feininger, Gunta Stölzl, Oskar Schlemmer.

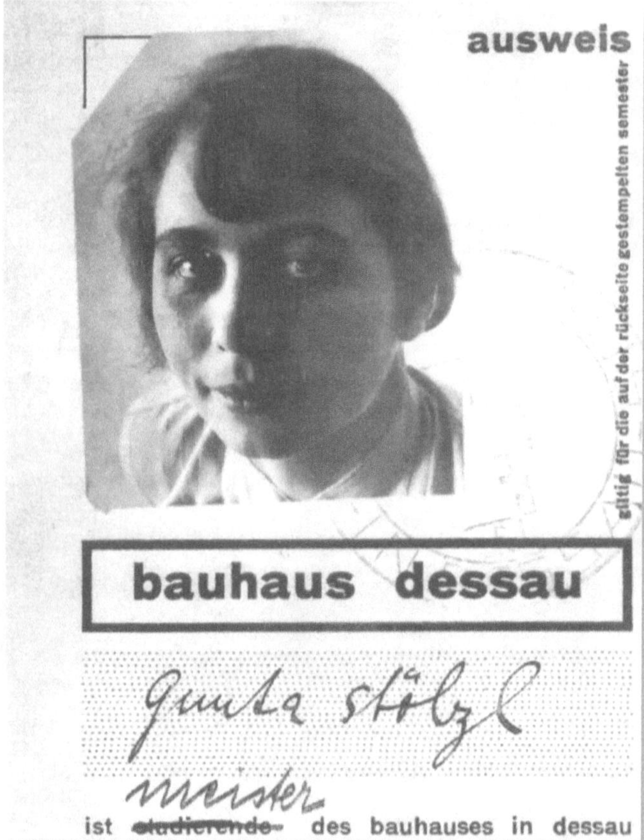

ausweis
gültig für die auf der rückseite gestempelten semester
bauhaus dessau
gunta stölzl
meister
ist studierende des bauhauses in dessau

Research mutation: Gunta Stölzl

Gunta Stölzl (1897–1983) was a German textile artist who played a fundamental role in the development of the Bauhaus school's weaving workshop. As the Bauhaus' only female master she created enormous change within the weaving department as it transitioned from individual pictorial works to modern industrial designs. Her textile work is thought to typify the distinctive style of Bauhaus textiles. She joined the Bauhaus as a student in 1920, became a junior master in 1927 and a full master the next year. She was dismissed for political reasons in 1931, two years before the Bauhaus closed under pressure from the Nazis.

"As the Bauhaus' only female master she created enormous change"

The textile department was a neglected part of the Bauhaus when Ms. Stölzl began her career, and its active masters were weak on the technical aspects of textile production. She soon became a mentor to other students and reopened the Bauhaus dye studios in 1921. After a brief departure, Stölzl became the school's weaving director in 1925 when it relocated from Weimar to Dessau and expanded the department to increase its weaving and dyeing facilities. She applied ideas from modern art to weaving, experimented with synthetic materials, and improved the department's technical instruction to include courses in mathematics. The Bauhaus weaving workshop became one of its most successful facilities under her direction.

Early life

Stölzl was born in Munich, Bavaria. She attended a high school for the daughters of professionals, graduating in 1913. She began her studies at the Kunstgewerbeschule (School of Applied Arts) in 1914, where she studied glass painting, decorative arts and ceramics under the well known director Richard Riemerschmid. In 1917 Stölzl's studies were interrupted by the ongoing war and she volunteered to work as a nurse for the Red Cross, behind the front lines until the end of World War I in 1918. Upon her return home she re-immersed herself in her studies at the Kunstgewerbeschule in Munich, where she participated in the school's curriculum reform. It was during this time that Stölzl encountered the Bauhaus manifesto. Having decided to continue her studies at the newly formed Bauhaus school, Stölzl spent the summer of 1919 in the glass workshop and mural painting classes of the Bauhaus to earn her trial acceptance into Johannes Itten's preliminary

Klee Mutations

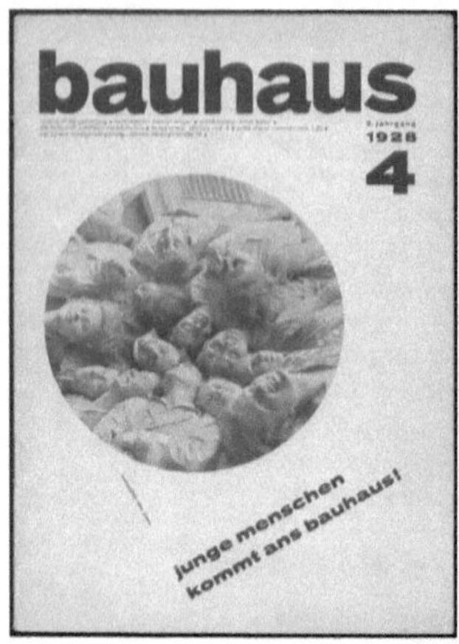

The Bauhaus journal: *zeitschrift für gestaltung*, featuring Gunta Stölzl on the front cover (1928).

course. By 1920, Stölzl had not only been fully accepted into the Bauhaus school, but had received a scholarship to attend.

Student life

Within Stölzl's first year at the Bauhaus, she began what she referred to as the "women's department", which due to the underlying gender roles within the school, eventually became synonymous with the weaving workshop. Stölzl was very active within the weaving department and was immediately seen as a leader among the pack. At the time, the department was putting emphasis on artistic expression and individual works that reflected the teachings and philosophies of the painters who served as Bauhaus masters. The Weimar Bauhaus had a very relaxed atmosphere that was almost wholly dependent on the students teaching themselves and one another. Unfortunately, Georg Muche, who was the head of the weaving workshop at the time, had very little interest in the craft itself. He saw weaving and other textile arts as 'women's work' and thus was of very little help with the technical processes involved. This meant the students were left to their own devices to figure out all technical aspects of a craft most had little experience working in. Due to this set-up, it is important to look at the Weimar era works visually as opposed to technically.

In 1921 Stölzl and two of her friends made a trip to Italy to view the art and architecture they had studied for further inspiration. After passing her journeyman's examination as a weaver and taking courses in textile dyeing at a school in Krefeld, Stölzl was able to reopen the previously abandoned dye studios. It was becoming obvious that she was giving direction to the other students, though unofficially, as neither Muche, the form master nor Helene Börner, the crafts master, could really teach and promote the students in technical aspects. In 1921, Stölzl collaborated with Marcel Breuer on the African Chair – made of painted wood with a colorful textile weave. The first official Bauhaus exhibition took place in September 1923 in the Haus am Horn building. The building itself, primarily designed by Georg Muche, was a simplistic, highly modern cube structure made largely of steel and concrete. Each room of the house was designed around its specific function and had specially made furniture, hardware etc., which had been produced in the Bauhaus workshops. The weaving workshop participated by creating rugs, wall hangings and other objects for various rooms all of which won favorable reviews. With this exhibition, Walter Gropius released an essay titled 'Art and Technology – A New Unity' which seemed to have a great impact on the women of the weaving workshop. Despite the favorable reviews of their works, the women began to move away from the pictorial imagery and traditional methods they had been working with up to this point and began working abstractly, attempting to make objects more in line with Kandinsky's teachings of the 'inner self'.

she was not officially made a junior master until 1927, it was clear both the organization and content of the workshop were under her control. It was obvious from the start, the pairing of Muche and Stölzl was not enjoyed by either side, and resulted in Stölzl running the workshop almost single-handedly from 1926 onward.

The new Dessau campus was equipped with a greater variety of looms and much improved dyeing facilities, which allowed Stölzl to create a more structured environment. Georg Muche brought in Jacquard looms to help intensify production. He saw this as especially important now as the workshops were the school's main source of funding for the new Dessau Bauhaus. The students rejected this and were not happy with the way Muche had used the schools funds.

"Don't shrink from chaos .. take from it things that seem to represent life, and give shape to them." —Gunta Stölzl, diary entry, Bauhaus Weimar

Bauhaus master

In April 1925, the Weimar Bauhaus closed and reopened in Dessau in 1926. Stölzl, who had previously left the Bauhaus upon graduating to help Itten set up Ontos Weaving Workshops in Herrliberg, near Zurich, Switzerland, returned to become the weaving studio's technical director, replacing Helene Börner, and work with Georg Muche, who would remain the form master. Although

This, among other smaller events, instigated a student uprising within the weaving department. On March 31, 1927, despite some staff objections, Muche left the Bauhaus. With his departure, Stölzl took over both as form master and master crafts person of the weaving studio. She was assisted by many other key Bauhaus women, including Anni Albers, Otti Berger and Benita Otte.

Stölzl began trying to move weaving away from its

Klee Mutations

'woman's work' connotations
by applying the vocabulary
used in modern art, moving
weaving more and more in the
direction of industrial design.
By 1928, the need for practical
materials was highly stressed
and experimentation with
materials such as cellophane
became more prominent. Stölzl
quickly developed a curriculum
which emphasized the use
of handlooms, training in the
mechanics of weaving and
dyeing, and taught classes in
math and geometry, as well as
more technical topics such as
weave techniques and workshop
instruction. The earlier Bauhaus
methods of artistic expression
were quickly replaced by a design
approach which emphasized
simplicity and functionality.
Stölzl considered
the workshop a place for
experimentation and encouraged
improvisation. She and her
students, especially Anni
Albers, were very interested
in the properties of a fabric
and in synthetic fibers. They
tested materials for qualities
such as color, texture, structure,
resistance to wear, flexibility, light
refraction and sound absorption.
Stölzl believed the challenge
of weaving was to create an
aesthetic that was appropriate
to the properties of the material.
In 1930, Stölzl issued the first
ever Bauhaus weaving workshop
diplomas and set up the first
joint project between the
Bauhaus and the Berlin Polytex
Textile company which wove
and sold Bauhaus designs. In
1931 she published an article
entitled "The Development of the
Bauhaus Weaving Workshop",
in the Bauhaus Journal spring
issue. Stölzl's ability to translate
complex formal compositions into
hand woven pieces combined
with her skill of designing for
machine production made her
by far the best instructor the
weaving workshop was to have.
Under Stölzl's direction, the
weaving workshop became one of
the most successful faculties of
the Bauhaus.

Dismissal

The school was constantly
under attack as the Nazi Party
gained more power, and the
school's sacrifices to remain
open were beginning to break
its own ideology. During Mies
van der Rohe's directorship
there was intense pressure from
the community for Stölzl to be
let go. Van der Rohe required
her resignation in 1931, not due
to incompetence but because
of the surrounding political
atmosphere. The students were
so opposed to this unjust action
they dedicated an entire issue
of the school journal to Stölzl
upon her dismissal. The Dessau
campus of the Bauhaus was
closed in 1932 by the Nazis, and
the Bauhaus itself, which had
moved from Dessau to Berlin,
officially dissolved, by vote of the
faculty, on 19 July 1933.[2]

Drawing is not the reproduction
of what is seen, but making
whatever one senses through
external stimulus flow through
one's entire body . . .

"The students were so opposed to this unjust action they dedicated an entire issue of the school journal to Stölzl upon her dismissal."

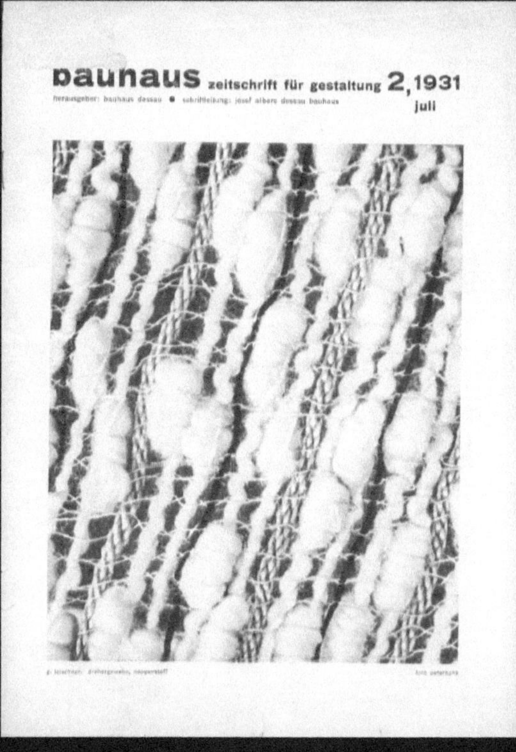

The Bauhaus' *zeitschrift für gestaltung*, students dedicated an entire issue to Stölzl upon her controversial dismissal in 1931

am 1. oktober d. j. verläßt frau gunta sharon-stölzl das bauhaus. mit ihr verliert unsere weberei-werkstatt ihre langjährige leiterin, der sie aufbau, entscheidende entwicklung und erfolg verdankt. daß man von bauhausstoffen spricht, ist ihr verdienst.

---

die entwicklung
der bauhausweberei
von gunta sharon-stölzl.

bauhausmädchen der ersten zeiten versuchten sich in jeder werkstatt: tischlerei, wandmalerei, metallwerkstatt, töpferei, buchbinderei.

bald zeigte sich, daß der schwere hobel, das harte metall, das anstreichen von wänden für manche nicht die betätigung war, die den psychischen und physischen kräften entsprach. die seele blieb dabei hungrig! handwerk mußte es sein! wir kamen ja fast alle von akademien und kunstgewerbeschulen und wollten uns befreien von dem trockenen mal- und zeichenleben. wir wollten lebendige dinge schaffen für unser heutiges dasein, für eine neue lebensgestaltung. wir gründeten eine frauenklasse. unsere ersten taten waren kinderspielzeuge, aus bunten lappen, holz, draht, glasperlen und knöpfen, stroh, gummischwämmchen und pelzresten bastelten wir flammend begeistert „urtiere und urmenschen" zusammen. die fanatik — die starke ausdruckskraft maximal kontrastierender materie hatte es uns angetan! unsere fantasiestrotzenden werke haben wir mit anderen ersten bauhauskuriositäten zusammen in einer „dadabude" auf dem weihnachtsmarkt von weimar einer jubelnden kinderschar für einen groschen verkauft.

das spielen mit der materie wurde ernster — wir versuchten mit neueroberten elementen bildmäßig zu komponieren, wandbelebende fläche, wandbild zu schaffen. die verschiedenen materialien mußten geordnet werden nach ihren werten: struktur, farbe, plastik, helldunkel, griffwerten wie weich — hart, rauh — glatt. sie mußten aus der sphäre des unbewußten gelöst werden, um brauchbare elemente neuer gestaltung zu sein. für dieses schaffen, dieses umwerten von erlebnissen gab es keine schablone der vergangenheit, kein technisches, kein geistiges rezept. wir suchten mit der neuen generation der bauhausmaler in dem wirbelnden chaos von kunstwerten herum, voll begeisterung für unsere taten, voll hoffnung für unseren selbständigen weg.

die materialnot der ersten nachkriegsjahre fing an sich aufzulockern, wir konnten uns endlich rohmaterial beschaffen. damit endeten im allgemeinen die flickenkompositionen. wir wandten uns der weberei zu. inhalt und ziel war auch auf diesem neuen arbeitsgebiet das „wandbild" — der gobelin. mit einem großen unterschied: bisher kombinierten wir vorhandene, festbegrenzte werte zu einem einheitlichen ganzen, während wir jetzt sozusagen an die q u e l l e der elemente, die zur gewebten fläche führen, gelangten. um die kümmerlichen reste einer bildwirkerei-tradition brauchten wir uns nicht zu kümmern — denn vor uns lag ein riesiges experimentierfeld. es galt, unsere vorstellungswelt zu präzisieren, unsere erlebnisse zu gestalten durch material, rhythmus, proportion, farbe form. allein schon die farbe, die in jedem material (wolle, seide, leinen) ein anderes ganz spezielles leben hat, stellte uns vor die tiefsten und umfassendsten probleme. diese spekulative arbeit am gobelin führte uns ganz natürlich

dazu, unsere erfahrungen für die praktische weberei auszuwerten. der schritt vom hochwebstuhl zum flachwebstuhl — vom gobelinstopfen zum weben — bedeutete eine große erweiterung unserer möglichkeiten.

das weben ist ein altes handwerk, das seine gesetzmäßigkeiten entwickelt hat, auf dem auch der mechanische webstuhl heute noch aufbauen muß. handwerkliche geschicklichkeit, können und wissen, müssen gründlich erlernt werden und sind nicht, wie beim gobelin, aus einfallskraft und künstlerischem empfinden zu ernähren. die auseinandersetzung mit dem flachwebstuhl hatte ganz natürlich zur folge: beschränkung der materialien, mäßigung der farbe, bindung der form an den webvorgang. umgekehrt beschränkt und bindet der zweck eines stoffes die wahl der elemente. funktionsfolgerungen sind immer abhängig von der auffassung des lebens und wohnens. 1922—23 hatten wir eine wesentlich andere wohnvorstellung als heute. unsere stoffe durften noch ideenschwere dichtungen, blumiges dekor, individuelles erlebnis sein! sie fanden auch außerhalb der bauhausmauern rasch anklang in ziemlich breiter öffentlichkeit — sie waren die leichtverständlichsten, auf grund der materie die einschmeichelndsten produkte dieser wildrevolutionierenden bauhauserzeugnisse.

allmählich trat eine wandlung ein. wir fühlten, wie anspruchsvoll diese selbständigen einzelstücke seien: decke, vorhang, wandbehang. der reichtum von farbe und form wurde uns zu selbstherrlich, er fügte sich nicht ein, er ordnete sich dem wohnen nicht unter. wir suchten uns zu vereinfachen, unsere mittel zu disziplinieren, materialgerechter, zweckbestimmter zu werden. damit kamen wir zu meterstoffen, die eindeutig dem raum, dem wohnproblem dienen konnten. die parole dieser neuen epoche: „modelle für die industrie!"

mit dem übergang nach dessau bekam die weberei, wie alle anderen werkstätten und abteilungen, neue gesündere voraussetzungen. die verschiedensten webstuhl-systeme — kontermarsch — schaftmaschine — jacquardmaschine — teppichknüpfstuhl konnten angeschafft werden. dazu alle zur einrichtung der webstühle nötigen apparaturen — eine eigene färberei. gründliche technische und theoretische schulung (ausbildung von gesellen) wurden festgelegt. ziel der allgemeinen ausbildung war, den lernenden aufzulockern, ihm eine möglichst breite basis und die richtung für einen systematischen aufbau seiner arbeit zu geben.

von jetzt ab trennen sich zwei gebiete der pädagogik, anfänglich miteinander verschmolzen, scharf und endgültig voneinander:

d i e e n t w i c k l u n g z u m g e b r a u c h s s t o f f für den innenausbau (typen für die industrie) und
s p e k u l a t i v e a u s e i n a n d e r s e t z u n g mit materie, form, farbe in gobelin und teppich.

gebrauchsstoffe unterliegen zwangsläufig exakten technischen und begrenzten, aber immerhin variablen gestaltungsforderungen. die technischen forderungen: reißfestigkeit, scheuerfestigkeit, elastizität, dehnbarkeit, lichtdurchlässigkeit oder undurchlässigkeit, farbenechtheit,

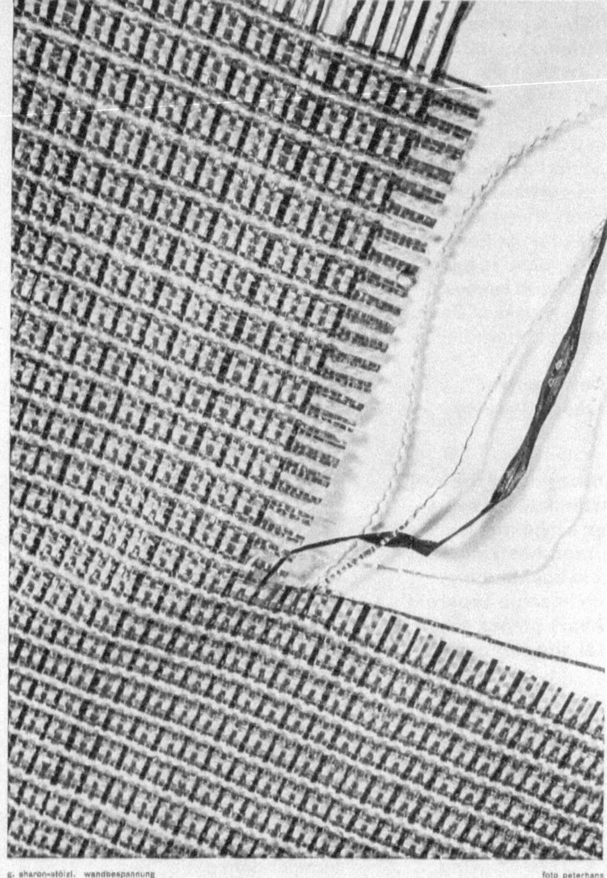

g. sharon-stölzl. wandbespannung   foto peterhans

Research mutation: Translation of *zeitschrift für gestaltung* for Stölzl

*Bauhaus Magazine
for Design*, July 1931
Bauhaus Dessau
Josef Albers

On the 1st October, Gunta Sharon-Stölzl left the Bauhaus. With her departure, our weaving workshop loses its longtime leader; its founder who was so crucial to its development and success. That anyone speaks of Bauhaus textiles is to her merit.

*The Development
of Bauhaus Weaving*
Gunta Stölzl

The Bauhaus girls of the early times participated in every workshop: carpentry, wall painting, metalworking, pottery and bookbinding.

It soon became apparent that the heavy planer, the hard metal, the painting of walls, was not, for some, the activity corresponding to their psychical and physical forces. The soul was hungry! It must have a craft! Almost all of us came from academies and art colleges and wanted to free ourselves from the dry painting and life-drawing. We wanted to create living things for our present day. For a new lifestyle. We founded a women's class. Our first creations were children's toys, made of colored laps, wood, wire, glass beads and buttons, straw, rubber wicks and fur rests, we were blazingly enthusiastic "primordial animals and primordial beings" working together. The fanatics – the strong expressive power of maximum contrast-render matter had changed us! At the Christmas Market of Weimar, we sold our imaginative-bursts in a "dadabude" together with other early Bauhaus-curiosities, earning ourselves a jubbling children's coffin of groschen."

Working with textiles became more serious - we attempted to create a new image with new elements, a wall-creating surface: wall-painting. The various textiles had to be ordered according to their values: structure, color, plastic, light – dark, grip values like soft – hard, rough – smooth. They had to be detached from the sphere of the unconscious, in order to be useful elements of a new form. For these creations, we needed to re-evaluate our experience: there was no template of the past, no instructions and no mental recipe. Side by side with a new generation of Bauhaus students, we were looking around for artifacts in the chaos, full of enthusiasm for our endevours, full of hope for our independent path.

The scarcity of textiles during the first years of the war began to loosen up, we were finally able to procure raw materials. Thus usually ending the flip-flop positions.

We turned to weaving. Our content and goal was the "wall-painting" – the tapestry – so far, in this new field of work: we have combined existing, fixed values into one uniform whole, while now we are exploring the processes of elements that lead to woven fabric. We did not have to worry about the miserable remnants of a tradition of image or sculpture, because before us lay a huge field of experimentation, it was our aim to create our world of ideas, to shape our experiences through material, rhythm, proportion, color and form. The color, which has a special, different life in every material (wool, silk, linen), presented us with the deepest and most comprehensive problems. This speculative work with tapestry led us, of course, to use our experience for practical weaving. A shift from the loom to the flat loom – from the gobelin plug to weaving – meant a great expansion our possibilities.

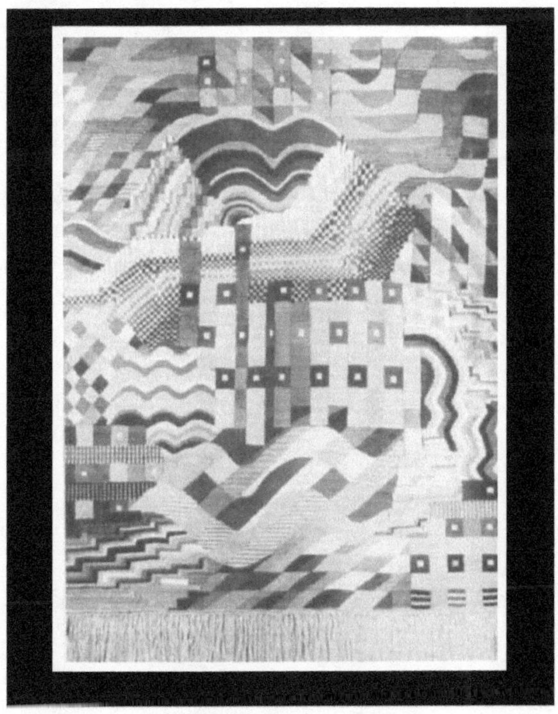

Guntha Sharon-Stözl Tapestry, 1927

A RETURN TO THE FOUNT OF MUTANT PEDAGOGY

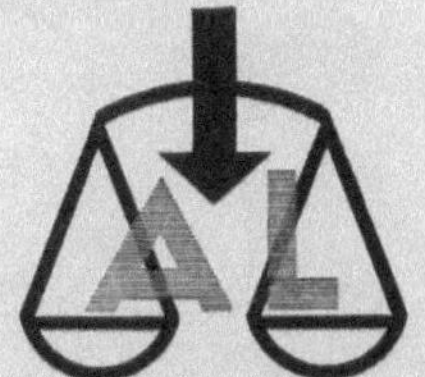

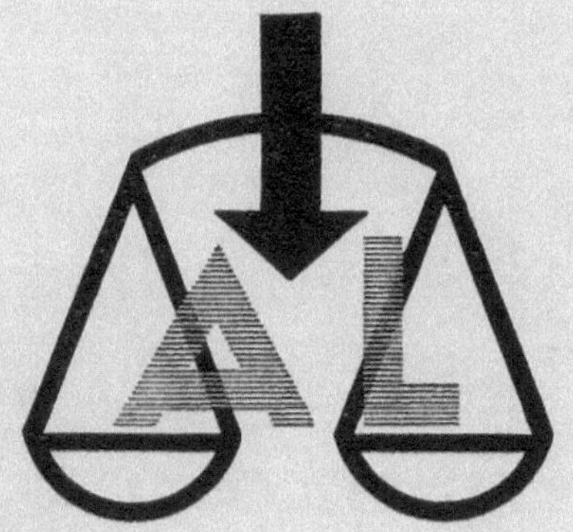

The logomark on the opening page of *Pädagogisches Skizzenbuch*

Research mutation: The A.L. Logo

The logomark which appears on page one of *Pädagogisches Skizzenbuch* belongs to the German publisher, Albert Langen Verlag München, founded by Albert Langen (1869 – 1909).

Langen was also founder of the satirical publication *Simplicissimus*; the most prominent German political-satirical weekly of the time. The name stands for the anticlerical, antifeudal and fundamentally democratic criticism of the domestic and foreign policy of the imperial empire and the Weimar Republic, as well as for pointed criticism of the average German citizen. For literary, historical and sociological questions in the context of the two world wars, the magazine offers an irreplaceable source material. Founded on April 1, 1896 the magazine soon became a forum for the artistic and literary avant-garde of the time.[1]

Early years

Langen was the third of four children born to Antwerp industrialist Friedrich Albert Langen and Ida Goeters. After the death of Langen's grandfather, Johann Jacob Langen, the family moved to Cologne on Jacordenstrasse, where Langen and his siblings grew up and where his younger sister, Elizabeth, was born.

After a clerical apprenticeship, Langen moved to Paris in 1890 to be trained as a painter. There, he became acquainted with many French writers, including Henry Becque, Abel Hermant, Paul Hervieu, Octave Mirbeau, and Émile Zola, as well as artists including Théophile Alexandre Steinlen (then a chief illustrator for Parisian literary periodical *Gil Blas Illustré*), who was to become a lifelong friend.

Langen also found a mentor in the Dane Julius Rudolph Wilhelm Petersen, who had lived in Paris since 1890 under the name Willy Gretor. Gretor was an outgoing adventurer and con man, who was a painter, poet, art dealer, and forger.

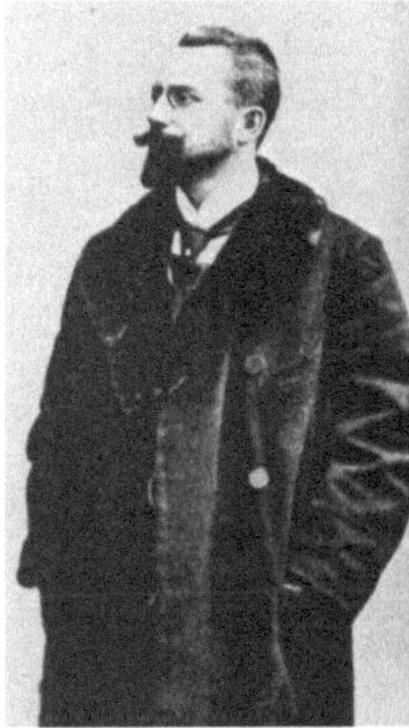

Albert Langen, circa 1894-1898

Klee Mutations

Langen took over Gretor's grandiose apartment on the Boulevard Malesherbes, along with expensive furniture and an extensive collection of images (including some, it was said, of dubious authenticity). Inspired by Gretor, Langen considered opening an art gallery, but an encounter with the author Knut Hamsun, whom he also met through Gretor, led him in a different direction. Hamsun's novel *Mysterien* had been rejected by S. Fischer Verlag, but Langen was so moved by a German translation of the work (by Marie von Borch) that he offered to pay Samuel Fischer for the printing costs.

When this still failed, Langen founded a publishing house to bring out the work himself. Hamsum's *Mysteries*, thus, came out in 1894 as the first title under the Langen imprint.

The following year, the publisher first moved to Leipzig and then to Munich. In addition to Scandinavian authors such as Bjørnstjerne Bjørnson, Georg Brandes, and Sven Lange, Langen also expanded into contemporary French and German literature.

His first German title, *Wedekind's Der Erdgeist (The Earth Spirit)*, was published in 1895. He was especially successful with paperback editions with signature bindings of, at first primarily French, artists such as Jules Chéret, Théophile Alexandre Steinlen, and especially Thomas Theodor Heine.[2]

Exile

In 1898 Kaiser Wilhelm's objections to being ridiculed on the cover of *Simplicissimus* resulted in the magazine

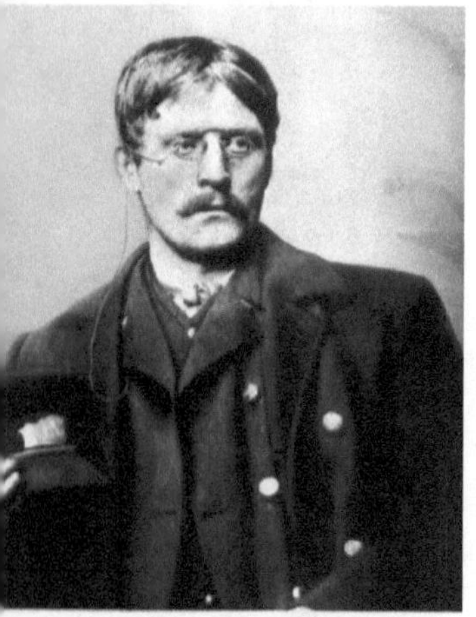

Knut Hamsun in 1884

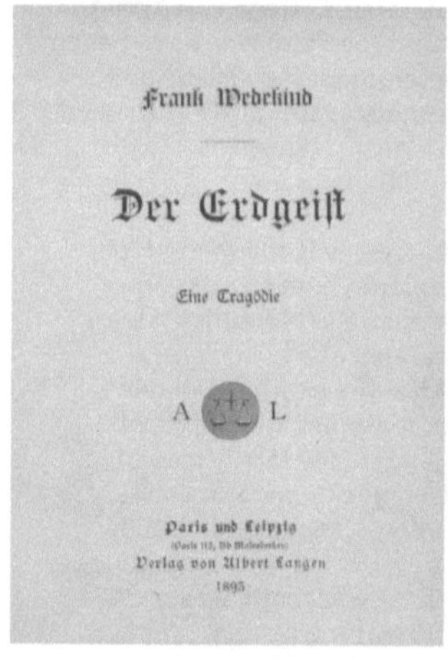

Wedekind's Der Erdgeist, 1895

being suppressed. Langen, the publisher, spent five years' exile in Switzerland and was fined 30,000 German gold marks. A six-month prison sentence was given to the cartoonist Heine, and seven months to the writer Frank Wedekind. Again in 1906 the editor Ludwig Thoma was imprisoned for six months for attacking the clergy. These controversies only served to increase circulation, which peaked at about 85,000 copies. Upon Germany's entry into World War I, the weekly dulled its satirical tone, began supporting the war effort and considered closing down. Thereafter, the strongest political satire expressed in graphics became the province of artists George Grosz and Käthe Kollwitz (who were both contributors) and John Heartfield.[3]

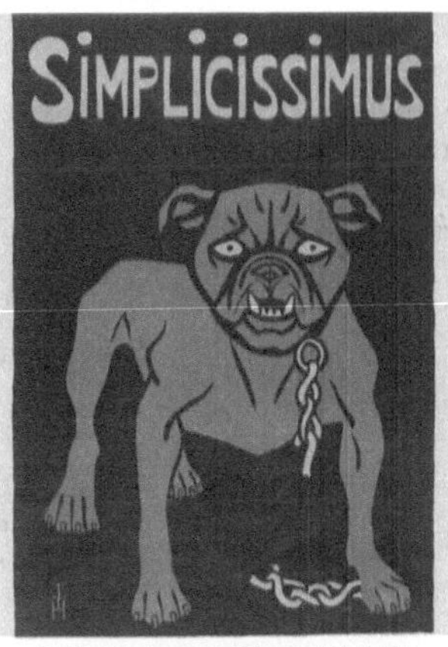

Bulldog Poster (Mops-Plakat) by Thomas Theodor Heine for *Simplicissimus*, **1896**

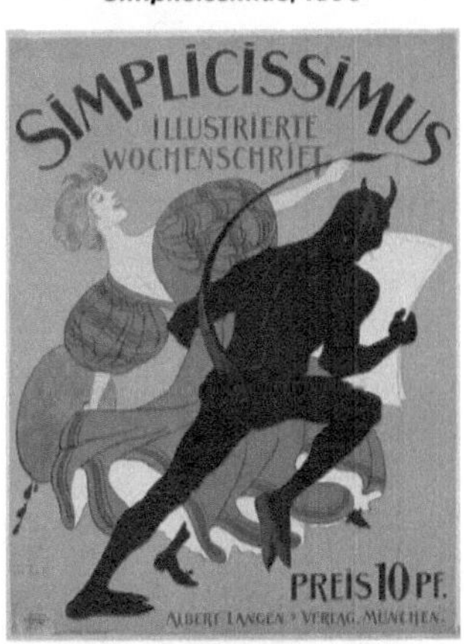

***Simplicissimus*, 1896 cover by Thomas Theodor Heine**

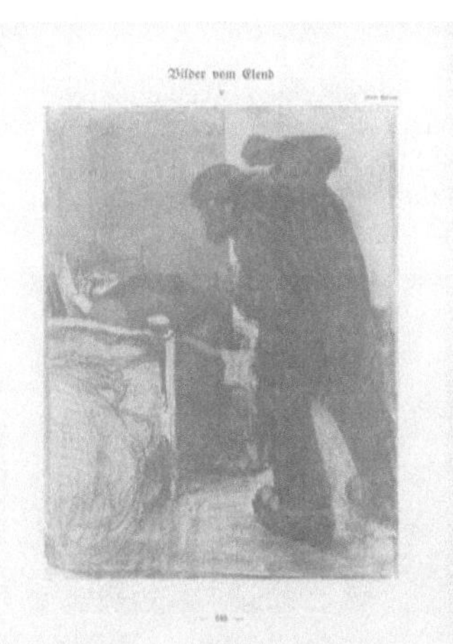

'Pictures of the Misery V' by Käthe Kollwitz for *Simplicissimus*, **1910**

Legacy

Langen is especially known for his contribution to modern book design. Heine and Bruno Paul were his most important book artists (designing the covers, dust jackets, vignettes, and illustrations), but both worked quite differently. Heine's drawing style was very fluid, whereas Paul presented strong blocking of surfaces and colors. Both artists were clearly influenced by the Art Nouveau. Other illustrators included Ferdinand von Reznicek, Eduard Thöny and the Norwegian Olaf Gulbransson who joined the firm in 1902 and whose minimalist drawing style eventually became as indispensable for *Simplicissimus* as Heine's.

Langen was not a typical publisher, in that he ran the company not only out of economic considerations, but also with a cultural-political mission. His main Kulturverleger rival at the time, Samuel Fischer, also chose modernity as a focal point. Several writers (including Henrik Ibsen, Jakob Wasserman, and Ludwig Thoma) briefly published with Langen but then returned to S. Fischer, whose earlier entry into the market (in 1886) proved insurmountable.

Within ten years, Langen had published 389 books by 117 authors.[4] In 1904, a catalogue was published promoting forthcoming titles and the back catalogue, featuring caricatures of the authors by Thomas Theodor Heine and Olaf Gulbransson – and author biographies which Langen had the authors write themselves.

On April 30, 1909, Albert Langen died – in his will, Langen had employed four long-term collaborators (Otto Friedrich, Reinhold Geheeb , August Gommel and Korfiz Holm) as curators for the publishing house. They operated the enterprise and eventually acquired it in 1918. In the 1920s the Bauhausbüchers (edited by Walter Gropius and Lászlo Moholy-Nagy) were published by Langen Verlag

In 1931, the publisher entered into a partnership with Georg Müller Verlag and the following year merged into Langenmüller Verlag.

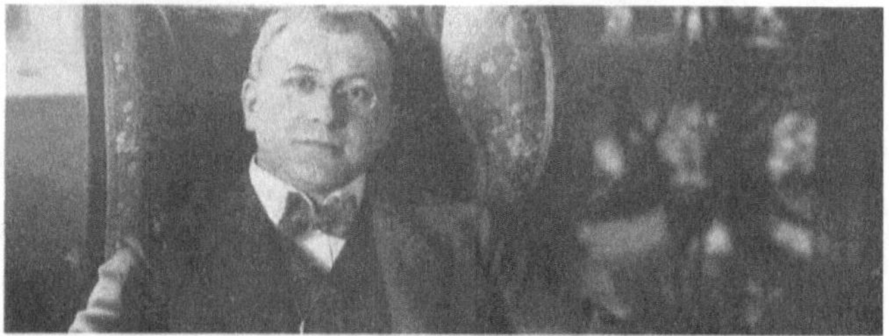

Albert Langen (1869-1909) in the volume of *Hermann Hesse: A chronicle in pictures* (1909, Stadtarchiv München)

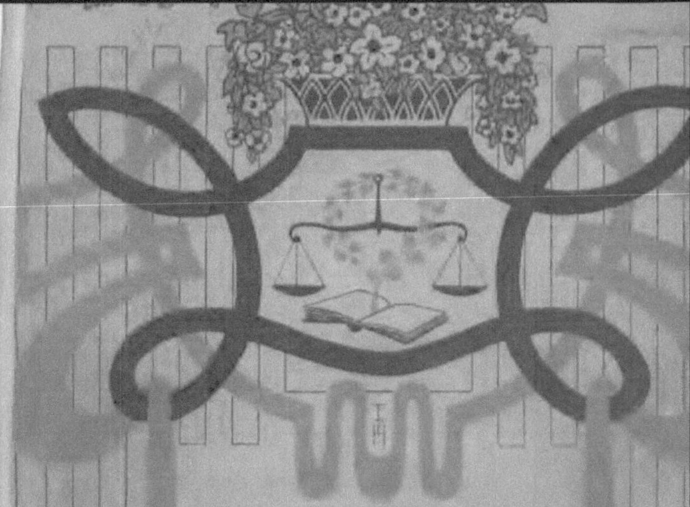

Albert Langens

Verlags=Katalog

1894 — 1904

36 Selbstbiographien der Verlagsautoren

57 Karikaturen
von O. Gulbransson und Th. Th. Heine

Ausgabe auf besserem Papier, Preis 2 Mark

52

Werke von Friedrich Hahn

Dämonen
> Erzählung
> Geheftet 2 Mark, gebunden 3 Mark

Fremdenblatt, Wien: Dieses ... Buch führt uns in meisterhaften Strichen die Geschichte eines Irren vor. Sie ist fesselnd, mit scharf treffender Psychologie geschrieben und das Milieu bei allem Dämonenhaften von einem ganz besonderen Reiz. Im ganzen ein interessantes Buch, das gelesen zu werden verdient.

Knut Hamsun

Ich bitte Sie, so freundlich zu sein, die Biographie selbst zu schreiben. Beginnen Sie mit dem 4. August 1860, wo ich geboren wurde, und fahren Sie mit vielen schönen Worten fort bis zu diesem Jahre.

Denn: was soll ich eigentlich sagen? Ich glaube, daß die Leute todmüde sind von all den Biographien und Bildern sämtlicher Autoren der Welt. Und unsrer sind so viele ...

Werke von Knut Hamsun

Hunger
> Roman
> Berechtigte Übersetzung von Maria von Borch
> Umschlagzeichnung von Th. Th. Heine
> Dritte Auflage
> Geheftet 3.50 Mark, gebunden 4.50 Mark

Berliner Neueste Nachrichten: ... Auch diesem Buche ist der Erfolg zu gönnen. Hamsun zählt lange schon zu den interessantesten Autoren, die uns die skandinavische Schule geschenkt hat. Seine Werke zeichnen sich durch eine so feine Detailzeichnung aus bei einer oft starken dramatisch bewegten Handlung, daß man sich der Stimmung, die dieser Dichter auszugießen versteht, nicht entziehen kann.

Mysterien
> Roman
> Berechtigte Übersetzung von Maria von Borch
> Zweite, durchgesehene Auflage
> Geheftet 4 Mark, gebunden 5 Mark

Frankfurter Zeitung: ... Es gibt in der modernen Litteratur kein ähnliches Bild einer genialischen Natur, über die der Wahnsinn beständig seine Schatten zu breiten sucht ... Ein großer Dichter, ein glänzender und scharfsinniger Geist hat diese „Mysterien" geschaffen.

Knut Hamsun's biographical contribution to *Verlagskatalog*:

I beg of you [Albert Langen], as kindly as possible, to write the biography for me. Begin with the 4th of August 1860, when I was born, and continue with very few words up to this year.

For what am I supposed to say? I believe that people are dead tired of all the biographies and pictures of authors of the world. We find so many ...

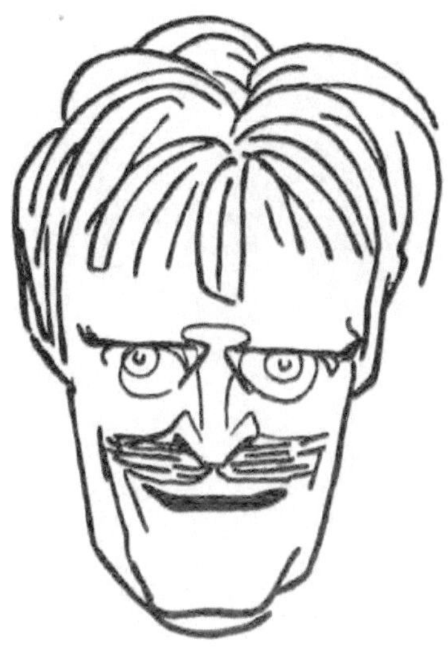

The accompanying author illustration by Olaf Gulbransson

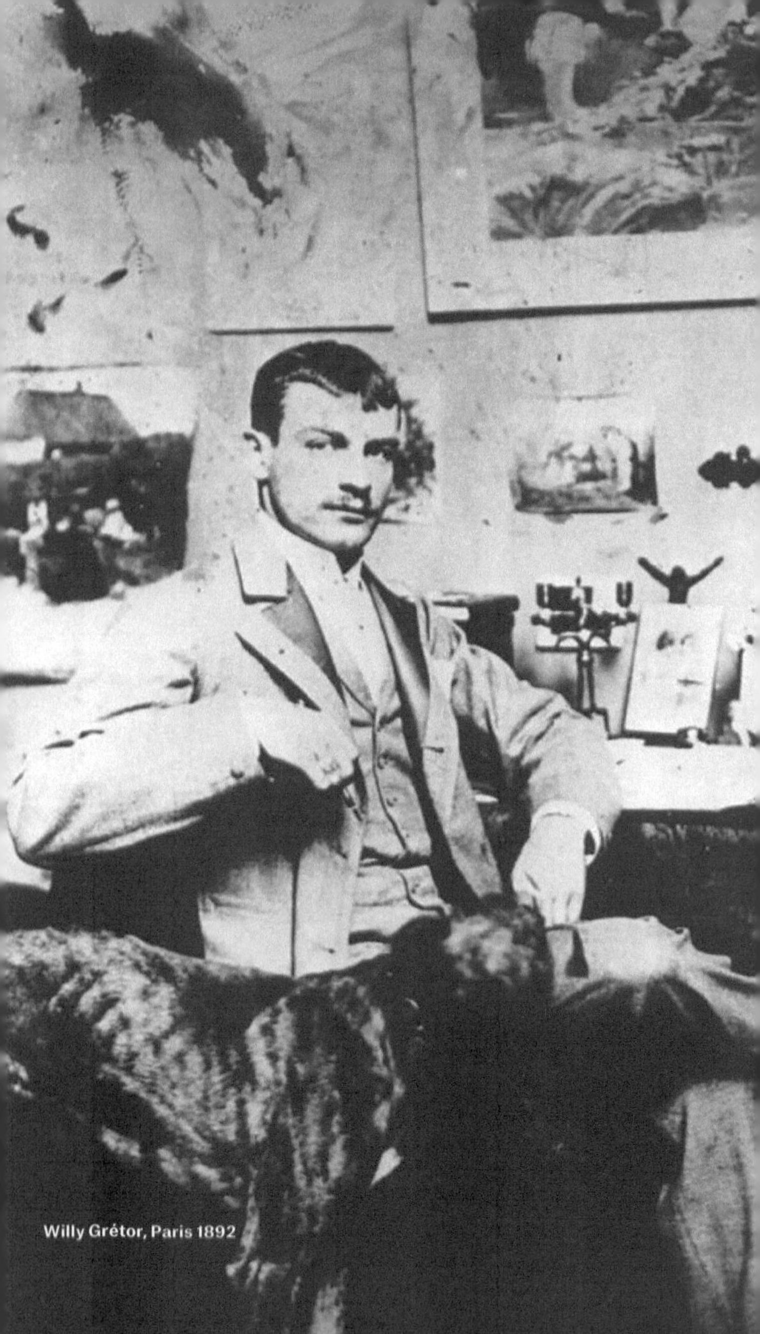

Willy Grétor, Paris 1892

Research mutation: Willy Grétor

Albert Langen found a mentor in Paris by the name of Willy Grétor, aka Dane Julius Rudolph Wilhelm Petersen.

"Grétor was an outgoing adventurer and con man who was a painter, poet, art dealer, and forger that depicted many images."[5]

For a time, the German playwright, Frank Wedekind, was employed as secretary by Grétor – and served as the inspiration behind the Marquis in Wedekind's 1898 play, *Der Marquis von Keith* – considered Wedekind's masterpiece. In the words of the play's publisher, Smith & Kraus, the play concerns the dealings of:

> a would-be entrepreneur who is caught between two ethical premises:
> the life of the pleasure-seeking sensualist and that of the idealistic moralist.
> Keith, the free-and-easy, light-hearted insouciant, is done in by a system
> and a bourgeois society of ambiguous morality that is corrupt to the core.
> He is, of course, no angel himself; rather, he is as unscrupulous a schemer
> as is to be found, gulling highly regarded, albeit morally vague, Munich
> industrialists into putting up the money for a fabulous project . . .
> His modus operandi is, of course, unrelenting ruthlessness. He is, alas,
> also an imposter; and, his philistine industrialist friends being better
> businessmen than he, his fraudulent fleecing scheme to line his own
> pockets is revealed and duly taken over by the bourgeois industrialists.
> The play is a biting indictment of a hypocritical social order.[6]

Gretor also appeared in the Jacob Wassermann novel *Der goldene Spiegel* (S. Fischer Verlag, 1912) as the charactor Riccardo Troyer[7] – and once more as Harry Andersen in Rosa Pfäffinger's post-humously published autobiographical novel, *Der Erbfeind oder ein Anti-Puppenheim* (*The Hereditary Enemy or an Anti-Doll House*)[8], which appears in annotated form in *Die Pariser Bohème* (*The Parisian Bohemia, 1889–1895: An Autobiographical Account by the Painter Rosa Pfäffinger*) edited by Ulrike Wolff-Thomsen, 2007. Beti Žerovc, the Slovene art historian, summarises Pfäffinger's book as follows[9]:

> It begins with a circle of friends – young women studying painting in Munich
> all twenty years of age or a little older. One of them, Maria Slavona, returns
> to her native Lübeck and there meets a handsome and multi-skilled artist:
> the *fin-de-siècle* decadent and, above all, swindler, Willy Gretor. He lures
> her to Paris – at the expense of the book's author, Rosa Pfäffinger, who had
> recently become a wealthy heiress and, from a mix of kind-heartedness and
> socialist ideas, had decided to use her inheritance to support her financially
> less secure friends. In Paris, Slavona becomes Gretor's lover and gets
> pregnant. Fearing the loss of such fine economic support, Gretor goes to
> Munich to see Pfäffinger. She too becomes his lover and moves to Paris,
> where she too soon gives birth to Gretor's child.

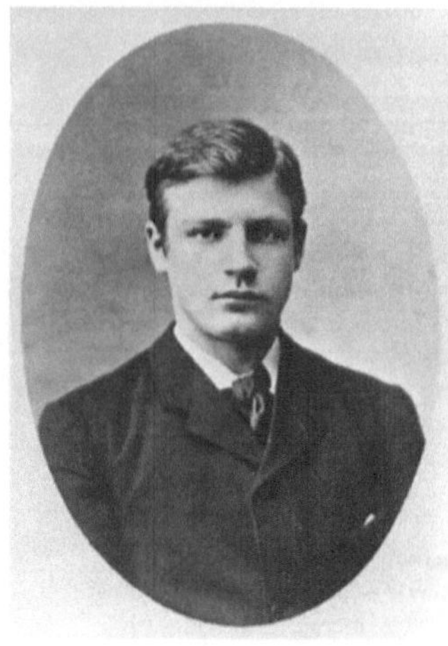

Willy Gretor, 16 years old, 1884.

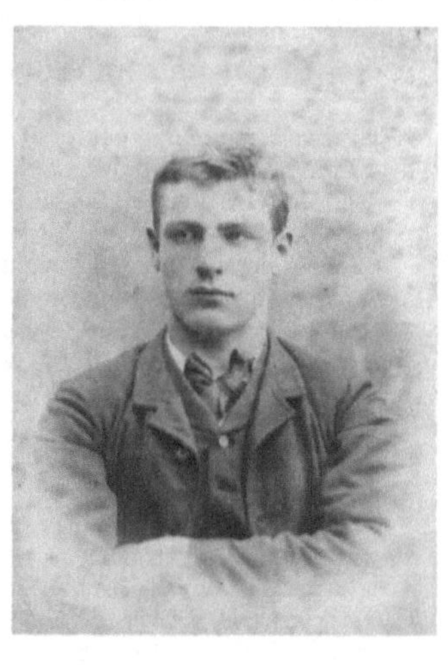

Willy Gretor, Copenhagen, 1886

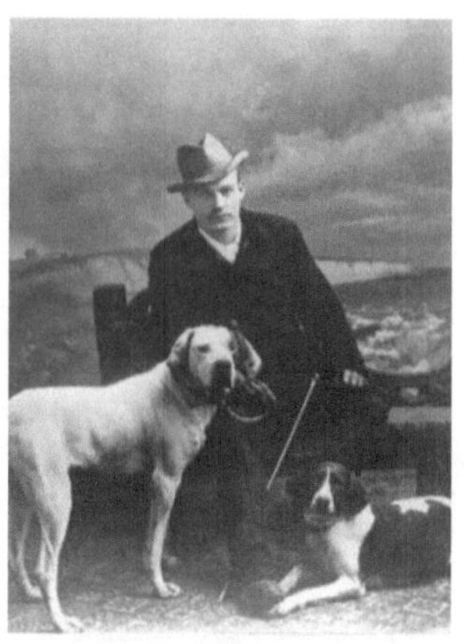

Willy Gretor sitting on a bench with
two dogs, 1890, Copenhagen

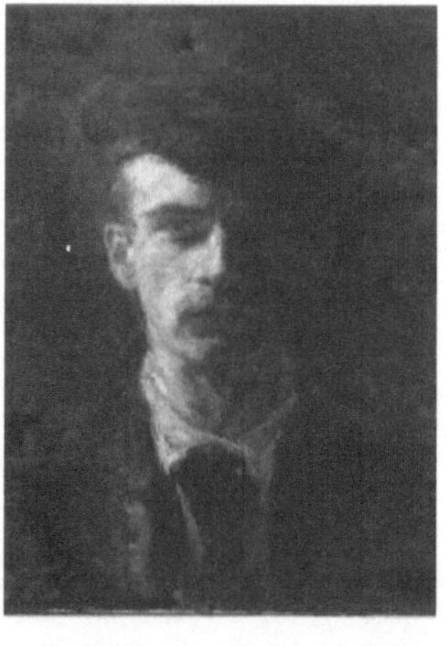

Willy Gretor self-portrait, probably
painted in Paris at the beginning of
the 1890s

In Paris, with Pfäffinger paying all the bills, a remarkable community is formed, a kind of commune, where Gretor's women, the two children, and other artists all live in a large shared apartment. Pfäffinger also pays for separate studios for some of them. Gretor himself has his own separate quarters, coming and going from the common apartment as he pleases.

Pfäffinger also finances the apartment and rich lifestyle of Gretor's "main" mistresses, initially the then very popular Italian singer Severina and, after her, the no less acclaimed dancer Polaire. Gretor also supports many other artists on Pfäffinger's money, including, for instance, August Strindberg. In the early 1890s, already recognizing their greatness, Gretor also begins to buy a large number of works by Gauguin, Van Gogh, and Cézanne. And so it goes until it reaches the point when this sort of communal living becomes unbearable and, most importantly, the fabulous inheritance runs out.

Grétor is also the subject of two German-language biographies, *Willy Grétor født Petersen* by Ernst Mentze written in 1965, and *Willy Grétor (1868-1923)* by Ulrike Wolff-Thomsen, written in 2006. The latter author studies Gretor's character in five themes: Gretor's self-creation as influenced by Nietzsche's *Übermensch* philosophy; his role as a bohemian, as an artist, a patron, and finally, as an art dealer.[10]

As an art-dealer, for a time Grétor represented August Strindberg, the Swedish playwright, novelist, poet, essayist and painter. However things ended disastrously[11]:

"[Grétor and Langen] were to play an important role in the onset of [Strindberg's] *Inferno* crisis ... [who] worried about the 'pack of fakers', who were quite capable of murder if rumour were to be believed ... "

Research mutation: August Strindberg

Johan August Strindberg (1849–1912) was a Swedish playwright, novelist, poet, essayist and painter. A prolific writer who often drew directly on his personal experience, Strindberg's career spanned four decades, during which time he wrote over sixty plays and more than thirty works of fiction, autobiography, history, cultural analysis, and politics. A bold experimenter and iconoclast throughout, he explored a wide range of dramatic methods and purposes, from naturalistic tragedy, monodrama, and history plays, to his anticipations of expressionist and surrealist dramatic techniques. From his earliest work, Strindberg developed innovative forms of dramatic action, language, and visual composition. He is considered the "father" of modern Swedish literature and his *The Red Room* has frequently been described as the first modern Swedish novel.

During the 1890s Strindberg engaged in scientific experiments and studies of the occult. Strindberg moved to Paris in the autumn of 1894, and continued painting there. He came into contact with the Danish painter and art dealer, Willy Grétor, who offered to back Strindberg as an artist. Strindberg was lent an exclusive flat in Paris-Passy by Gretor, and while living there started to work on a series of paintings intended for an exhibition ... the planned exhibition never took place: instead Strindberg broke off all connections with Grétor, who was suspected of dealing in forgeries.[12]

A series of psychotic attacks between 1894 and 1896 (referred to as his "*Inferno* crisis") led to his hospitalization and return to Sweden. Under the influence of the ideas of Swedenborg, he resolved after his recovery to become "the Zola of the Occult". He wrote *Inferno*, an autobiographical novel. The book is concerned with Strindberg's life both in and after he lived in Paris, and explores his various obsessions, including alchemy, occultism, and Swedenborgianism – and shows signs of paranoia and neuroticism.

The narrator spends most of the novel in Paris, isolated from his wife, children, and friends. He associates with a circle of Parisian artists and writers (including Paul Gauguin and Edvard Munch), but often fears they are ridiculing and persecuting him. In his isolation, Strindberg successfully attempts alchemical experiments, and has his work published in prominent journals. He fears, however, that his secrets will be stolen, and his persecution mania worsens, believing that his enemies are attacking him with 'infernal machines.'

Through this newfound imagery, Strindberg sees his life as a living hell, hence the novel's title.[13]

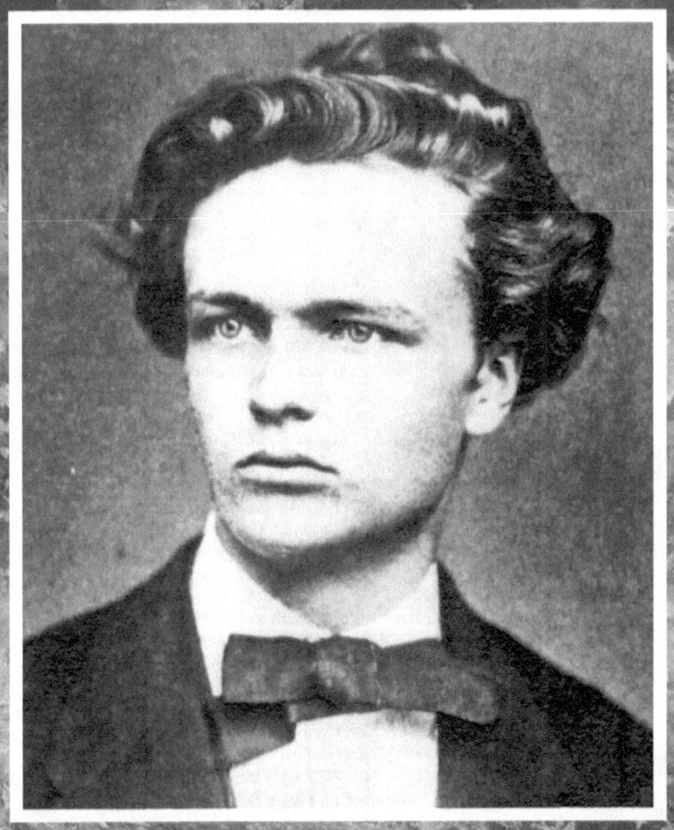

"There are
poisons that
blind you, and
poisons that
open your eyes."

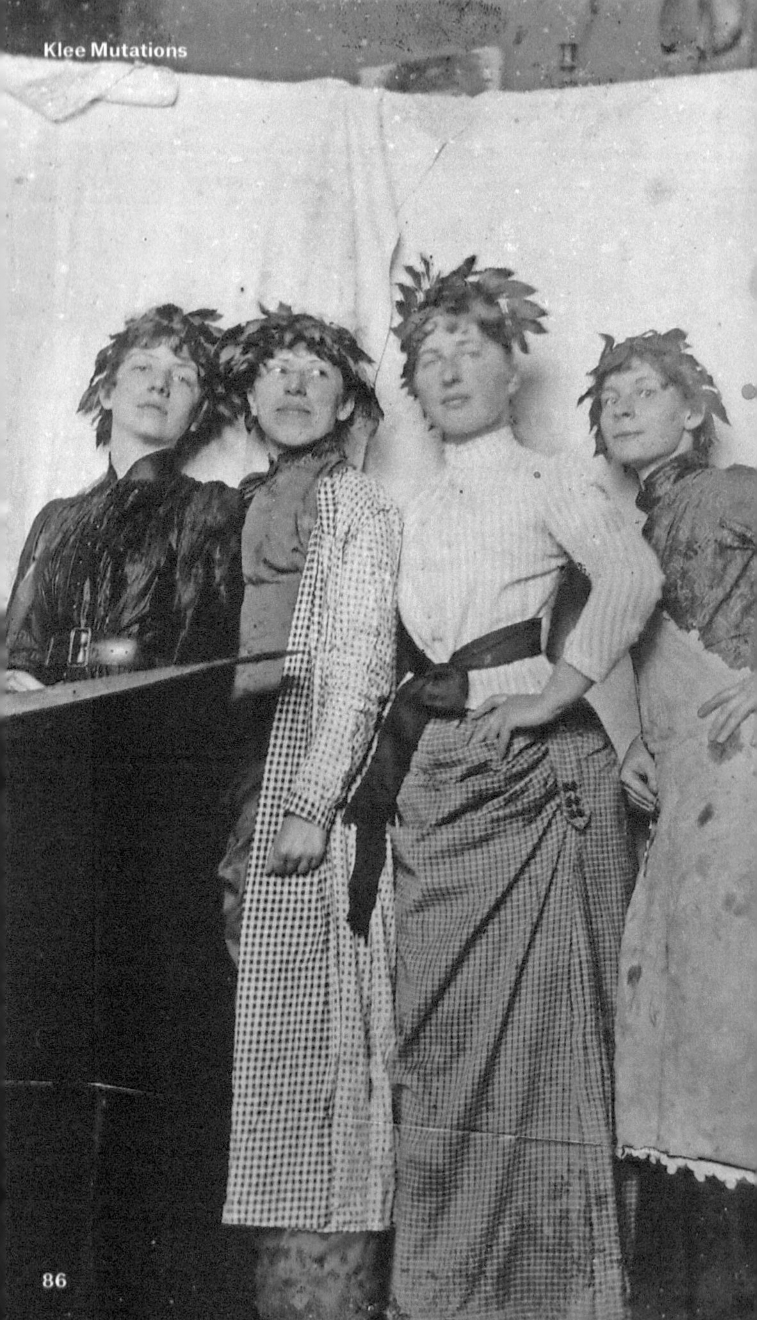

Research mutation: Rosa Pfäffinger

Rosa Pfäffinger (1866–1949) was an Austrian painter, patroness and bohemian. After the death of her wealthy father in 1872 and her sister in 1888, Pfäffinger received a generous inheritance. In 1888 she became acquainted with fellow artists Maria Slavona, Marie von Geyso and Käthe Schmidt (Käthe Kollwitz) while studying painting. Dissatisfied with the possibilities of training in Germany, Maria Slavona went to Paris in 1890, followed shotly after by Rosa Pfäffinger. There they studied the Impressionists and learned as autodidacts.

Despite their initial intention only for several months in Paris, they remained in France for a decade, sharing a six-room apartment with Willy Gretor, the Danish sculptor Hans Brichdahlerup, and Slovenian Impressionist Ivana Kobilca. It was an experiment with new forms of life, in which they undertook an attempt in free love in order to "break up the surviving, rigid, but affective, subjectivist house, family, and mind system." Slavona, Kobilca and Gretor became lovers – Slavona soon fell pregnant and gave birth to a daughter. Pfäffinger became the next lover of Willy Gretor, and gave birth to a son.

It was Rosa Pfaffinger who paid all the bills for the Bohème lifestyle in the apartment, with chambermaids, nurses and cooks, plus the rented studios in the neighborhood. Pfaffinger also financed Gretor's own apartment, his rich lifestyle and his mistresses. With Pfäffinger's money, Gretor bought art and supported many artists, including August Strindberg, who had moved into Rosa's studio in Passy. Life in the commune lasted until Pfaeffinger's inheritance was depleted.

Pfäffinger and Slavona remained friends, and as single-parents they moved to the Paris suburb of Meudon, sharing child care and time in the studio. Their new form of life offered the only possibility to remain active as professional artists. Under severe financial constraints and psychological stress, both women were able to counteract the social repressions, that were less intense in France than in Germany.

Pfaeffinger, once wealthy was now impoverished, lived alternately in Paris and Berlin, where Käthe Kollwitz was raising her son.

Slavona became acquainted with the Swiss art dealer, Otto Ackermann, in Paris. In 1901, she exhibited as a member of the Secession in Berlin, and in 1904 participated in the first joint exhibition with the Munich Secession. After receiving recognition as an artist, Slavona was able to support the impoverished Rosa Pfaffinger.

After the dissolution of the commune, Albert Langen took over the apartment, and founded his publishing practice in Paris.[14]

Research mutation: Bruno Paul

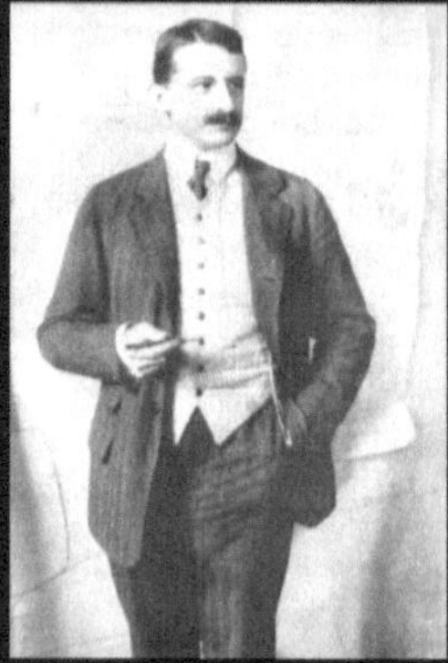

Bruno Paul circa 1907

One of the notable artist/designers Albert Langen Verlag worked with was Bruno Paul (1874–1968), the German illustrator, interior designer, furniture designer and architect. In 1907, Paul contributed to the founding of the Deutscher Werkbund. His work as an architect began in 1908 with the "Haus Westend" in Berlin. He developed the first prefab house with a flat roof for the German Workshops in Dresden-Hellerau in 1924. With the department store building, Macy's in New York, Bruno Paul also achieved international fame in 1925.[14]

At the dawn of the 20th century, Bruno Paul stood like a colossus astride the landscape of an emerging Modernism. As an illustrator, architect and educator his influence was unequalled. Arguably the most important German designer of his generation, his work was ubiquitous in the technical and professional publications of his day. For five decades, Paul's reputation was unparalleled among progressive German artists. As a young man he was a member of the Munich avant-garde responsible for the creation of the Jugendstil. As a designer of furniture and interiors, he achieved a commercial success unmatched by his illustrious contemporaries. In the light of his professional accomplishments, he was the most influential German architect of his generation, a figure of international significance. Ludwig Miss van der Rohe, Adolf Meyer and Kern Weber were among his students, and their work developed from the practices of his atelier, indeed, as director of the Vereinigte Staatsschulen fur freie und angewandte Kunst in Berlin he presided over an institution that rivaled the Bauhaus as a center of progressive instruction in the arts.

Despite the renown he enjoyed at the height of his career, Paul's name has been largely absent from the standard histories of the modern movement . . .

— William Owen Harrod, *Bruno Paul: The Life And Work of a Pragmatic Modernist*[15]

Inset: Illustration for *Simplicissimus*. By 1906, Paul had produced about five hundred cartoons.

"Kathreiner-Hochhaus" in Berlin, building designed by the architect Bruno Paul. Built in 1928/1930.

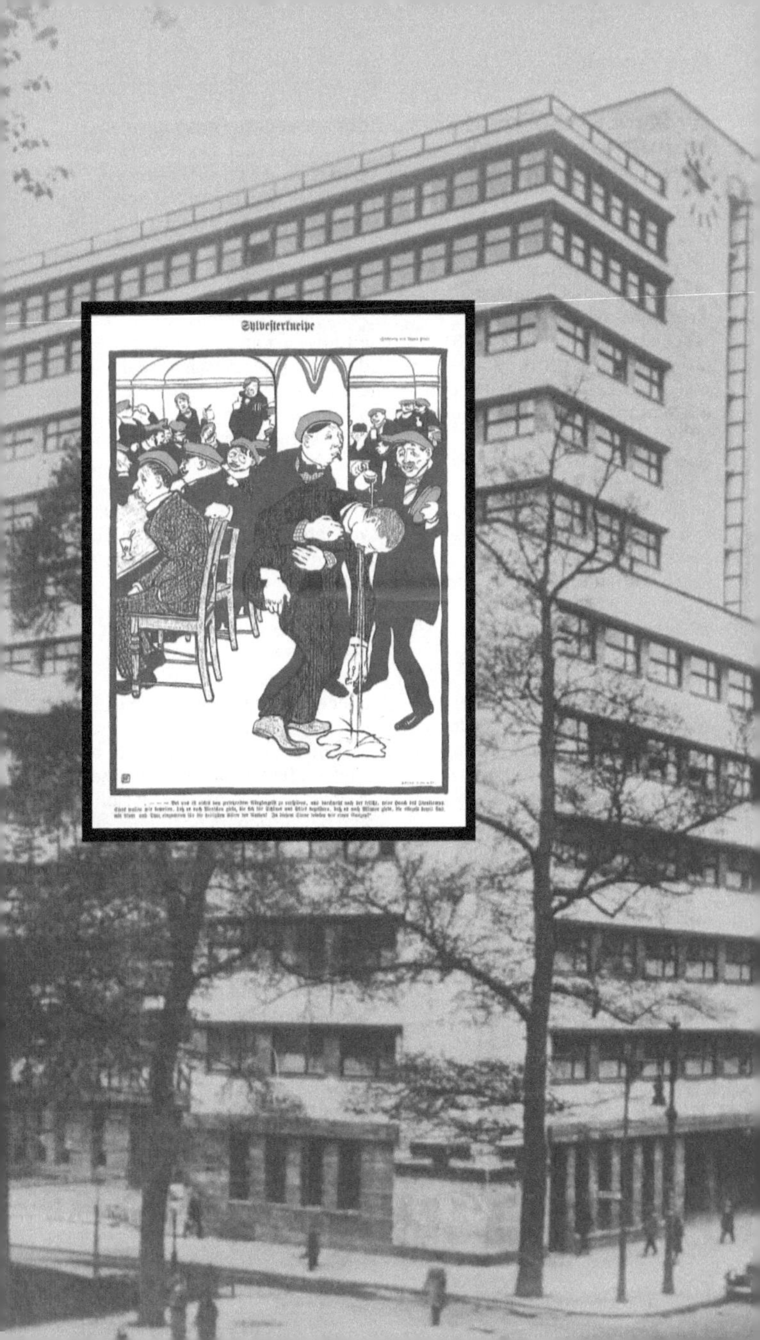

Sylvesterkneipe

A return to the fount of mutant pedagogy: *Pedagogical Sketchbook*

Pedagogical Sketchbook is a book by Paul Klee. It is based on his extensive lectures on visual form at Bauhaus Staatliche Art School where he was a teacher in between 1921-1931. Originally handwritten – as a pile of working notes he used in his lectures – it was eventually edited by Walter Gropius, designed by László Moholy-Nagy and published in 1925 as a Bauhaus student manual (Bauhausbucher No.2, as the second in the series of the fourteen Bauhaus books) under the original title, *Pädagogisches Skizzenbuch*. It was translated into English by Sibyl Moholy-Nagy in 1953..

Along with other Bauhaus books such as *Theory of Color* by Johannes Itten and *Point and Line to Plane* by Wassily Kandinsky, *Pedagogical Sketchbook* is a legacy of teaching methods on art theory and practice at Bauhaus Staatliche Art School.

During his teaching career at Bauhaus, Klee reflected on his own working methods and techniques. "When I came to be teacher", he wrote, "I had to account explicitly for what I had been used to doing unconsciously." He left over 3000 handwritten pages developed as a theoretical basis for his lectures, some of which are still unpublished.

From the same period comes another one of his books, *The Thinking Eye*, dealing with the same issues as *Pedagogical Sketchbook*, but much more extensive in scope. However, this book was published and translated later, after his death.

Teaching concept

Pedagogical Sketchbook is an intuitive art investigation of dynamic principles in visual arts. Klee takes his students on an 'adventure in seeing' guiding them step-by-step through a challenging conceptual framework. Objects are rendered in a complex relation to physical and intellectual space concepts. It is an exercise in modern art thinking.

In her introduction, Sibyl Moholy-Nagy divides the book into four different parts corresponding to the four conceptual frameworks. The starting chapter concerns 'Line and Structure'. A dot goes for a walk . . . freely and without a goal. A dot is a "point of progression" and by shifting its position forward becomes a line. Line variations lead to even more complex structures. It can move freely in a calligraphic stroke, or circumscribe, act as a planar definition, as a mathematical structural element (as in Golden Section) or as a path in motion (when it coordinates kinetic movements such as in muscle contraction). The artist's world is dynamic – in the state of becoming – rather than static.

In 'Dimension and Balance', the line is related to psychological and social concepts of space. Klee explains subjectivity of our perception by comparing examples of optical illusion with horizon and perspective. We use them as orientation points within the space. Klee evokes our reality as constructed and arbitrary. "Dimension is in itself nothing but an arbitrary expansion of form into height, width, depth and time". By challenging conventional perception of his students, Klee shows them a way 'beyond' the physical realm, into the world of metaphysical and spiritual. It is an invitation to approach art intuitively, since outer perception can be deceptive (socially constructed).

The third part is about "Gravitational Curve". A very first drawing of a strong black arrow pointing downwards postulates man (sic) as a tragic figure always brought down by a plummet of a gravitational force. However, Klee also points out that water and atmosphere are transitional regions, where the spirit gets lighter and breaks free. This is a spiritual space open to dynamic positions, new symbols and imaginative co-relations of visual elements (mechanical law of nature versus imaginative vision rendering of an object in art).

In the final part of the manual, 'Kinetic and Chromatic Energy', Klee gives examples of 'creative kinetics' defying gravitational force such as centripetal force in pendulum and spinning tops, or a 'feathered arrow'. He continues with a 'symbolic' arrow illustrating similar efforts of a man (sic) to move 'a bit further than customary – further than possible'.[16]

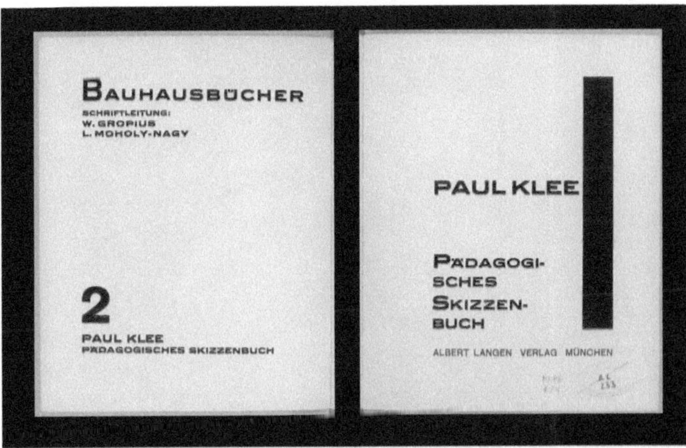

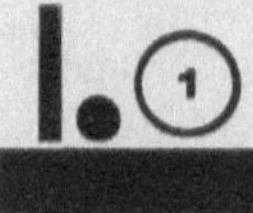

Eine **aktive** Linie, die sich frei ergeht, ein Spaziergang um seiner selbst willen, ohne Ziel. Das agens ist ein Punkt, der sich verschiebt (Fig. 1):

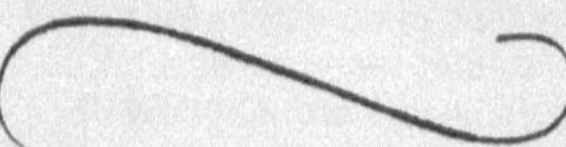

Fig. 1

Dieselbe Linie mit Begleitungsformen (Fig. 2 und 3):

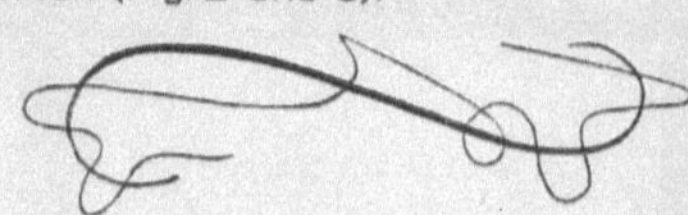

Fig. 2

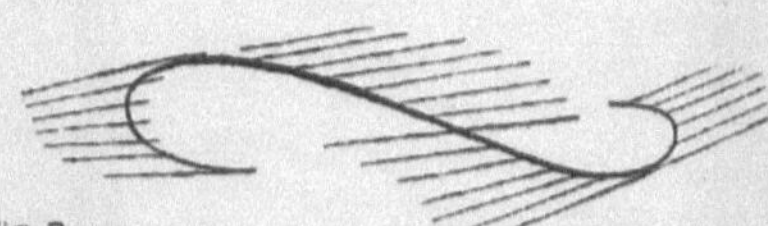

Fig. 3

6

An active line
        that goes free
a walk for itself
        without a goal

The agent is
        a point
        that moves

The same line
        with clothing

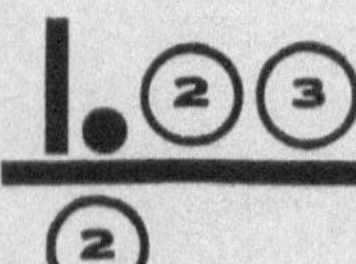

Eine **aktive** Linie, die, befristet, sich zwischen bestimmten Punkten bewegt (Fig. 6):

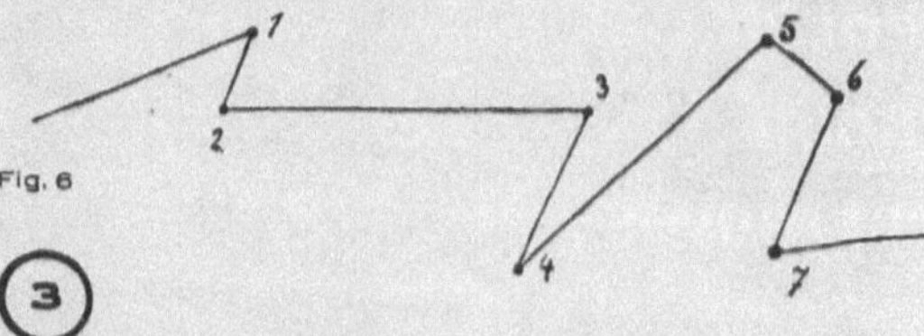

Fig. 6

Eine **mediale** Linie, welche zwischen Punktbewegung und Flächen-wirkung steht (Fig. 7):

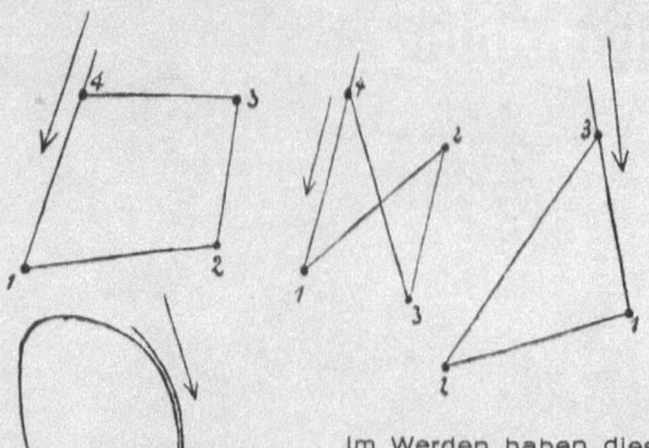

Fig. 7

Im Werden haben diese Figuren linearen Charakter; zu Ende geformt aber wird diese lineare Eigenschaft von der Flächenvor-stellung unverzüglich abgelöst.

8

An active line
      which
for a limited time
      moves between
certain points

A medial line, soft
      between point movement
and flat action

These figures
      are linear in character
      but   this linear
property
      is
      immediately   detached
from
      the surface

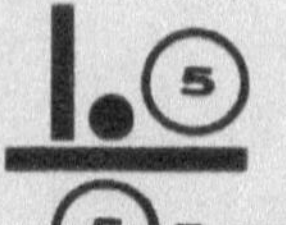

(5) **Zusammengefaßt** (Fig. 9—12):

ERSTER FALL:

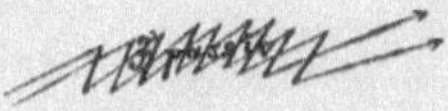

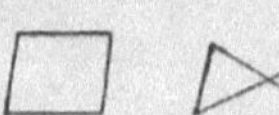

Fig. 9

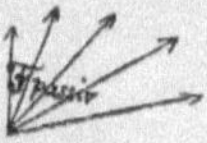

Fig. 9 a

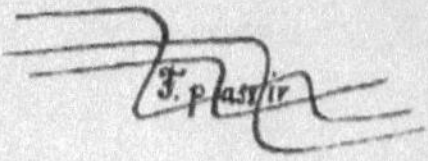

Fig. 9 b

Aktive Linien, passive Flächen; lineare Energie (Ursache), linearer Effekt (Wirkung), Flächen-Nebenwirkung.

ZWEITER FALL:

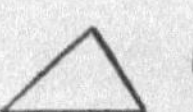 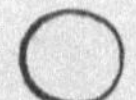

Fig. 10

Mediale Linien; lineare Energie (Ursache), Flächeneffekt (Wirkung).

DRITTER FALL:

 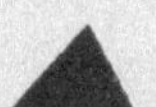 

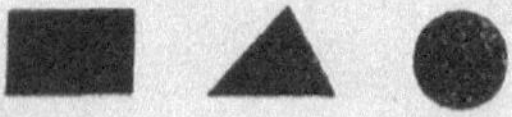

Fig. 11

Aktive Fläche, passive Linie; Flächenenergie (Ursache), Flächenwirkung und lineare Nebenwirkung.

10

First case:

Active lines, passive surfaces;
        linear energy (cause)
linear effect (effect)
        surface side-effect

Second case:

Medial Lines,
        Linear Energy (cause)
Flat Effect (effect)

Third case:

Active flat passive line,
        flat energy (cause),
flat effect and linear
        side-effect

Research mutation: Paul Klee

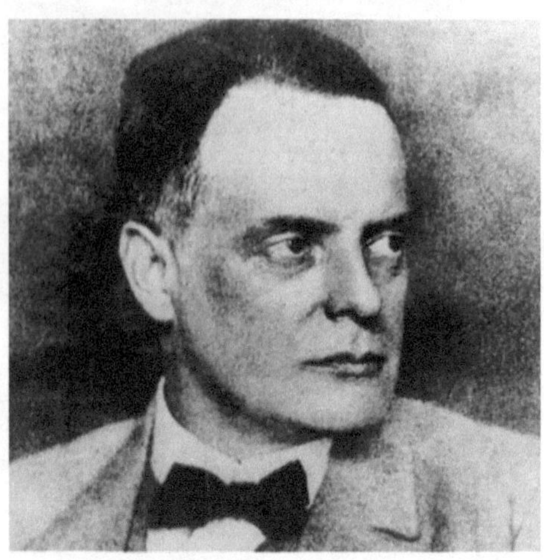

Paul Klee was born on December 18, 1879, in Münchenbuchsee, Switzerland, into a family of musicians. His childhood love of music was always to remain profoundly important in his life and work. From 1898 to 1901 Klee studied in Munich, first with Heinrich Knirr, then at the Kunstakademie under Franz von Stuck. Upon completing his schooling, he traveled to Italy. It was the first in a series of trips abroad that nourished his visual sensibilities. He settled in Bern in 1902. A series of his satirical etchings was exhibited at the Munich Secession in 1906. That same year Klee married Lily Stumpf, a pianist, and moved to Munich. There he gained exposure to Modern art. Klee's work was shown at the Kunstmuseum Bern in 1910 and at Moderne Galerie, Munich, in 1911.

Klee met Alexej Jawlensky, Vasily Kandinsky, August Macke, Franz Marc, and other avant-garde figures in 1911; he participated in important shows of advanced art, including the second Blaue Reiter (Blue Rider) exhibition at Galerie Hans Goltz, Munich, in 1912, and the *Erste deutsche Herbstsalon* at the Der Sturm Gallery, Berlin, in 1913. In 1912 he visited Paris for the second time, where he saw the work of Georges Braque and Pablo Picasso, and met Robert Delaunay. Klee helped found the Neue Münchner Secession in 1914. Color became central to his art only after a revelatory trip to Tunisia in 1914.

In 1920 a major Klee retrospective was held at the Galerie Hans Goltz, Munich; his *Schöpferische Konfession* was published; he was also appointed to the faculty of the Bauhaus. Klee taught at the Bauhaus in Weimar from 1921 to 1926 and in Dessau from 1926 to 1931.[17]

—The Solomon R. Guggenheim Foundation

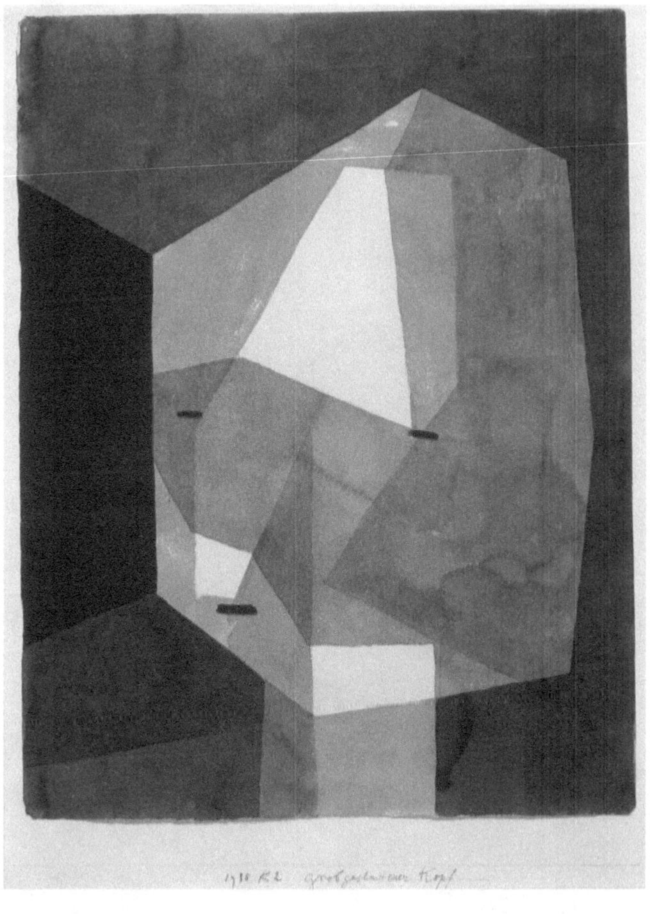

Rough Cut Head
(Paul Klee, 1935)

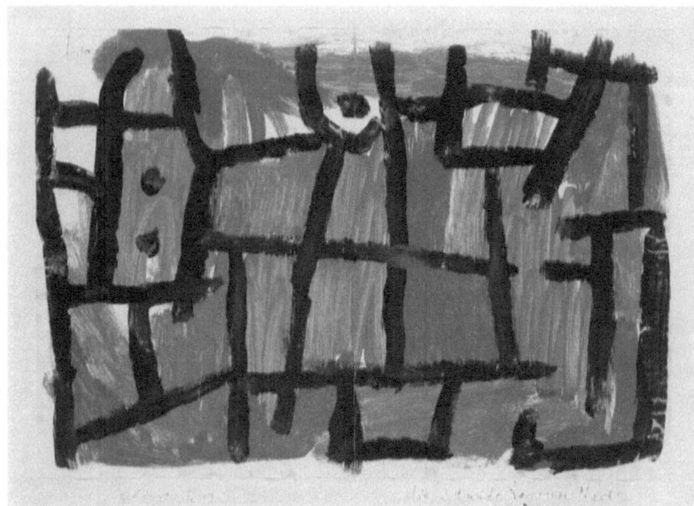

The Hour Before One Night (1940)

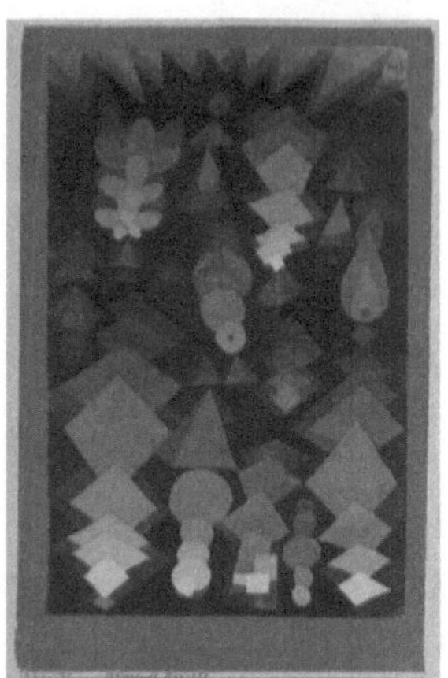

Tower in Orange and Green (1922)

Suspended Fruit (1921)

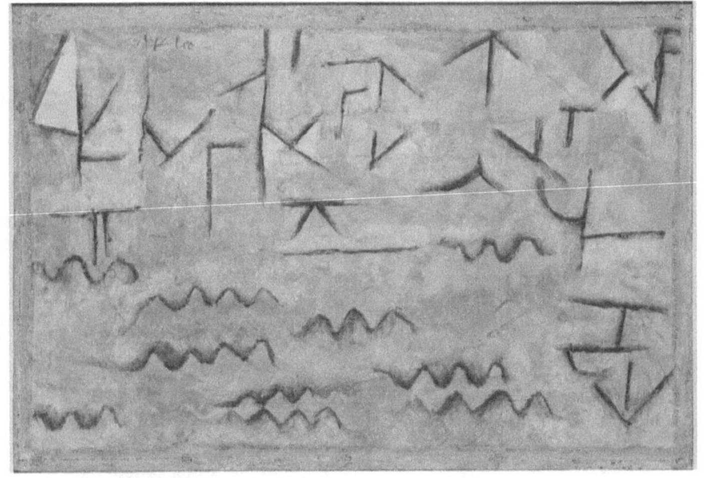

The Rhine at Duisburg (1937)

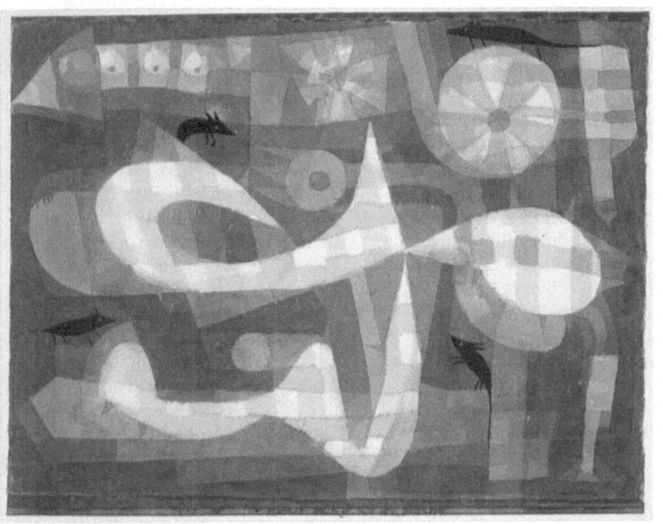

The Barbed Noose with the Mice (1923)

Research mutation: Color theory

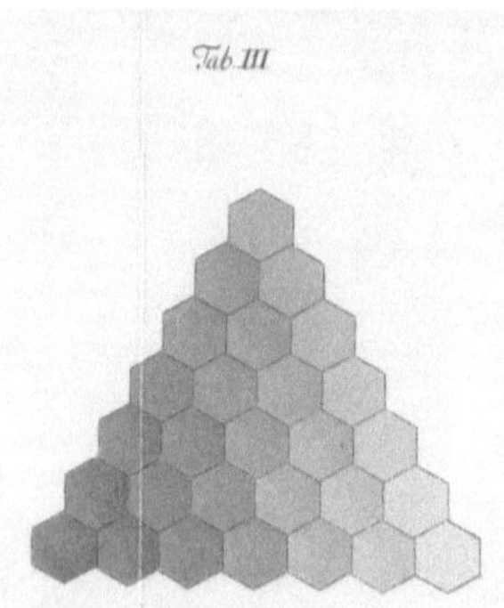

Tobias Mayer's colour triangle, first published in 1775

In the visual arts, color theory or colour theory is a body of practical guidance to color mixing and the visual effects of a specific color combination. There are also definitions (or categories) of colors based on the color wheel: primary color, secondary color and tertiary color. Although color theory principles first appeared in the writings of Leon Battista Alberti (c.1435) and the notebooks of Leonardo da Vinci (c.1490), a tradition of "colory theory" began in the 18th century, initially within a partisan controversy over Isaac Newton's theory of color (*Opticks*, 1704) and the nature of primary colors. From there it developed as an independent artistic tradition with only superficial reference to colorimetry and vision science.

Color abstractions

The foundations of pre-20th-century color theory were built around "pure" or ideal colors, characterized by sensory experiences rather than attributes of the physical world. This has led to a number of inaccuracies in traditional color theory principles that are not always remedied in modern formulations.

The most important problem has been a confusion between the behavior of light mixtures, called additive color, and the behavior of paint, ink, dye, or pigment mixtures, called subtractive color. This problem arises because the absorption of light by material substances follows different rules from the perception of light by the eye.

A second problem has been the failure to describe the very important effects of strong luminance (lightness) contrasts in the appearance of colors reflected from a surface (such as paints or inks) as opposed to colors of light; "colors" such as browns or ochres cannot appear in mixtures of light. Thus, a strong lightness contrast between a mid-valued yellow paint and a surrounding bright white makes the yellow appear to be green or brown, while a strong brightness contrast between a rainbow and the surrounding sky makes the yellow in a rainbow appear to be a fainter yellow, or white.

A third problem has been the tendency to describe color effects holistically or categorically, for example as a contrast between "yellow" and "blue" conceived as generic colors, when most color effects are due to contrasts on three relative attributes that define all colors:

1. lightness (light vs. dark, or white vs. black),
2. saturation (intense vs. dull), and
3. hue (e.g. red, orange, yellow, green, blue or purple).

Thus, the visual impact of "yellow" vs. "blue" hues in visual design depends on the relative lightness and saturation of the hues.

These confusions are partly historical, and arose in scientific uncertainty about color perception that was not resolved until the late 19th century, when the artistic notions were already entrenched. However, they also arise from the attempt to describe the highly contextual and flexible behavior of color perception in terms of abstract color sensations that can be generated equivalently by any visual media.

Many historical "color theorists" have assumed that three "pure" primary colors can mix all possible colors, and that any failure of specific paints or inks to match this ideal performance is due to the impurity or imperfection of the colorants. In reality, only imaginary "primary colors" used in colorimetry can "mix" or quantify all visible (perceptually possible) colors: but to do this, these imaginary primaries are defined as lying outside the range of visible colors; i.e., they cannot be seen. Any three real "primary" colors of light, paint or ink can mix only a limited range of colors, called a gamut, which is always smaller (contains fewer colors) than the full range of colors humans can perceive.

Historical background

Color theory was originally formulated in terms of three "primary" or "primitive" colors – red, yellow and blue (RYB) – because these colors were believed capable of mixing all other colors. This color mixing behavior had long been known to printers, dyers and painters, but these trades preferred pure pigments to primary color mixtures, because the mixtures were too dull (unsaturated).

The RYB primary colors became the foundation of 18th century theories of color vision, as the fundamental sensory qualities that are blended in the perception of all physical colors and equally in the physical mixture of pigments or dyes. These theories were enhanced by 18th-century investigations of a variety of purely psychological color effects, in particular the contrast between "complementary" or opposing hues that are produced by color afterimages and in the contrasting shadows in colored light. These ideas and many personal color observations were summarized in two founding documents in color theory: the *Theory of Colours* (1810) by the German poet and government minister Johann Wolfgang von Goethe, and *The Law of Simultaneous Color Contrast* (1839) by the French industrial chemist Michel Eugène Chevreul. Charles Hayter published *A New Practical Treatise on the Three Primitive Colours Assumed as a Perfect System of Rudimentary Information* (London 1826), in which he described how all colours could be obtained from just three.

Subsequently, German and English scientists established in the late 19th century that color perception is best described in terms of a different set of primary colors – red, green and blue violet (RGB) – modeled through the additive mixture of three monochromatic lights. Subsequent research anchored these primary colors in the differing responses to light by three types of color receptors or cones in the retina (trichromacy). On this basis the quantitative description of color mixture or colorimetry developed in the early 20th century, along with a series of increasingly sophisticated models of color space and color perception, such as the opponent process theory.

Across the same period, industrial chemistry radically expanded the color range of lightfast synthetic pigments, allowing for substantially improved saturation in color mixtures of dyes, paints and inks. It also created the dyes and chemical processes necessary for color photography. As a result, three-color printing became aesthetically and economically feasible in mass printed media, and the artists' color theory was adapted to primary colors most effective in inks or photographic dyes: cyan, magenta, and yellow (CMY). (In printing, dark colors are supplemented by a black ink, known as the CMYK system; in both printing and photography, white is provided by the color of the paper.) These CMY primary colors were reconciled with the RGB primaries, and subtractive color mixing with additive color mixing, by defining the CMY primaries as substances that absorbed only one of the retinal primary colors: cyan absorbs only red (−R+G+B), magenta only green (+R−G+B), and yellow only blue violet (+R+G−B). It is important to add that the CMYK, or process, color printing is meant as an economical way of producing a wide range of colors for printing, but is deficient in reproducing certain colors, notably orange and slightly deficient in reproducing purples. A wider range of color can be obtained with the addition of other colors to the printing process, such as in Pantone's Hexachrome printing ink system (six colors), among others.

For much of the 19th century artistic color theory either lagged behind scientific understanding or was augmented by science books written for the lay public, in particular *Modern Chromatics* (1879) by the American physicist Ogden Rood, and early color atlases developed by Albert Munsell (*Munsell Book of Color*, 1915) and Wilhelm Ostwald (*Color Atlas*, 1919). Major advances were made in the early 20th century by artists teaching or associated with the German Bauhaus, in particular Wassily Kandinsky, Johannes Itten, Paul Klee, Faber Birren and Josef Albers, whose writings mix speculation with an empirical or demonstration-based study of color design principles.

Traditional color theory
Complementary colors

For the mixing of colored light, Isaac Newton's color wheel is often used to describe complementary colors, which are colors which cancel each other's hue to produce an achromatic (white, gray or black) light mixture. Newton offered as a conjecture that colors exactly opposite one another on the hue circle cancel out each other's hue; this concept was demonstrated more thoroughly in the 19th century.

A key assumption in Newton's hue circle was that the "fiery" or maximum saturated hues are located on the outer circumference of the circle, while achromatic white is at the center. Then the saturation of the mixture of two spectral hues was predicted by the straight line between them; the mixture of three colors was predicted by the "center of gravity" or centroid of three triangle points, and so on.

According to traditional color theory based on subtractive primary colors and the RYB color model, which is derived from paint mixtures, yellow mixed with violet, orange mixed with blue, or

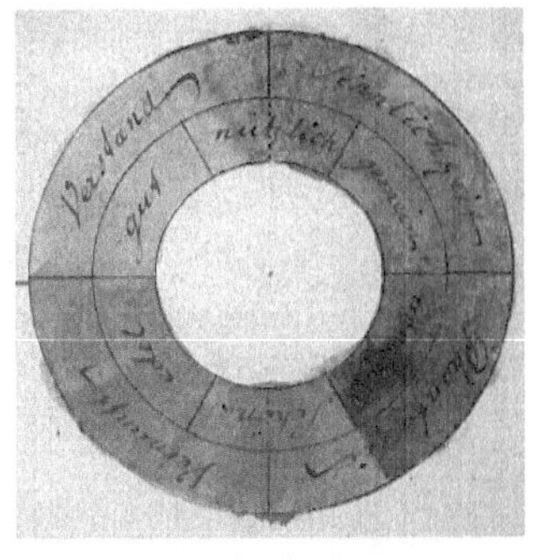

Goethe's color wheel from his 1810 *Theory of Colours*

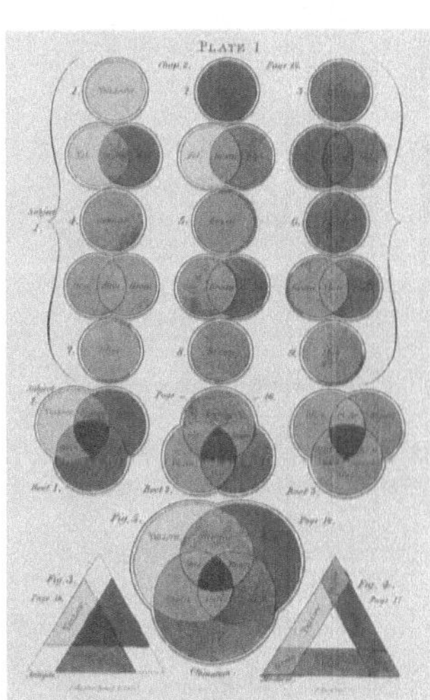

A page from *A New Practical Treatise on the Three Primitive Colours Assumed as a Perfect System of Rudimentary Information* by Charles Hayter (1826)

red mixed with green produces an equivalent gray and are the painter's complementary colors. These contrasts form the basis of Chevreul's law of color contrast: colors that appear together will be altered as if mixed with the complementary color of the other color. Thus, a piece of yellow fabric placed on a blue background will appear tinted orange, because orange is the complementary color to blue.

However, when complementary colors are chosen based on definition by light mixture, they are not the same as the artists' primary colors. This discrepancy becomes important when color theory is applied across media. Digital color management uses a hue circle defined according to additive primary colors (the RGB color model), as the colors in a computer monitor are additive mixtures of light, not subtractive mixtures of paints.

One reason the artist's primary colors work at all is that the imperfect pigments being used have sloped absorption curves, and thus change color with concentration. A pigment that is pure red at high concentrations can behave more like magenta at low concentrations. This allows it to make purples that would otherwise be impossible. Likewise, a blue that is ultramarine at high concentrations appears cyan at low concentrations, allowing it to be used to mix green. Chromium red pigments can appear orange, and then yellow, as the concentration is reduced. It is even possible to mix very low concentrations of the blue mentioned and the chromium red to get a greenish color. This works much better with oil colors than it does with watercolors and dyes.

So the old primaries depend on sloped absorption curves and pigment leakages to work, while newer scientifically derived ones depend solely on controlling the amount of absorption in certain parts of the spectrum.

Another reason the correct primary colors were not used by early artists is that they were not available as durable pigments. Modern methods in chemistry were needed to produce them.

Warm vs. cool colors

The distinction between "warm" and "cool" colors has been important since at least the late 18th century. The contrast, as traced by etymologies in the Oxford English Dictionary, seems related to the observed contrast in landscape light, between the "warm" colors associated with daylight or sunset, and the "cool" colors associated with a gray or overcast day. Warm colors are often said to be hues from red through yellow, browns and tans included; cool colors are often said to be the hues from blue green through blue violet, most grays included. There is historical disagreement about the colors that anchor the polarity, but 19th-century sources put the peak contrast between red orange and greenish blue.

Color theory has described perceptual and psychological effects to this contrast. Warm colors are said to advance or appear more active in a painting, while cool colors tend to recede; used in interior design or fashion, warm colors are said to arouse or stimulate the viewer, while cool colors calm and relax. Most of these effects, to the extent they are real, can be attributed to the higher saturation and lighter value of warm pigments in contrast to cool pigments. Thus, brown is a dark, unsaturated warm color that few people think of as visually active or psychologically arousing.

Contrast the traditional warm-cool association of color with the color temperature of a theoretical radiating black body, where the association of color with temperature is reversed. For instance, the hottest stars radiate blue light (i.e., with shorter wavelength and higher frequency), and the coolest radiate red.

Achromatic colors

Any color that lacks strong chromatic content is said to be unsaturated, achromatic, near neutral, or neutral. Near neutrals include browns, tans, pastels and darker colors. Near neutrals can be of any hue or lightness. Pure achromatic, or neutral colors include black, white and all grays.

Near neutrals are obtained by mixing pure colors with white, black or grey, or by mixing two complementary colors. In color theory, neutral colors are easily modified by adjacent more saturated colors and they appear to take on the hue complementary to the saturated color; e.g.: next to a bright red couch, a gray wall will appear distinctly greenish.

Black and white have long been known to combine "well" with almost any other colors; black decreases the apparent saturation or brightness of colors paired with it, and white shows off all hues to equal effect.

Tints and shades

When mixing colored light (additive color models), the achromatic mixture of spectrally balanced red, green and blue (RGB) is always white, not gray or black. When we mix colorants, such as the pigments in paint mixtures, a color is produced which is always darker and lower in chroma, or saturation, than the parent colors. This moves the mixed color toward a neutral color - a gray or near-black. Lights are made brighter or dimmer by adjusting their brightness, or energy level; in painting, lightness is adjusted through mixture with white, black or a color's complement.

It is common among some painters to darken a paint color by adding black paint - producing colors called shades - or lighten a color by adding white - producing colors called tints. However it is not always the best way for representational painting, as an unfortunate result is for colors to also shift in hue. For instance, darkening a color by adding black can cause colors such as yellows, reds and oranges, to shift toward the greenish or bluish part of the spectrum. Lightening a color by adding white can cause a shift towards blue when mixed with reds and oranges. Another practice when darkening a color is to use its opposite, or complementary, color (e.g. purplish-red added to yellowish-green) in order to neutralize it without a shift in hue, and darken it if the additive color is darker than the parent color. When lightening a color this hue shift can be corrected with the addition of a small amount of an adjacent color to bring the hue of the mixture back in line with the parent color (e.g. adding a small amount of orange to a mixture of red and white will correct the tendency of this mixture to shift slightly towards the blue end of the spectrum).

Split primary colors

In painting and other visual arts, two-dimensional color wheels or three-dimensional color solids are used as tools to teach beginners the essential relationships between colors. The organization of colors in a particular color model depends on the purpose of that model: some models show relationships based on human color perception, whereas others are based on the color mixing properties of a particular medium such as a computer display or set of paints.

This system is still popular among contemporary painters, as it is basically a simplified version of Newton's geometrical rule that colors closer together on the hue circle will produce more vibrant mixtures. However, with the range of contemporary paints available, many artists simply add more paints to their palette as desired for a variety of practical reasons. For example, they may add a scarlet, purple and/or green paint to expand the mixable gamut; and they include one or more dark colors (especially "earth" colors such as yellow ochre or burnt sienna) simply because they are convenient to have premixed. Printers commonly augment a CMYK palette with spot (trademark specific) ink colors.

Color harmony

It has been suggested that "Colors seen together to produce a pleasing affective response are said to be in harmony". However, color harmony is a complex notion because human responses to color are both affective and cognitive, involving emotional response and judgment. Hence, our responses to color and the notion of color harmony is open to the influence of a range of different factors. These factors include individual differences (such as age, gender, personal preference, affective state, etc.) as well as cultural, sub-cultural and socially-based differences which gives rise to conditioning and learned responses about color. In addition, context always has an influence on responses about color and the notion of

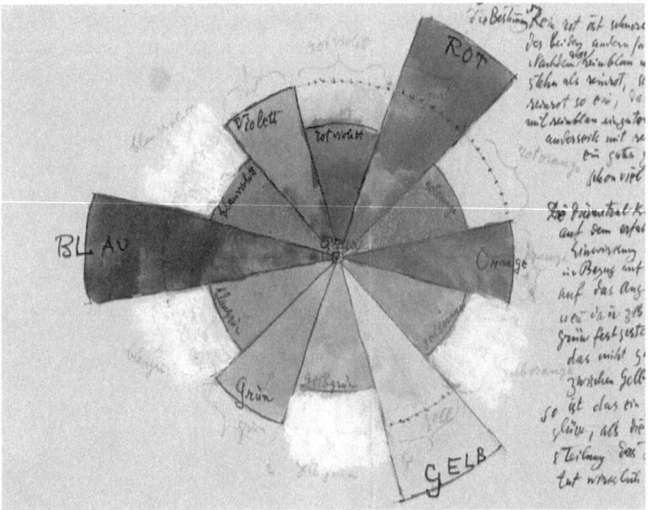

Paul Klee's color chart, from his *Schöpferische Konfession* (1920)

color harmony, and this concept is also influenced by temporal factors (such as changing trends) and perceptual factors (such as simultaneous contrast) which may impinge on human response to color. The following conceptual model illustrates this 21st century approach to color harmony:

Color harmony =
f (Col1,2,3,...,n) ·
(ID+CE+CX+P+T)

Wherein color harmony is a function (f) of the interaction between color/s (Col 1, 2, 3,..., n) and the factors that influence positive aesthetic response to color: individual differences (ID) such as age, gender, personality and affective state; cultural experiences (CE), the prevailing context (CX) which includes setting and ambient lighting; intervening perceptual effects (P) and the effects of time (T) in terms of prevailing social trends.

Current status

Color theory has not developed an explicit explanation of how specific media affect color appearance: colors have always been defined in the abstract, and whether the colors were inks or paints, oils or watercolors, transparencies or reflecting prints, computer displays or movie theaters, was not considered especially relevant. Josef Albers investigated the effects of relative contrast and color saturation on the illusion of transparency, but this is an exception to the rule.[18]

Research mutation: Walter Gropius

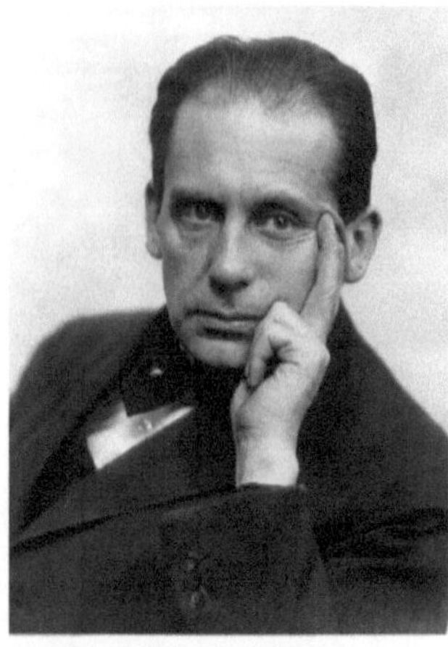

Walter Gropius (c. 1919)

Walter Adolph Georg Gropius (1883–5 1969) was a German architect and founder of the Bauhaus School, who, along with Ludwig Mies van der Rohe, Le Corbusier and Frank Lloyd Wright, is widely regarded as one of the pioneering masters of modernist architecture.

Early career (1908–14)

Walter Gropius was drafted August 1914 and served as a sergeant and then as a lieutenant in the signal corps in the First World War. He survived being buried under rubble and dead bodies, and shot out of the sky with a dead pilot. Gropius then, like his father and his great-uncle Martin Gropius before him, became an architect. Gropius could not draw, and was dependent on collaborators and partner-interpreters throughout his career. In school he hired an assistant to complete his homework for him. In 1908, after studying architecture in Munich and Berlin for four semesters, Gropius joined the office of the renowned architect and industrial designer Peter Behrens, one of the first members of the utilitarian school. His fellow employees at this time included Ludwig Mies van der Rohe, Le Corbusier, and Dietrich Marcks.

In 1910 Gropius left the firm of Behrens and together with fellow employee Adolf Meyer established a practice in Berlin. Together they share credit for one of the seminal modernist buildings created during this period: the Faguswerk in Alfeld-an-der-Leine, Germany, a shoe last factory. Although Gropius and Meyer only designed the facade, the glass curtain walls of this building demonstrated both the modernist principle that form reflects function and Gropius's concern with providing healthful conditions for the working class. The factory is now regarded as one of the crucial founding monuments of European modernism. Gropius was commissioned in 1913 to design a car for the Prussian Railroad Locomotive Works in Königsberg. This locomotive was unique and the first of its kind in Germany and perhaps in Europe. Other works of this early period include the office and factory building for the Werkbund Exhibition (1914) in Cologne.

Generative Mistranslation as Pedagogical Design Strategy

In 1913, Gropius published an article about "The Development of Industrial Buildings," which included about a dozen photographs of factories and grain elevators in North America. A very influential text which had a strong influence on other European modernists, including Le Corbusier and Erich Mendelsohn, both of whom reprinted Gropius's grain elevator pictures between 1920 and 1930.

Gropius's career was interrupted by the outbreak of World War I in 1914. Called up immediately as a reservist, Gropius served as a sergeant major at the Western front during the war years and was wounded and almost killed. Gropius was awarded an Iron Cross ("when it still meant something," he confided to his friend Chester Nagel) while fighting for four years for Germany on the Western Front.

Bauhaus period (1919–28)

Gropius's career advanced in the postwar period. Henry van de Velde, the master of the Grand-Ducal Saxon School of Arts and Crafts in Weimar was asked to step down in 1915 due to his Belgian nationality. His recommendation for Gropius to succeed him led eventually to Gropius's appointment as master of the school in 1919. It was this academy which Gropius transformed into the world-famous Bauhaus, attracting a faculty that included Paul Klee, Johannes Itten, Josef Albers, Herbert Bayer, László Moholy-Nagy, Otto Bartning and Wassily Kandinsky. In principle, the Bauhaus represented an opportunity to extend beauty and quality to every home through well designed industrially produced objects.

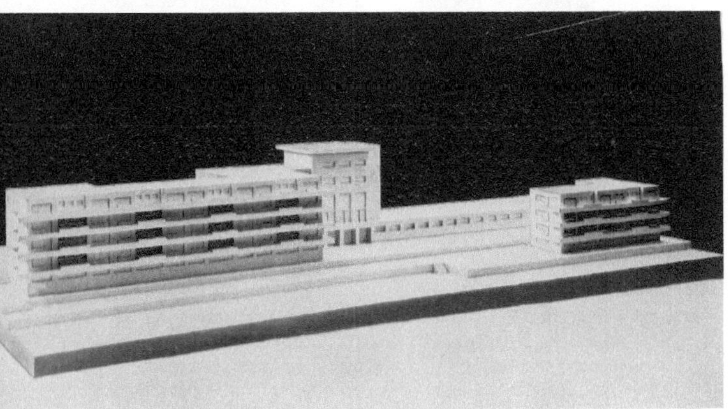

Walter Gropius, Dessau, Anhalt mit Adolf Meyer   Modell zu einem Internationalen Philisophenheim auf dem Burgberg in Erlangen. 1923.

Klee Mutations

In 1919, Gropius was involved in the Glass Chain utopian expressionist correspondence under the pseudonym "Mass." Usually more notable for his functionalist approach, the "Monument to the March Dead," designed in 1919 and executed in 1920, indicates that expressionism was an influence on him at that time.

Walter Gropius designed the newly constructed school building in 1925 on behalf of the city of Dessau. Gropius collaborated with Carl Fieger, Ernst Neufert and others within his private architectural practice. He also designed large-scale housing projects in Berlin, Karlsruhe and Dessau in 1926–32 that were major contributions to the New Objectivity movement, including a contribution to the Siemensstadt project in Berlin.

Gropius left the Bauhaus in 1928 and moved to Berlin. Hannes Meyer took over the role of Bauhaus director.

Post Bauhaus (1933–45)

The rise of Hitler in the 1930s would soon drive Gropius out of Germany. With the help of the English architect Maxwell Fry, Gropius was able to leave Nazi Germany in 1934, on the pretext of making a temporary visit to Italy for a film propaganda festival; he then fled to Britain to avoid the fascist powers of Europe. He lived and worked in Britain, as part of the Isokon group with Fry and others and then moved on to the United States with his family. Walter Gropius and his second wife, Ise Gropius, arrived in the United States in February 1937, while their twelve-year-old daughter, Ati, finished the school year in England. Though built in 1938, the Gropiuses believed their house could embody architectural qualities similar to those practiced today, such as simplicity, economy, and aesthetic beauty. In designing his house, Gropius used the approach developed at the Bauhaus. The house the Gropiuses built for themselves in Lincoln, Massachusetts (now known as Gropius House), was influential in bringing International Modernism to the U.S., but Gropius disliked the term: "I made it a point to absorb into my own conception those features of the New England architectural tradition that I found still alive and adequate." Helen Storrow, a banker's wife and philanthropist, became Gropius's benefactor when she invested a portion of her land and wealth for the architect's home. She was so satisfied with the result that she gave more land and financial support to four other professors, two of whom Gropius designed homes for. With the Bauhaus philosophy in mind, every aspect of the homes and their surrounding landscapes were planned for maximum efficiency and simplicity.

Gropius and his Bauhaus protégé Marcel Breuer both moved to Cambridge, Massachusetts, to teach at the Harvard Graduate School of Design (1937–1952) and collaborate on projects including The Alan I W Frank House in Pittsburgh and the company-town Aluminum City Terrace project in New Kensington, Pennsylvania, before their professional split. In 1938 he was appointed chairman of the Department of Architecture, a post he held until his retirement in 1952. Gropius also sat on the Massachusetts Institute of Technology (MIT) Visiting Committee at the end of his career.[19]

Research mutation: László Moholy-Nagy

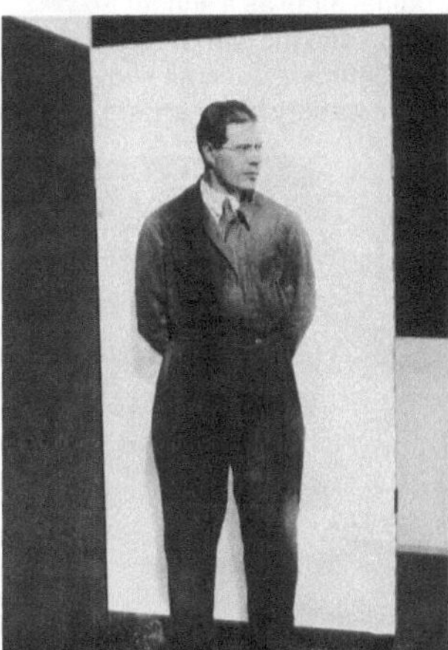

Moholy-Nagy at the Bauhaus in Dessau, wearing his customary uniform of the red coveralls. Photo by Lucia Moholy, 1926

László Moholy-Nagy (1895 – 1946) was a Hungarian painter and photographer as well as a professor in the Bauhaus school. He was highly influenced by

constructivism and a strong advocate of the integration of technology and industry into the arts.

Early life

Moholy-Nagy was born László Weisz in Bácsborsód to a Jewish family. He changed his German-Jewish surname to the Magyar surname of his mother's Christian lawyer friend Nagy, who supported the family and helped raise László and his brothers when their Jewish father, Lipót Weisz left the family. Later, he added "Moholy" to his

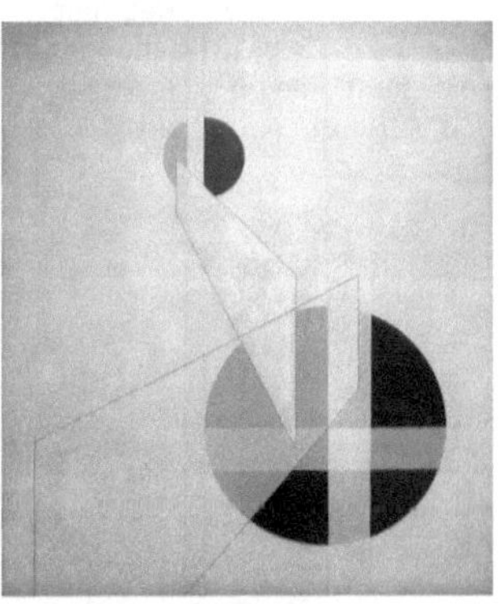

Laszlo Moholy-Nagy, composizione A.XX, 1924

surname, after the name of the town of Mohol (today in Serbia) in which he grew up. One part of his boyhood was spent in the family home near Mohol.

In 1918, he formally converted to the Hungarian Reformed Church; his godfather was his Roman Catholic university friend, the art critic

Klee Mutations

Ivan Hevesy. Immediately before and during World War I, he studied law in Budapest and served in the war, where he sustained a serious injury. In Budapest, on leave and during convalescence, Moholy-Nagy became involved first with the journal *Jelenkor* (*The Present Age*), edited by Hevesy, and then with the "Activist" circle around Lajos Kassák's journal *Ma* (*Today*). After his discharge from the Austro-Hungarian army in October 1918, he attended the private art school of the Hungarian Fauve artist Róbert Berény. He was a supporter of the Hungarian Soviet Republic, declared early in 1919, though he assumed no official role in it. After the defeat of the Communist regime in August, he withdrew to Szeged. An exhibition of his work was held there, before he left for Vienna around November 1919. He left for Berlin early in 1920.

At the Bauhaus

In 1923, Moholy-Nagy took over Johannes Itten's role co-teaching the Bauhaus preliminary course with Josef Albers and also replaced Itten as Head of the Metal Workshop. This effectively marked the end of the school's expressionistic leanings and moved it closer towards its original aims as a school of design and industrial integration. The Bauhaus became known for the versatility of its artists, and

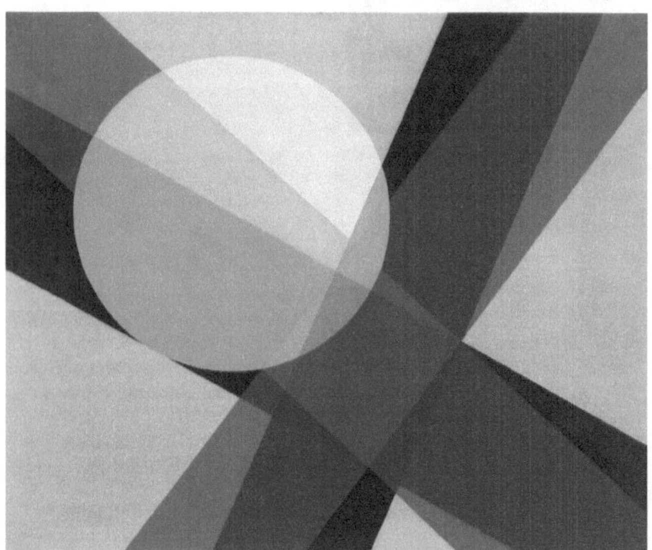

Laszlo Moholy-Nagy, composizione A.XX, 1924

Moholy-Nagy was no exception. Throughout his career, he became proficient and innovative in the fields of photography, typography, sculpture, painting, printmaking, and industrial design. One of his main focuses was photography. He coined the term *Neues Sehen* (New Vision) for his belief that photography could create a whole new way of seeing the outside world that the human eye could not. His theory of art and teaching is summed up in his book *The New Vision, from Material to Architecture*. He experimented with the photographic process of exposing light sensitive paper with objects overlain on top of it, called photogram. His teaching practice covered a diverse range of media, including painting, sculpture, photography, photomontage and metal.

He left the Bauhaus in 1928 and established his own design studio in Berlin. Marianne Brandt took over his role as Head of the Metal Workshop.

Later career

Perhaps his most enduring achievement is the construction of the "Lichtrequisit einer elektrischen Bühne" [Light Prop for an Electric Stage] (completed 1930), a device with moving parts meant to have light projected through it in order to create mobile light reflections and shadows on nearby surfaces. Made with the help of the Hungarian architect Istvan Seboek for the Deutscher Werkbund exhibition held in Paris during the summer of 1930, it is often interpreted as a kinetic sculpture. After his death, it was dubbed the "Light-Space Modulator" and was seen as a pioneer achievement of kinetic sculpture. It might more accurately be seen as one of the earliest examples of Light Art. Moholy-Nagy was photography editor of the Dutch avant-garde magazine *International Revue i 10* from 1927 to 1929. He designed stage sets for successful and controversial operatic and theatrical productions, designed exhibitions and books, created ad campaigns, wrote articles and made films. His studio employed artists and designers such as Istvan Seboek, Gyorgy Kepes and Andor Weininger. After the Nazis came to power in Germany in 1933, and, as a foreign citizen, he was no longer allowed to work, he operated for a time in the Netherlands (doing mostly commercial work) before moving to London in 1935.

In England, Moholy-Nagy formed part of the circle of émigré artists and intellectuals who based themselves in Hampstead. Moholy-Nagy lived for a time in the Isokon building with Walter Gropius for eight months and then settled in Golders Green. Gropius and Moholy-Nagy planned to establish an English version of the Bauhaus but could not secure backing, and then Moholy-Nagy was turned down for a teaching job at the Royal College of Art. Moholy-Nagy made his way in London by taking on various design jobs including

Klee Mutations

Imperial Airways and a shop display for men's underwear. He photographed contemporary architecture for the Architectural Review where the assistant editor was John Betjeman who commissioned Moholy-Nagy to make documentary photographs to illustrate his book *An Oxford University Chest*. In 1936, he was commissioned by fellow Hungarian film producer Alexander Korda to design special effects for *Things to Come*. Working at Denham Studios, Moholy-Nagy created kinetic sculptures and abstract light effects, but they were rejected by the film's director. At the invitation of Leslie Martin, he gave a lecture to the architecture school of Hull School of Art.

In the US

In 1937, at the invitation of Walter Paepcke, the Chairman of the Container Corporation of America, Moholy-Nagy moved to Chicago to become the director of the New Bauhaus. The philosophy of the school was basically unchanged from that of the original, and its headquarters was the Prairie Avenue mansion that architect Richard Morris Hunt designed for department store magnate Marshall Field.

Unfortunately, the school lost the financial backing of its supporters after only a single academic year, and it closed in 1938. Moholy-Nagy was also the Art Advisor for the mail-order house of Spiegel in Chicago

Paepcke, however, continued his own support, and in 1939,

Moholy-Nagy opened the School of Design. In 1944, this became the Institute of Design. In 1949 the Institute of Design became a part of Illinois Institute of Technology and became the first institution in the United States to offer a PhD in design. Moholy-Nagy authored an account of his efforts to develop the curriculum of the School of Design in his book *Vision in Motion*.[20]

Research mutation: Lucia Moholy

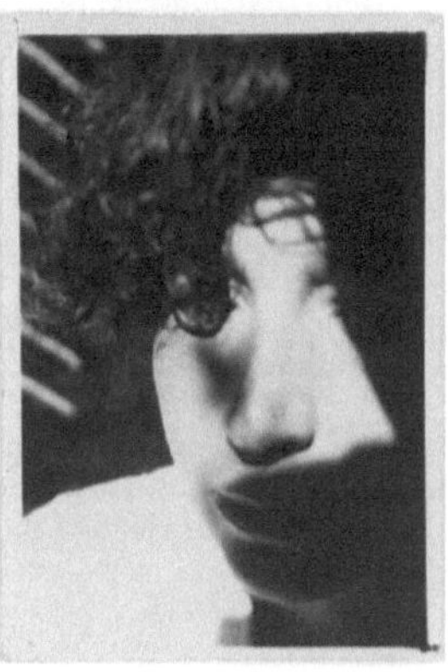

Lucia Moholy, circa. 1924–28

Lucia Moholy, born Lucia Schulz (1894–1989) was a photographer, artist, art critic and photographic historian. Her photography documented the architecture and products of the Bauhaus and introduced their work to a post-World War II audience. However, Moholy was seldom credited for her work, which was often attributed to László Moholy-Nagy or Walter Gropius.

Generative Mistranslation as Pedagogical Design Strategy

In the early 1910s Lucia Moholy studied philosophy, philology, and art history, at the University of Prague. In 1915 she shifted her attention to publishing and worked as an editor for several publishing houses in Germany. In 1919 she published radical, Expressionist literature under the pseudonym Ulrich Steffen. She met Hungarian artist László Moholy-Nagy in 1920 in Berlin and married him on her 27th birthday in January 1921.The two

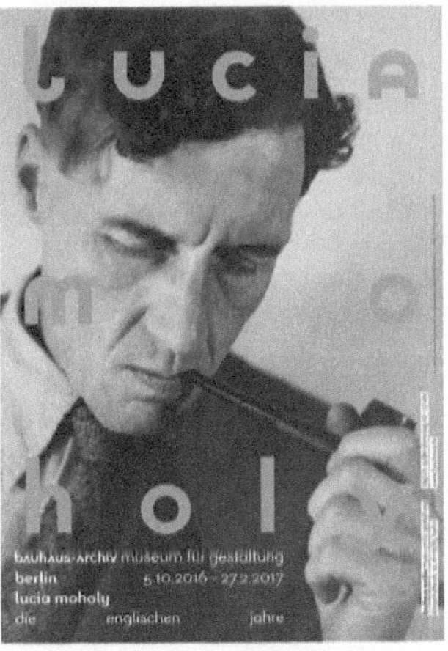

Poster for a 2016 Lucia Moholy exhibition at the Bauhaus-Archiv

would spend five years at the Bauhaus, where Lucia Moholy would explore her affinity with photography.

Her husband became a master at the Bauhaus in 1923 with Lucia Moholy as his primary darkroom technician and an important collaborator. She also became an apprentice in Otto Eckner's Bauhaus photography studio. Moholy studied at the Leipzig Academy for Graphic and Book Arts (Academy of Visual Arts, Leipzig) where she became a skilled photographer. Together the couple lived in Weimar and Dessau and she would produce images and portraits associated with that school. Moholy documented the interior and exterior of the Bauhaus architecture, its facilities, as well as the students and teachers. Her aesthetic was part of the *Neue Sachlichkeitm* (New Objectivity) which focused on documentation from a straightforward perspective. Moholy's Bauhaus photographs helped construct the identity of the school and created its image.

Lucia Moholy and her husband experimented with different processes in the darkroom, such as photogram. In numerous publications, all of the experimentation the couple had done was credited solely to László Moholy-Nagy, such as the book *Malerei, Photografie, Film* (1925; *Painting, Photography, Film*), which was published only under her husband's name.

In 1929 the couple separated. That same year Lucia Moholy was included in the landmark exhibition in Stuttgart, *Film and Foto*. It featured artists working in the New Vision aesthetic ("Precisionism").

She then taught photography at a private art school in Berlin directed by Johannes Itten. In 1933 when the National Socialist German Workers Party rose to power she emigrated to London to flee from World War II. There, she focused on commercial photography and teaching. She also published a book, *A Hundred Years of Photography, 1839-1939*, written in English, which discussed in depth the history of the medium.

Recognition

Lucia Moholy struggled to receive recognition for her work. Her images were used for marketing and in the Bauhaus school's sales catalogs, as well as Bauhaus books that she edited. In 1933 Moholy was dating a Communist Member of Parliament, who was arrested in her apartment one day when she was out. She fled to Prague and stayed with family, and then to Switzerland, then Austria, then Paris, and finally settled in London. She had left everything behind in Berlin, including glass negatives of her photographs of the Bauhaus. They ended up in the hands of Walter Gropius.

While she resided in London, an interest in the Bauhaus started to grow, and she saw numerous catalogs of the Bauhaus printed with her lost images. Gropius had been using her photographs without crediting her. In an exhibition on the Bauhaus at the Museum of Modern Art (MoMA) in 1938, Gropius used nearly 50 of Moholy's images for the exhibition and the accompanying catalogue without crediting her once. She repeatedly reached out to Walter Gropius to reclaim her images and he would continuously protest. Moholy resulted to hiring a lawyer to retrieve her work.

Letters from Walter Gropius and Lucia Moholy were retrieved in which Moholy stated, "These negatives are irreplaceable documents which could be extremely useful, now more than ever" to which Gropius replied, ". . . long years ago in Berlin, you gave all these negatives to me. You will imagine that these photographs are extremely useful to me and that I have continuously made use of them; so I hope you will not deprive me of them." Lucia Moholy responded, "Surely you did not expect me to delay my departure in order to draw up a formal contract stipulating date and conditions of return? No formal agreement could have carried more weight than our friendship. It is a friendship I have always relied on, and which, also, I am now invoking."

Moholy did not get a hold of her original material until the 1960s, even then she only retrieved a number of them. Her 1972 publication, *Moholy-Nagy Notes*, was an attempt to reclaim her work that was printed without permission.

Research mutation: Sibyl Moholy-Nagy

Sibyl Moholy-Nagy (1903–1971) was an architectural and art historian. Originally a German citizen, she accompanied her husband, László Moholy-Nagy, in his move to the United States. She is the author of one of the most important studies of his work, *Moholy-Nagy: Experiment in Totality*, plus several other books on architectural history.

Sibylle Pietzsch was born in Dresden on October 29, 1903 to architect Martin Pietzsch (Deutscher Werkbund) and Fanny Clauss Pietzsch. After attending the University of Dresden, she became an actress, performing in several films. She eventually became a scriptwriter,

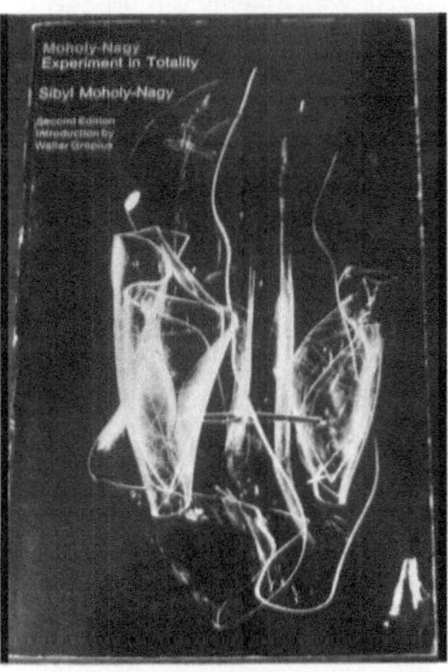

Moholy-Nagy: Experiment in Totality
by Sibyl Moholy-Nagy

and in the late 1920s, met László Moholy-Nagy while working on a film script. They were married in 1932. They had two daughters, Hattula (born 1933), and Claudia (1936–1971). After residing together in Germany for over a year and a half, they left due to the rise of Nazism. In 1934, they settled in Amsterdam, and then London for two years.

In 1937, the family emigrated

to the United States, settling in Chicago. Here, Moholy-Nagy assisted her husband in opening and the New Bauhaus, in October 1937. Moholy-Nagy also helped her husband and the New Bauhaus staff to run the school until its closure in 1938. Moholy-Nagy also helped her husband run the Chicago Institute of Design for several years. Her first, and only published novel, *Children's Children*, appeared in 1945.

After her husband's death in November, 1946, Moholy-Nagy decided she would become an architectural historian and teacher. Her first book, a biography on her husband, *Moholy-Nagy: Experiment in Totality*, established her as an academic. In 1951, after holding teaching positions in Chicago and San Francisco respectively, she got a job as associate professor of architecture history at the Pratt Institute in New York City. She taught courses on such subjects as urban history and design. She retired from being a full professor in 1969, and became a visiting professor at Columbia University until her death.

One her most important books, *Matrix of Man: An Illustrated History of Urban Environment*, appeared in 1968. She also made numerous contributions to architecture magazines, such as *Architectural Forum* and *Progressive Architecture*. She was also one of the first critics to study post-War Latin American architecture in-depth.

She died in New York City on January 8, 1971.[18]

Research mutation: Johannes Itten

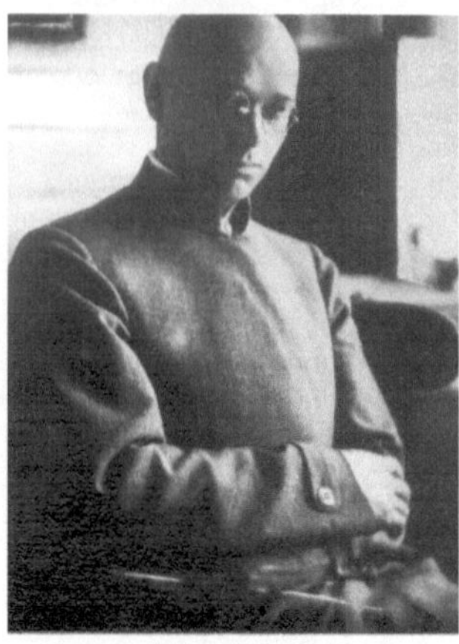

Johannes Itten

Johannes Itten (1888–1967) was a Swiss expressionist painter, designer, teacher, writer and theorist associated with the Bauhaus school. Under the direction of German architect Walter Gropius, Itten was part of the core of the Weimar Bauhaus.

Life and work

He was born in Südern-Linden, Switzerland. From 1904 to 1908 he trained as an elementary school teacher. Beginning in 1908 he taught using methods developed by the creator of the kindergarten concept, Friedrich Fröbel, and was exposed to the ideas of psychoanalysis.

Itten's studies at the Bern-Hofwil Teachers' Academy with Ernst Schneider proved seminal for his later work as a master at the Bauhaus. Itten adopted principles espoused by Schneider, including the practice of not correcting his students' creative work on an individual basis, for fear that this would crush the creative impulse. Rather, he selected certain common mistakes to correct for the class as a whole. In 1912, he returned to Geneva, where he studied under Eugène Gilliard, an abstract painter.

He was heavily influenced by Adolf Hölzel and Franz Cižek Itten opened a private art school in Vienna, using the work and textbook of Eugène Gilliard as a base. From Hölzel, Itten adopted a series of basic shapes (the line, the plane, the circle, the spiral) as a means from which to begin creation, and the use of gymnastic exercises to relax his students and prepare them for the experiences that were to occur in the class.

From 1919 to 1922, Itten taught at the Bauhaus, developing the innovative "preliminary course" which was to teach students the basics of material characteristics, composition, and color. Itten theorized seven types of color contrast and devised exercises to teach them. His color contrasts include: 1. Contrast by hue, 2. Contrast by value, 3. Contrast by temperature, 4. Contrast by complements (neutralization), 5. Simultaneous contrast (from Chevreuil, 6. Contrast by saturation (mixtures with gray), and 7. Contrast by extension (from Goethe). In 1920 Itten invited Paul Klee and

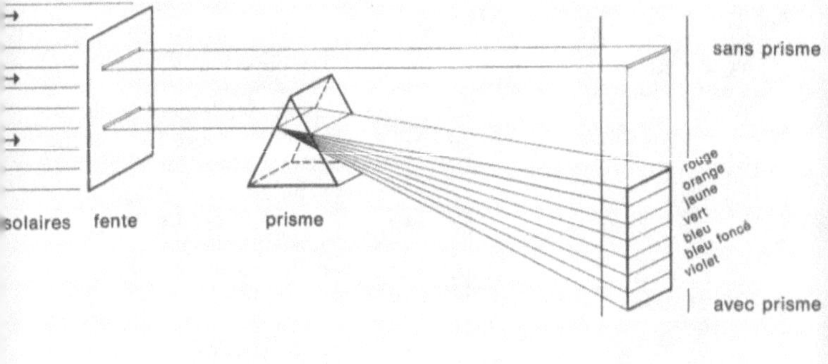

Detail from Itten's *The Art of Color*

Georg Muche to join him at the Bauhaus. He also published a book, *The Art of Color*, which describes these ideas as a furthering of Adolf Hölzel's color wheel. Itten's so called "color sphere" went on to include 12 colors. In 1924, Itten established the "Ontos Weaving Workshops" near Zurich, with the help of Bauhaus weaver Gunta Stölzl.

Itten was a follower of Mazdaznan, a fire cult originating in the United States that was largely derived from Zoroastrianism. He observed a strict vegetarian diet and practiced meditation as a means to develop inner understanding and intuition, which was for him the principal source of artistic inspiration and practice. Itten's mysticism and the reverence in which he was held by a group of the students, some of whom converted to Mazdaznan, created conflict with Walter Gropius who wanted to move the school in a direction that embraced mass production rather than solely individual artistic expression. The rift led to Itten's resignation from the Bauhaus and his prompt replacement by László Moholy-Nagy in 1923. From 1926 to 1934 he had a small art and architecture school in Berlin, in which Ernst Neufert, the former chief-architect of Walter Gropius at the Bauhaus, taught as well from 1932 to 1934.

Itten's works exploring the use and composition of color resemble the square op art canvases of artists such as Josef Albers, Max Bill and Bridget Riley, and the expressionist works of Wassily Kandinsky.

In 1955, Itten taught colour courses at the HfG Ulm (Hochschule für Gestaltung Ulm).[21]

Research mutation: Wassily Kandinsky

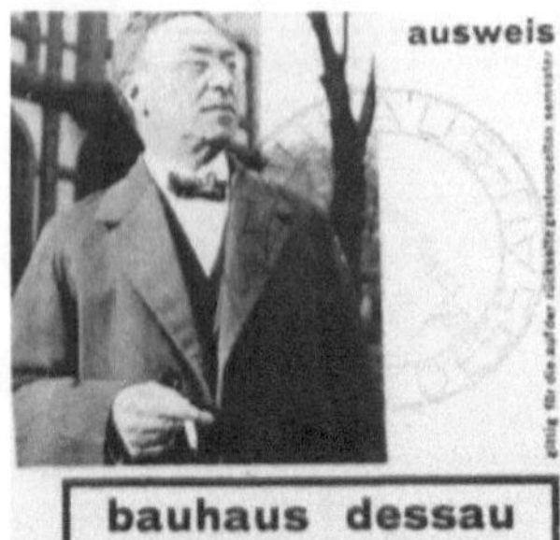

Kandinsky's Bauhaus identification card

Wassily Wassilyevich Kandinsky (1866–1944) was a Russian painter and art theorist.

He is credited with painting one of the first recognised purely abstract works. Born in Moscow, Kandinsky spent his childhood in Odessa, where he graduated at Grekov Odessa Art school. He enrolled at the University of Moscow, studying law and economics. Successful in his profession – he was offered a professorship (chair of Roman Law) at the University of Dorpat – Kandinsky began painting studies (life-drawing, sketching and anatomy) at the age of 30.

In 1896, Kandinsky settled in Munich, studying first at Anton Ažbe's private school and then at the Academy of Fine Arts. He returned to Moscow in 1914, after the outbreak of World War I.

Kandinsky was unsympathetic to the official theories on art in Communist Moscow, and returned to Germany in 1920. There, he taught at the Bauhaus school of art and architecture from 1922 until the Nazis closed it in 1933. He then moved to France, where he lived for the rest of his life, becoming a French citizen in 1939 and producing some of his most prominent art. He died at Neuilly-sur-Seine in 1944.

Artistic periods

Kandinsky's creation of abstract work followed a long period of development and maturation of intense thought based on his artistic experiences. He called this devotion to inner beauty, fervor of spirit, and spiritual desire inner necessity; it was a central aspect of his art.

Youth and inspiration (1866–1896)

Kandinsky was born in Moscow, the son of Lidia Ticheeva and Vasily Silvestrovich Kandinsky, a tea merchant. His family comprised German aristocrats, and from his maternal side he also had Tatar origins, to which he ascribed the "slight Mongolian trait in his features". Later in life, he would recall being fascinated and stimulated by colour as a child. His fascination with colour symbolism and psychology continued as he grew. In 1889, he was part of an ethnographic research group which travelled to the Vologda region north of

Generative Mistranslation as Pedagogical Design Strategy

Moscow. In *Looks on the Past*, he relates that the houses and churches were decorated with such shimmering colours that upon entering them, he felt that he was moving into a painting. This experience, and his study of the region's folk art (particularly the use of bright colours on a dark background), was reflected in much of his early work. A few years later he first likened painting to composing music in the manner for which he would become noted, writing, "Colour is the keyboard, the eyes are the hammers, the soul is the piano with many strings. The artist is the hand which plays, touching one key or another, to cause vibrations in the soul".

In 1896, at the age of 30, Kandinsky gave up a promising career teaching law and economics to enroll in the Munich Academy where his teachers would eventually include Franz von Stuck. He was not immediately granted admission, and began learning art on his own. That same year, before leaving Moscow, he saw an exhibit of paintings by Monet. He was particularly taken with the impressionistic style of Haystacks; this, to him, had a powerful sense of colour almost independent of the objects themselves. Later, he would write about this experience:

> That it was a haystack the catalogue informed me. I could not recognize it. This non-recognition was painful to me. I considered that the painter had no right to paint indistinctly.

> I dully felt that the object of the painting was missing. And I noticed with surprise and confusion that the picture not only gripped me, but impressed itself ineradicably on my memory. Painting took on a fairy-tale power and splendour.

Kandinsky was similarly influenced during this period by Richard Wagner's *Lohengrin* which, he felt, pushed the limits of music and melody beyond standard lyricism. He was also spiritually influenced by Madame Blavatsky, the best-known exponent of theosophy. Theosophical theory postulates that creation is a geometrical progression, beginning with a single point. The creative aspect of the form is expressed by a descending series of circles, triangles and squares. Kandinsky's book *Concerning the Spiritual In Art* (1910) and *Point and Line to Plane* (1926) echoed this theosophical tenet. Illustrations by John Varley in *Thought Forms* (1901) also influenced him visually.

Metamorphosis

In the summer of 1902, Kandinsky invited Gabriele Münter to join him at his summer painting classes just south of Munich in the Alps. She accepted, and their relationship became more personal than professional. Art school, usually considered difficult, was easy for Kandinsky. It was during this time that he began to emerge as an art theorist as well as a painter. The number of his existing paintings increased in the beginning of the 20th century; much remains of the landscapes and towns he painted, using broad swaths of colour and recognizable forms. For the most part, however, Kandinsky's paintings did not feature any human figures; an exception is *Sunday, Old Russia* (1904), in which Kandinsky recreates a highly colourful (and fanciful) view of peasants and nobles in front of the walls of a town. *Riding Couple* (1907) depicts a man on horseback, holding a woman with tenderness and care as they ride past a Russian town with luminous walls across a river. The horse is muted while the leaves in the trees, the town, and the reflections in the river glisten with spots of colour and brightness. This work demonstrates the influence of pointillism in the way the depth of field is collapsed into a flat, luminescent surface. Fauvism is also apparent in these early works. Colours are used to express Kandinsky's experience of subject matter, not to describe objective nature.

Perhaps the most important of his paintings from the first decade of the 1900s was *The Blue Rider* (1903), which shows a small cloaked figure on a speeding horse rushing through a rocky meadow. The rider's cloak is medium blue, which casts a darker-blue shadow. In the foreground are more amorphous blue shadows, the counterparts of the fall trees in the background. The blue rider in the painting is prominent (but not clearly defined), and the horse has an unnatural gait (which Kandinsky must have known). Some art historians believe that a second figure (perhaps a child) is being held by the rider, although this may be another shadow from the solitary rider. This intentional disjunction, allowing viewers to participate in the creation of the artwork, became an increasingly conscious technique used by Kandinsky in subsequent years; it culminated in the abstract works of the 1911–1914 period. In *The Blue Rider*, Kandinsky shows the rider more as a series of colours than in specific detail. This painting is not exceptional in that regard when compared with contemporary painters, but it shows the direction Kandinsky would take only a few years later.

From 1906 to 1908 Kandinsky spent a great deal of time travelling across Europe (he was an associate of the Blue Rose symbolist group of Moscow), until he settled in the small Bavarian town of Murnau. In 1908 he bought a copy of *Thought-Forms* by Annie Besant and Charles Webster Leadbeater. In 1909 he joined the Theosophical Society. *The Blue Mountain* (1908–1909) was painted at this time, demonstrating his trend toward abstraction. A mountain of blue is flanked by two broad trees, one yellow and one red. A procession, with three riders and several others, crosses at the bottom. The faces, clothing, and saddles of the riders are each a single colour, and neither they nor the walking figures display any real detail. The flat planes and the contours also are indicative of Fauvist influence. The broad use of colour in *The Blue Mountain* illustrates Kandinsky's inclination toward an art in which colour is presented independently of form, and which each colour is given equal attention. The composition is more planar; the painting is divided into four sections: the sky, the red tree, the yellow tree and the blue mountain with the three riders.

Blue Rider Period (1911-1914)

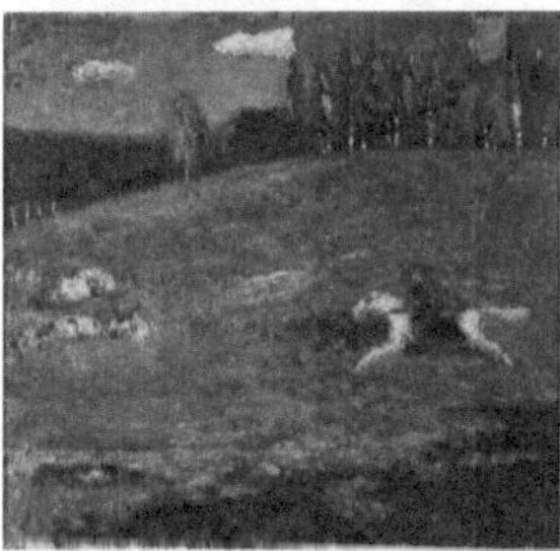

The Blue Rider. 1903

Kandinsky's paintings from this period are large, expressive coloured masses evaluated independently from forms and lines; these serve no longer to delimit them, but overlap freely to form paintings of extraordinary force. Music was important to the birth of abstract art, since music is abstract by nature – it does not try to represent the exterior world, but expresses in an immediate way the inner feelings of the soul. Kandinsky sometimes used musical terms to identify his works; he called his most spontaneous paintings "improvisations" and described more elaborate works as "compositions."

In addition to painting, Kandinsky was an art theorist; his influence on the history of Western art stems perhaps more from his theoretical works than from his paintings. He helped found the *Neue Künstlervereinigung München* (Munich New Artists' Association), becoming its president in 1909. However, the group could not integrate the radical approach of Kandinsky (and others) with conventional artistic concepts and the group dissolved in late 1911. Kandinsky then formed a new group, the Blue Rider (Der Blaue Reiter) with like-minded artists such as August Macke, Franz Marc, Albert Bloch, and Gabriele Münter. The group released an almanac (*The Blue Rider Almanac*) and held two exhibits. More of each were planned, but the outbreak of World War I in 1914 ended these plans and sent Kandinsky back to Russia via Switzerland and Sweden.

His writing in *The Blue Rider Almanac* and the treatise *On the Spiritual In Art* were both a defence and promotion of abstract art and an affirmation that all forms of art were equally capable of reaching a level of spirituality. He believed that colour could be used in a painting as something autonomous, apart from the visual description of an object or other form.

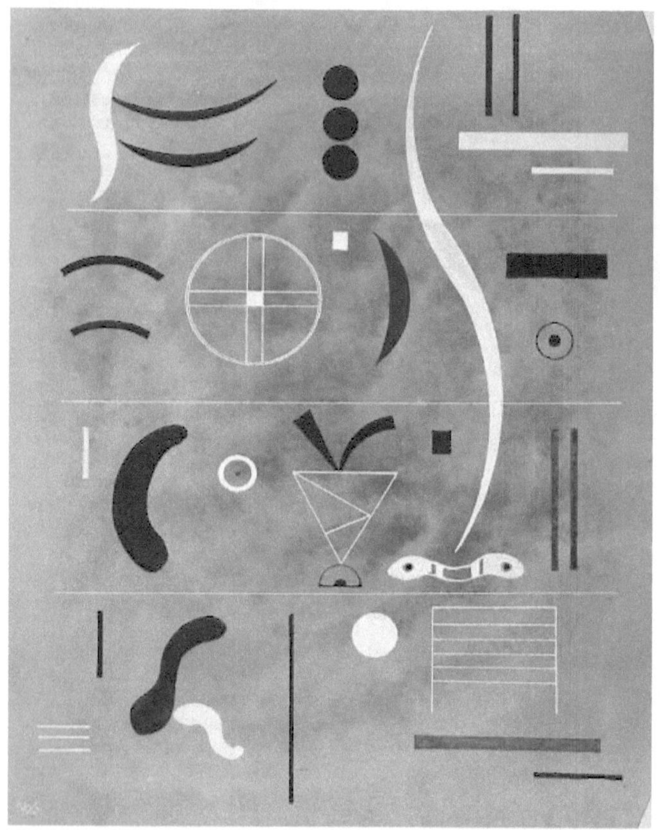

Four Parts, 1932
Gouache on paper, mounted on Masonite

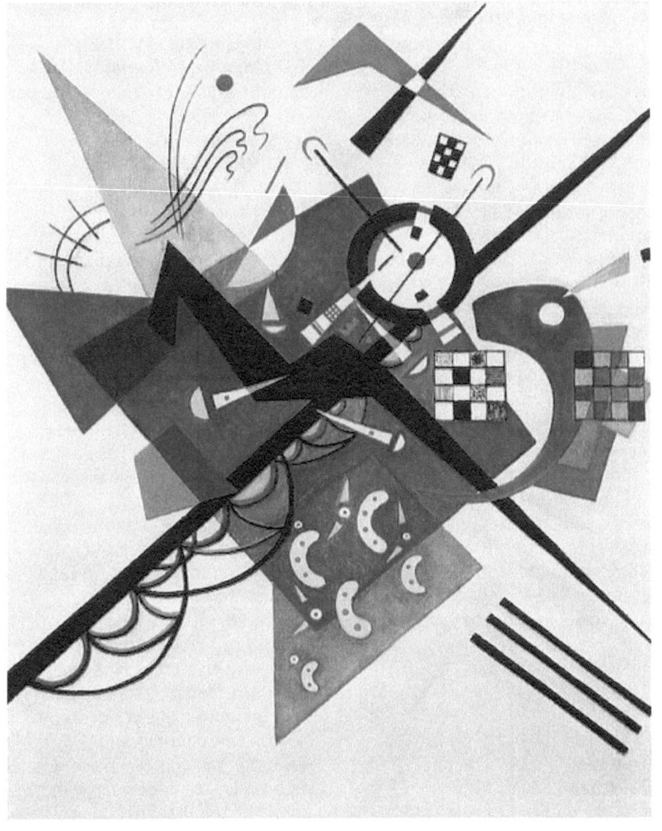

On White II. 1923
Gouache on paper, mounted on Masonite

Klee Mutations

These ideas had an almost-immediate international impact, particularly in the English-speaking world. As early as 1912, *On the Spiritual In Art* was reviewed by Michael Sadleir in the London-based *Art News*. Interest in Kandinsky grew apace when Sadleir published an English translation of *On the Spiritual In Art* in 1914. Extracts from the book were published that year in Percy Wyndham Lewis's periodical *Blast*, and Alfred Orage's weekly cultural newspaper *The New Age*. Sadleir's interest in Kandinsky also led to Kandinsky's first works entering a British art collection; Sadleir's father, Michael Sadler, acquired several woodprints and the abstract painting *Fragment for Composition VII* in 1913 following a visit by father and son to meet Kandinsky in Munich that year.

Return to Russia
(1914–1921)

From 1918 to 1921, Kandinsky dealt with the cultural politics of Russia and collaborated in art education and museum reform. He painted little during this period, but devoted his time to artistic teaching, with a program based on form and colour analysis; he also helped organize the Institute of Artistic Culture in Moscow. In 1916 he met Nina Andreievskaya, whom he married the following year. His spiritual, expressionistic view of art was ultimately rejected by the radical members of the Institute as too individualistic and bourgeois.

In 1921, Kandinsky was invited to go to Germany to attend the Bauhaus of Weimar by its founder, architect Walter Gropius.

Bauhaus
(1922–1933)

Kandinsky taught the basic design class for beginners and the course on advanced theory at the Bauhaus; he also conducted painting classes and a workshop in which he augmented his colour theory with new elements of form psychology. The development of his works on forms study, particularly on points and line forms, led to the publication of his second theoretical book, *Point and Line to Plane*, in 1926. His examinations of the effects of forces on straight lines, leading to the contrasting tones of curved and angled lines, coincided with the research of Gestalt psychologists, whose work was also discussed at the Bauhaus. Geometrical elements took on increasing importance in both his teaching and painting –particularly the circle, half-circle, the angle, straight lines and curves. This period was intensely productive. This freedom is characterised in his works by the treatment of planes rich in colours and gradations – as in *Yellow – red – blue* (1925), where Kandinsky illustrates his distance from the constructivism and suprematism movements influential at the time.

The two-meter-wide *Yellow – red – blue* of several main forms: a vertical yellow rectangle, an inclined red cross and a large dark blue circle; a multitude of straight (or sinuous) black lines, circular arcs, monochromatic circles and scattered, coloured checkerboards contribute to its delicate complexity. This simple visual identification of forms and the main coloured masses present on the canvas is only a first approach to the inner reality of the work, whose appreciation necessitates deeper observation – not only of forms and colours involved in the painting but their relationship, their absolute and relative positions on the canvas and their harmony.

Kandinsky was one of *Die Blaue Vier* (Blue Four), formed in 1923 with Klee, Feininger and von Jawlensky, which lectured and exhibited in the United States in 1924. After the Bauhaus's dissolution in July 1933, Kandinsky left Germany, settling in Paris.

Theoretical writings on art

Kandinsky's analyses on forms and colours result not from simple, arbitrary idea-associations but from the painter's inner experience. He spent years creating abstract, sensorially rich paintings, working with form and colour, tirelessly observing his own paintings and those of other artists, noting their effects on his sense of colour. This subjective experience is what French philosopher Michel Honry calls "absolute subjectivity" or the "absolute phenomenological life".

Concerning the spiritual in art

Published in 1912, Kandinsky's text, *Du Spirituel dans l'art*, defines three types of painting; impressions, improvisations and compositions. While impressions are based on an external reality that serves as a starting point, improvisations and compositions depict images emergent from the unconscious, though composition is developed from a more formal point of view. Kandinsky compares the spiritual life of humanity to a pyramid – the artist has a mission to lead others to the pinnacle with his work. The point of the pyramid is those few, great artists. It is a spiritual pyramid, advancing and ascending slowly even if it sometimes appears immobile. During decadent periods, the soul sinks to the bottom of the pyramid; humanity searches only for external success, ignoring spiritual forces.

Colours on the painter's palette evoke a double effect: a purely physical effect on the eye which is charmed by the beauty of colours, similar to the joyful impression when we eat a delicacy. This effect can be much deeper, however, causing a vibration of the soul or an "inner resonance" – a spiritual effect in which the colour touches the soul itself.

"Inner necessity" is, for Kandinsky, the principle of art and the foundation of forms and the harmony of colours. He defines it as the principle of efficient contact of the form with the human soul. Every form is the delimitation of a surface by another one; it possesses an inner content, the effect it produces on one who looks at it attentively. This inner necessity is the right of the artist to unlimited freedom, but this freedom becomes licence if it is not founded on such a necessity. Art is born from the inner necessity of the artist in an enigmatic, mystical way through which it acquires an autonomous life; it becomes an independent subject, animated by a spiritual breath.

The obvious properties we can see when we look at an isolated colour and let it act alone, on one side is the warmth or coldness of the colour tone, and on the other side is the clarity or obscurity of that tone. Warmth is a tendency towards yellow, and coldness a tendency towards blue; yellow and blue form the first great, dynamic contrast. Yellow has an eccentric movement and blue a concentric movement; a yellow surface seems to move closer to us, while a blue surface seems to move away. Yellow is a typically terrestrial colour, whose violence can be painful and aggressive. Blue is a celestial colour, evoking a deep calm. The combination of blue and yellow yields total immobility and calm, which is green.

Clarity is a tendency towards white, and obscurity is a tendency towards black. White and black form the second great contrast, which is static. White is a deep, absolute silence, full of possibility. Black is nothingness without possibility, an eternal silence without hope, and corresponds with death. Any other colour resonates strongly on its neighbors. The mixing of white with black leads to gray, which possesses no active force and whose tonality is near that of green. Gray corresponds to immobility without hope; it tends to despair when it becomes dark, regaining little hope when it lightens.

Red is a warm colour, lively and agitated; it is forceful, a movement in itself. Mixed with black it becomes brown, a hard colour. Mixed with yellow, it gains in warmth and becomes orange, which imparts an irradiating movement on its surroundings. When red is mixed with blue it moves away from man to become purple, which is a cool red. Red and green form the third great contrast, and orange and purple the fourth.

Point and Line to Plane

In his writings, Kandinsky analyzed the geometrical elements which make up every painting – the point and the line. He called the physical support and the material surface on which the artist draws or paints the basic plane, or BP. He did not analyze them objectively, but from the point of view of their inner effect on the observer.

A point is a small bit of colour put by the artist on the canvas. It is neither a geometric point nor a mathematical abstraction; it is extension, form and colour. This form can be a

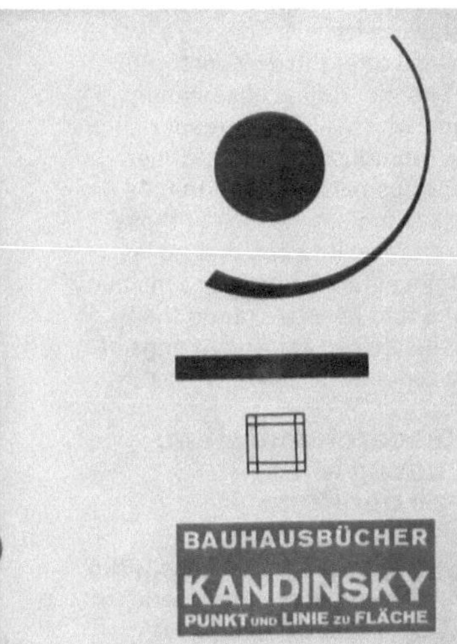

***Punkt und Linie zu Flache
(Point and Line to Plane) 1926.***

square, a triangle, a circle, a star or something more complex. The point is the most concise form but, according to its placement on the basic plane, it will take a different tonality. It can be isolated or resonate with other points or lines.

A line is the product of a force which has been applied in a given direction: the force exerted on the pencil or paintbrush by the artist. The produced linear forms may be of several types: a straight line, which results from a unique force applied in a single direction; an angular line, resulting from the alternation of two forces in different directions, or a curved (or wave-like) line, produced by the effect of two forces acting simultaneously. A plane may be obtained by condensation (from a line rotated around one of its ends).

The subjective effect produced by a line depends on its orientation: a horizontal line corresponds with the ground on which man rests and moves; it possesses a dark and cold affective tonality similar to black or blue. A vertical line corresponds with height, and offers no support; it possesses a luminous, warm tonality close to white and yellow. A diagonal possesses a more-or-less warm (or cold) tonality, according to its inclination toward the horizontal or the vertical.

A force which deploys itself, without obstacle, as the one which produces a straight line corresponds with lyricism; several forces which confront (or annoy) each other form a drama. The angle formed by the angular line also has an inner sonority which is warm and close to yellow for an acute angle (a triangle), cold and similar to blue for an obtuse angle (a circle), and similar to red for a right angle (a square).

The basic plane is, in general, rectangular or square. therefore, it is composed of horizontal and vertical lines which delimit it and define it as an autonomous entity which supports the painting, communicating its affective tonality. This tonality is determined by the relative importance of horizontal and vertical lines: the horizontals giving a calm, cold tonality to the basic plane while the verticals impart a calm, warm tonality. The artist intuits the inner effect of the canvas format and dimensions, which he chooses according to the tonality he wants to give to his work. Kandinsky considered the basic plane a living being, which the artist "fertilizes" and feels "breathing".

Each part of the basic plane possesses an affective colouration; this influences the tonality of the pictorial elements which will be drawn on it, and contributes to the richness of the composition resulting from their juxtaposition on the canvas. The above of the basic plane corresponds with looseness and to lightness, while the below evokes condensation and heaviness. The painter's job is to listen and know these effects to produce paintings which are not just the effect of a random process, but the fruit of authentic work and the result of an effort towards inner beauty.

This book contains many photographic examples and drawing from Kandinsky's works which offer the demonstration of its theoretical observations, and which allow the reader to reproduce in him the inner obviousness provided that he takes the time to look at those pictures with care, that he let them acting on its own sensibility and that he let vibrating the sensible and spiritual strings of his soul.[22]

Research mutation: Ludwig Mies van der Rohe

Ludwig Mies van der Rohe (1886–1969) was a German-American architect. He is commonly referred to and was addressed as Mies, his surname. Along with Le Corbusier, Walter Gropius and Frank Lloyd Wright, he is widely regarded as one of the pioneers of modernist architecture.

Mies, like many of his post-World War I contemporaries,

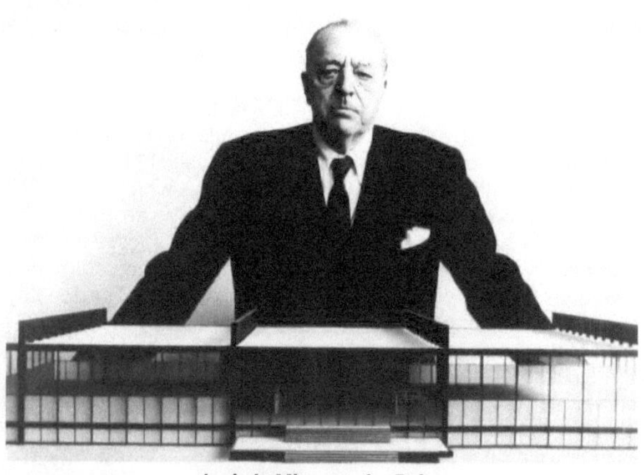

Ludwig Mies van der Rohe

sought to establish a new architectural style that could represent modern times just as Classical and Gothic did for their own eras. He created an influential twentieth-century architectural style, stated with extreme clarity and simplicity. His mature buildings made use of modern materials such as industrial steel and plate glass to define interior spaces. He strove toward an architecture with a minimal framework of structural order balanced against the implied freedom of unobstructed free-flowing open space. He called his buildings "skin and bones" architecture. He sought an objective approach that would guide the creative process of architectural design, but he was always concerned with expressing the spirit of the modern era. He is often associated with his quotation of the aphorisms, "less is more" and "God is in the details".

Early career

Mies was born March 27, 1886 in Aachen, Germany. He worked in his father's stone carving shop and at several local design firms before he moved to Berlin, where he joined the office of interior designer Bruno Paul. He began his architectural career as an apprentice at the studio of Peter Behrens from 1908 to 1912, where he was exposed to the current design theories and to progressive German culture, working alongside Le Corbusier and Walter Gropius. Mies served as construction manager of the Embassy of the German Empire in Saint Petersburg under Behrens.

His talent was quickly recognized and he soon began independent commissions, despite his lack of a formal college-level education. A physically imposing, deliberative, and reticent man, Ludwig Mies renamed himself as part of his rapid transformation from a tradesman's son to an architect working with Berlin's cultural elite, adding "van der" and his mother's surname "Rohe", using the Dutch "van der", because the German form "von" was a nobiliary particle legally restricted to those of genuine aristocratic lineage.

He began his independent professional career designing upper-class homes, joining the movement seeking a return to the purity of early 19th-century Germanic domestic styles. He admired the broad proportions, regularity of rhythmic elements, attention to the relationship of the man-made to nature, and compositions using simple cubic forms of the early nineteenth century Prussian Neo-Classical architect Karl Friedrich Schinkel. He rejected the eclectic and cluttered classical styles so common at the turn of the 20th century as irrelevant to the modern times.

Traditionalism to Modernism

After World War I, Mies began, while still designing traditional neoclassical homes, a parallel experimental effort. He joined his avant-garde peers in the long-running search for a new style that would be suitable for the modern industrial age. The weak points of traditional styles had been under attack by progressive theorists since the mid-nineteenth century, primarily for the contradictions of hiding modern construction technology with a facade of ornamented traditional styles.

The mounting criticism of the historical styles gained substantial cultural credibility after World War I, a disaster widely seen as a failure of the old world order of imperial leadership of Europe. The aristocratic classical revival styles were particularly reviled by many as the architectural symbol of a now-discredited and outmoded social system. Progressive thinkers called for a completely new architectural design process guided by rational problem-solving and an exterior expression of modern materials and structure rather than, what they considered, the superficial application of classical facades.

While continuing his traditional neoclassical design practice Mies began to develop visionary projects that, though mostly unbuilt, rocketed him to fame as an architect capable of giving form that was in harmony with the spirit of the emerging modern society. Boldly abandoning ornament altogether, Mies made a dramatic modernist debut with his stunning competition proposal for the faceted all-glass *Friedrichstraße* skyscraper in 1921, followed by

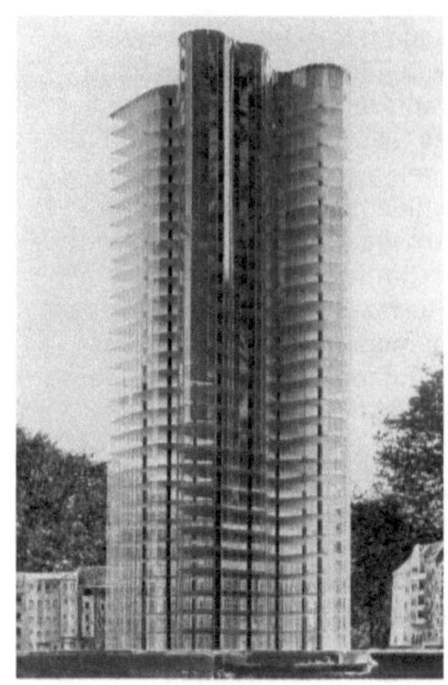

The Glass Skyscraper

a taller curved version in 1922 named the *Glass Skyscraper*.

He continued with a series of pioneering projects, culminating in his two European masterworks: the temporary German Pavilion for the Barcelona exposition (often called the Barcelona Pavilion) in 1929 (a 1986 reconstruction is now built on the original site) and the elegant Villa Tugendhat in Brno, Czech Republic, completed in 1930.

He joined the German avant-garde, working with the progressive design magazine *G* which started in July 1923. He developed prominence as architectural director of the Werkbund, organizing the influential Weissenhof Estate prototype modernist housing exhibition. He was also one of the founders of the architectural association *Der Ring*. He joined

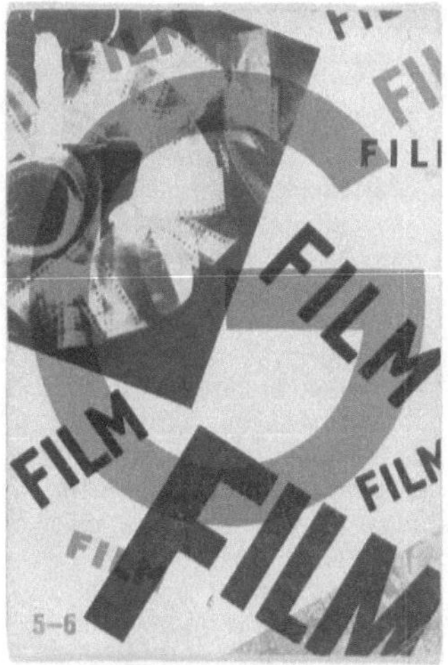

G magazine 5-6 (1926)

the avant-garde Bauhaus design school as their director of architecture, adopting and developing their functionalist application of simple geometric forms in the design of useful objects. He served as its last director.

Like many other avant-garde architects of the day, Mies based his architectural mission and principles on his understanding and interpretation of ideas developed by theorists and critics who pondered the declining relevance of the traditional design styles. He selectively adopted theoretical ideas such as the aesthetic credos of Russian Constructivism with their ideology of "efficient" sculptural assembly of modern industrial materials. Mies found appeal in the use of simple rectilinear and planar forms, clean lines, pure use of color, and the extension of space around and beyond interior walls expounded by the Dutch De Stijl group. In particular, the layering of functional sub-spaces within an overall space and the distinct articulation of parts as expressed by Gerrit Rietveld appealed to Mies.

The design theories of Adolf Loos found resonance with Mies, particularly the ideas of replacing elaborate applied artistic ornament with the straightforward display of innate visual qualities of materials and forms. Loos had proposed that art and crafts should be entirely independent of architecture, that the architect should no longer control those cultural elements as the Beaux Arts principles had dictated. Mies also admired his ideas about the nobility that could be found in the anonymity of modern life.

Emigration to the United States

Commission opportunities dwindled with the Great Depression after 1929. Starting in 1930, Mies served as the last director of the faltering Bauhaus, at the request of his colleague and competitor Walter Gropius. In 1932, Nazi political pressure forced the state-supported school to leave its campus in Dessau, and Mies moved it to an abandoned telephone factory in Berlin. By 1933, however, the continued operation of the school was untenable (it was raided by the Gestapo in April), and in July of that year, Mies and the faculty voted to close the Bauhaus. He built very little in these years (one built commission was Philip Johnson's New York apartment); the Nazis rejected his style as not "German" in character.

Frustrated and unhappy, he left his homeland reluctantly in 1937 as he saw his opportunity for any future building commissions vanish, accepting a residential commission in Wyoming and then an offer to head the department of architecture of the newly established Illinois Institute of Technology (IIT) in Chicago. There he introduced a new kind of education and attitude later known as Second Chicago School, which became very influential in the following decades in North America and Europe.[23]

Research mutation: Deutscher Werkbund

The Deutscher Werkbund (German Association of Craftsmen) is a German association of artists, architects, designers, and industrialists, established in 1907. The Werkbund became an important element in the development of modern architecture and industrial design, particularly in the later creation of the Bauhaus school of design. Its initial purpose was to establish a partnership of product manufacturers with design professionals to improve the competitiveness of German companies in global markets. The Werkbund was less an artistic movement than a state-sponsored effort to integrate traditional crafts and industrial

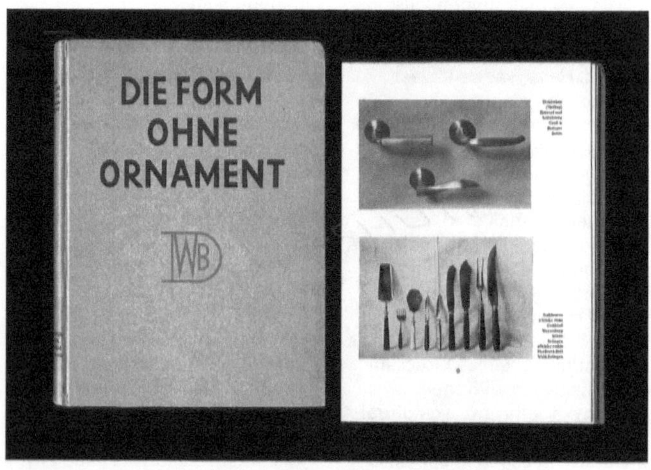

Die Form ohne Ornament, Deutscher Werkbund, 1924

mass production techniques, to put Germany on a competitive footing with England and the United States. Its motto *Vom Sofakissen zum Städtebau* (from sofa cushions to city-building) indicates its range of interest.

The Deutscher Werkbund emerged when the architect Joseph Maria Olbrich left Vienna for Darmstadt, Germany, in 1899, to form an artists' colony at the invitation of Ernest Louis, Grand Duke of Hesse. The Werkbund was founded by Olbrich, Peter Behrens, Richard Riemerschmid, Bruno Paul and others in 1907 in Munich at the instigation of Hermann Muthesius, existed through 1934, then re-established after World War II in 1950. Muthesius was the author of the exhaustive three-volume *The English House* of 1905, a survey of the practical lessons of the English Arts and Crafts movement. Muthesius was seen as something of a cultural ambassador, or industrial spy, between Germany and England.

The organization originally included twelve architects and twelve business firms. Among the Werkbund's more noted members was the architect Ludwig Mies Van der Rohe, who served as Architectural Director.[24]

The Deutscher Werkbund was a major influence on the early careers of Le Corbusier, Walter Gropius and Mies van der Rohe.[25]

Research mutation: Josef Albers

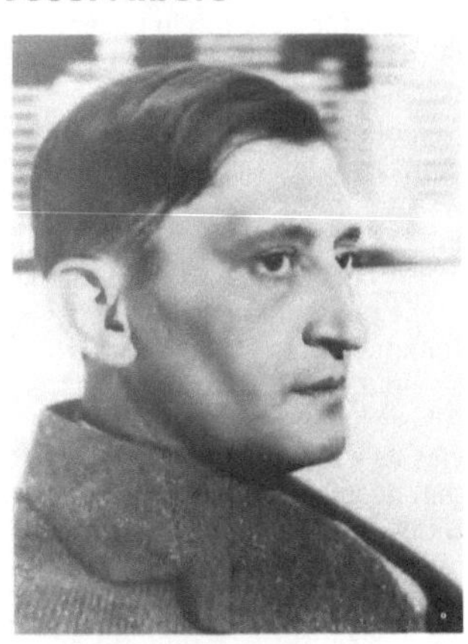

Albers in his Bauhaus studio, Dessau, 1928

Josef Albers (1888–1976) was a German-born American artist and educator whose work, both in Europe and in the United States, formed the basis of some of the most influential and far-reaching art education programs of the twentieth century.

Life and work

Albers was born into a Roman Catholic family of craftsmen in Bottrop, Westphalia, Germany. He worked from 1908 to 1913 as a schoolteacher in his home town; he also trained as an art teacher at Königliche Kunstschule in Berlin, Germany, from 1913 to 1915. From 1916 to 1919 he began his work as a printmaker at the Kunstgewerbschule in Essen. In 1918 he received his first public commission, *Rosa mystica ora pro nobis*, a stained-glass window for a church in Essen. In 1919 he went to Munich, Germany, to study at the Königliche Bayerische Akademie der Bildenden Kunst, where he was a pupil of Max Doerner and Franz Stuck.

Albers enrolled as a student in the preliminary course of Johannes Itten at the Weimar Bauhaus in 1920. Although Albers had studied painting, it was as a maker of stained glass that he joined the faculty of the Bauhaus in 1922, approaching his chosen medium as a component of architecture and as a stand-alone art form. The director and founder of the Bauhaus, Walter Gropius, asked him in 1923 to teach in the preliminary course 'Werklehre' of the department of design to introduce newcomers to the principles of handicrafts, because Albers came from that background and had appropriate practice and knowledge.

In 1925, Albers was promoted to professor, the year the Bauhaus moved to Dessau. At this time, he married Anni Albers (née Fleischmann) who was a student there. His work in Dessau included designing furniture and working with glass. As a younger art teacher, he was teaching at the Bauhaus among artists who included Oskar Schlemmer, Wassily Kandinsky, and Paul Klee. The so-called form master, Klee taught the formal aspects in the glass workshops where Albers was the crafts master; they cooperated for several years.

With the closure of the Bauhaus under Nazi pressure in 1933 the artists dispersed, most leaving the country. Albers emigrated to the United States. The architect Philip Johnson, then a curator at the Museum of Modern Art, arranged for Albers to be offered a job as head of a new art school, Black Mountain College, in North Carolina. In November 1933, he joined the faculty of the college where he was the head of the painting program until 1949.

At Black Mountain, his students included Ruth Asawa, Ray Johnson, Robert Rauschenberg, Cy Twombly, and Susan Weil. He also invited important American artists such as Willem de Kooning, to teach in the summer seminar. Weil remarked that, as a teacher, Albers was "his own academy" and she said that Albers claimed that "when you're in school, you're not an artist, you're a student", although he was very supportive of self-expression when one became an artist and began their journey.

In 1950, Albers left Black Mountain to head the department of design at Yale University in New Haven, Connecticut. While at Yale, Albers worked to expand the nascent graphic design program (then called "graphic arts"), hiring designers Alvin Eisenman, Herbert Matter, and Alvin Lustig Albers worked at Yale until he retired from teaching in 1958. At Yale, Richard Anuszkiewicz, Eva Hesse, Neil Welliver, and Jane Davis Doggett were notable students.

Generative Mistranslation as Pedagogical Design Strategy

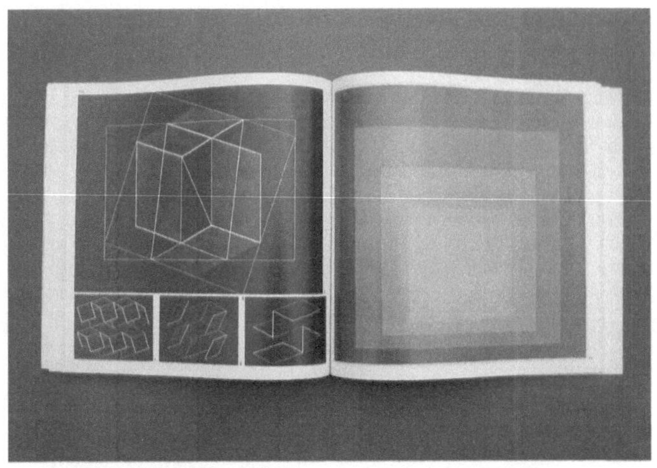

Josef Albers exhibiition catalogue, Stuttgart 1974

In 1963, Albers published *Interaction of Color* which presented his theory that colors were governed by an internal and deceptive logic. The very rare first edition has a limited printing of only 2,000 copies and contained 150 silk screen plates. Also during this time, he created the abstract album covers of band leader Enoch Light's *Command* LP records. His album cover for Terry Snyder and the All Stars 1959 album, *Persuasive Percussion*, shows a tightly packed grid or lattice of small black disks from which a few wander up and out as if stray molecules of some light gas. He was elected a Fellow of the American Academy of Arts and Sciences in 1973. Albers continued to paint and write, staying in New Haven with his wife, textile artist, Anni Albers, until his death in 1976.

Homage to the Square

Accomplished as a designer, photographer, typographer, printmaker, and poet, Albers is best remembered for his work as an abstract painter and theorist. He favored a very disciplined approach to composition. Most famous of all are the hundreds of paintings and prints that make up the series, Homage to the Square. In this rigorous series, begun in 1949, Albers explored chromatic interactions with nested squares. Usually painting on Masonite, he used a palette knife with oil colors and often recorded the colors he used on the back of his works. Each painting consists of either three or four squares of solid planes of color nested within one another, in one of four different arrangements and in square formats ranging from 406×406 mm to 1.22×1.22 m.

Black Mountain College

Black Mountain College, a school founded in 1933 in Black Mountain, North Carolina, was a new kind of college in the United States in which the study of art was seen to be central to a liberal arts education, and in which John Dewey's principles of education played a major role. Many of the school's students and faculty were influential in the arts or other fields, or went on to become influential. Although notable even during its short life, the school closed in 1957 after only 24 years.

History

Founded in 1933 by John Andrew Rice, Theodore Dreier, Frederick Georgia, and Ralph Lounsbury, all dismissed faculty members of Rollins College, Black Mountain was experimental by nature and committed to an interdisciplinary approach, attracting a faculty that included many of America's leading visual artists, composers including John Cage, poets, and designers, like Buckminster Fuller, who developed the geodesic dome.

Operating in a relatively isolated rural location with little budget, Black Mountain College inculcated an informal and collaborative spirit and over its lifetime attracted a venerable roster of instructors. Some of the innovations, relationships, and unexpected connections formed at Black Mountain would prove to have a lasting influence on the postwar American art scene, high culture, and eventually pop culture.

Buckminster Fuller met student Kenneth Snelson at Black Mountain, and the result was their first geodesic dome (improvised out of Venetian blind slats in the school's back yard); Merce Cunningham formed his dance company; and John Cage staged his first happening (the term itself is traceable to Cage's student Allan Kaprow, who applied it later to such events).

Not a haphazardly conceived venture, Black Mountain College was a consciously directed liberal arts school that grew out of the progressive education movement. The College was an important incubator for the American avant garde.

For the first eight years, the college rented the YMCA Blue Ridge Assembly buildings south of Black Mountain, North Carolina. In 1941, it moved across the valley to its own campus at Lake Eden where it remained until its closing in 1956.

Research mutation: Buckminster Fuller

Richard Buckminster "Bucky" Fuller (1895–1983) was an American architect, systems theorist, author, designer, and inventor.

Fuller published more than 30 books, coining or popularizing terms such as ephemeralization, and synergetic. He also developed numerous inventions, mainly architectural designs, and popularized the widely known geodesic dome.

Generative Mistranslation as Pedagogical Design Strategy

Depression and epiphany

Buckminster Fuller recalled 1927 as a pivotal year of his life. His daughter Alexandra had died in 1922 of complications from polio and spinal meningitis just before her fourth birthday. Fuller dwelled on her death, suspecting that it was connected with the Fullers' damp and drafty living conditions. This provided motivation for Fuller's involvement in Stockade Building Systems, a business which aimed to provide affordable, efficient housing.

In 1927, at age 32, Fuller lost his job as president of Stockade. The Fuller family had no savings, and the birth of their daughter Allegra in 1927 added to the financial challenges. Fuller drank heavily and reflected upon the solution to his family's struggles on long walks around Chicago. During the autumn of 1927, Fuller contemplated suicide, so that his family could benefit from a life insurance payment.

Fuller said that he had experienced a profound incident which would provide direction and purpose for his life. He felt as though he was suspended several feet above the ground enclosed in a white sphere of light. A voice spoke directly to Fuller, and declared:

> From now on you need never await temporal attestation to your thought. You think the truth. You do not have the right to eliminate yourself. You do not belong to you. You belong to Universe. Your significance will remain forever obscure to you, but you may assume that you are fulfilling your role if you apply yourself to converting your experiences to the highest advantage of others.

Fuller stated that this experience led to a profound re-examination of his life. He ultimately chose to embark on "an experiment, to find what a single individual [could] contribute to changing the world and benefiting all humanity."

Recovery

In 1927 Fuller resolved to think independently which included a commitment to "the search for the principles governing the universe and help advance the evolution of humanity in accordance with them ... finding ways of doing more with less to the end that all people everywhere can have more." By 1928, Fuller was living in Greenwich Village and spending much of his time at the popular café Romany Marie's, where he had spent an evening in conversation with Marie and Eugene O'Neill several years earlier. Fuller accepted a job decorating the interior of the café in exchange for meals, giving informal lectures several times a week, and models of the Dymaxion house were exhibited at the café. Isamu Noguchi arrived during 1929 – Constantin Brâncuși, an old friend of Marie's, had directed him there – and Noguchi and Fuller were soon collaborating on several projects, including the modeling of the Dymaxion car based on recent work by Aurel Persu. It was the beginning of their lifelong friendship.

Geodesic domes

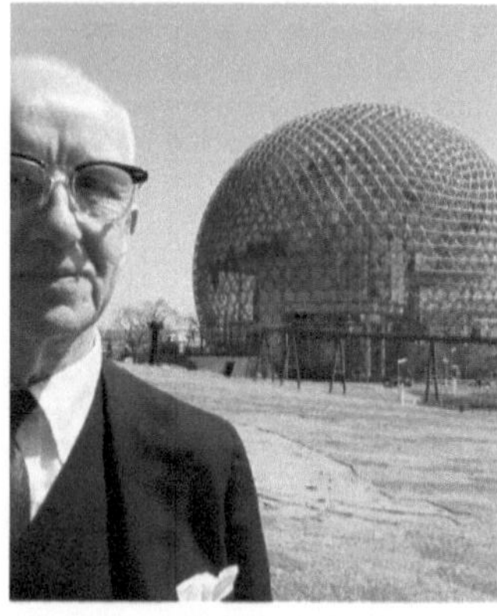

Fuller and dome, Expo 67, Montreal

Fuller taught at Black Mountain College in North Carolina during the summers of 1948 and 1949, serving as its Summer Institute director in 1949. There, with the support of a group of professors and students, he began reinventing a project that would make him famous: the geodesic dome.

> [Fuller's] obsession with this particular type of structure emerged from his interests in material efficiency, structural integrity, and modularity, the key ingredients of what he hoped would become a sustainable, easily replicable design intervention.

Fuller began working with architect Shoji Sadao in 1954, and in 1964 they co-founded the architectural firm Fuller & Sadao Inc., whose first project was to design the large geodesic dome for the U.S. Pavilion at Expo 67 in Montreal. This building is now the "Montreal Biosphère".

Fuller believed human societies would soon rely mainly on renewable sources of energy, such as solar- and wind-derived electricity. He hoped for an age of "omni-successful education and sustenance of all humanity." Fuller referred to himself as "the property of universe" and during one radio interview he gave later in life, declared himself and his work "the property of all humanity". For his lifetime of work, the American Humanist Association named him the 1969 Humanist of the Year.

Housing

Fuller's energy-efficient and inexpensive Dymaxion house garnered much interest, but only two prototypes were ever produced. Here the term "Dymaxion" is used in effect to signify a "radically strong and light tensegrity structure". One of Fuller's Dymaxion Houses is on display as a permanent exhibit at the Henry Ford Museum in Dearborn, Michigan. Designed and developed during the mid-1940s, this prototype is a round structure (not a dome), shaped something like the flattened "bell" of certain jellyfish. It has several innovative features, including revolving dresser drawers, and a fine-mist shower that reduces water consumption. According to Fuller biographer Steve Crooks, the house was designed to be delivered in two cylindrical packages, with interior color panels available

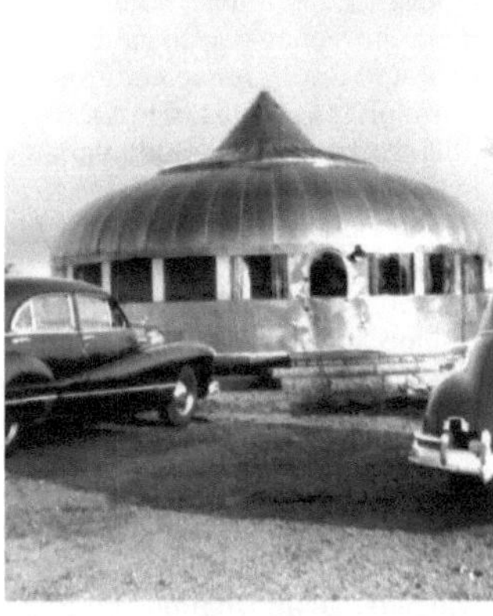

Fuller's "Wichita House", 1948

at local dealers. A circular structure at the top of the house was designed to rotate around a central mast to use natural winds for cooling and air circulation.

Conceived nearly two decades earlier, and developed in Wichita, Kansas, the house was designed to be lightweight, adapted to windy climates, cheap to produce and easy to assemble.

It looked ultramodern at the time, built of metal, and sheathed in polished aluminum. The basic model enclosed 90 m2 (970 sq ft) of floor area. Due to publicity, there were many orders during the early Post-War years, but the company that Fuller and others had formed to produce the houses failed due to management problems.

Dymaxion sleep

In the 1920s, Fuller experimented with polyphasic sleep, which he called Dymaxion sleep. Inspired by the sleep habits of animals such as dogs and cats, Fuller worked until he was tired, and then slept short naps. This generally resulted in Fuller sleeping 30-minute naps every 6 hours. This allowed him "twenty-two thinking hours a day", which aided his work productivity.

Fuller reportedly kept this Dymaxion sleep habit for two years, before quitting the routine because it conflicted with his business associates' sleep habits

Despite no longer personally partaking in the habit, in 1943 Fuller suggested Dymaxion sleep as a strategy that the United States could adopt to win World War II.

Research mutation: John Cage

John Milton Cage Jr. (1912–1992) was an American composer, music theorist, writer, philosopher, and artist. A pioneer of indeterminacy in music, electroacoustic music, and non-standard use of musical instruments, Cage was one of the leading figures of the post-war avant-garde. Critics have lauded him as one of the most influential composers of the 20th century. He was also instrumental in the development of modern dance, mostly through his association

Klee Mutations

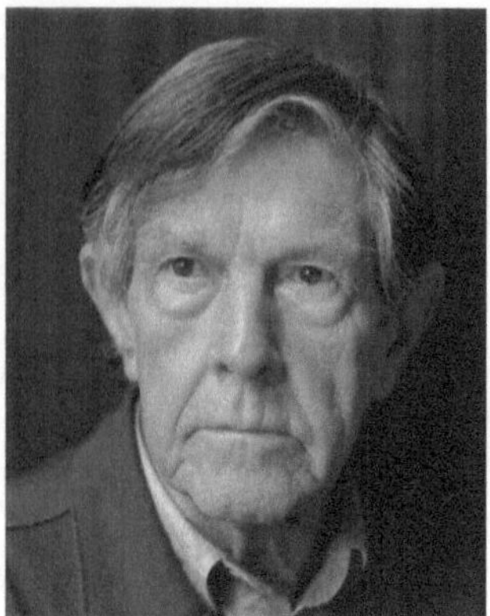

**John Cage, 1988 (Bogaerts, Rob /
Anefo - Fotocollectie Anefo)**

with choreographer Merce
Cunningham, who was also
Cage's romantic partner for most
of their lives.

Cage is perhaps best known
for his 1952 composition 4'33",
which is performed in the
absence of deliberate sound;
musicians who present the work
do nothing aside from being
present for the duration specified
by the title. The content of the
composition is not "four minutes
and 33 seconds of silence," as
is often assumed, but rather
the sounds of the environment
heard by the audience during
performance.

The work's challenge to
assumed definitions about
musicianship and musical
experience made it a popular
and controversial topic
both in musicology and the
broader aesthetics of art and
performance. Cage was also a
pioneer of the prepared piano (a
piano with its sound altered by

objects placed between or on its
strings or hammers), for which he
wrote numerous dance-related
works and a few concert pieces.

His teachers included
Henry Cowell (1933) and
Arnold Schoenberg (1933–35),
both known for their radical
innovations in music, but Cage's
major influences lay in various
East and South Asian cultures.
Through his studies of Indian
philosophy and Zen Buddhism
in the late 1940s, Cage came to
the idea of aleatoric or chance-
controlled music, which he
started composing in 1951. The
I Ching, an ancient Chinese
classic text on changing events,
became Cage's standard
composition tool for the rest
of his life. In a 1957 lecture,
Experimental Music, he described
music as "a purposeless play"
which is "an affirmation of life
– not an attempt to bring order
out of chaos nor to suggest
improvements in creation, but
simply a way of waking up to the
very life we're living".

Research mutation:
Anni Albers

Annelise Albers (1899–1994)
was a German textile artist and
printmaker. She is perhaps the
best known textile artist of the
20th century.

Albers was born Annelise
Else Frieda Fleischmann in
Berlin of Jewish descent. Her
mother was from a family in
the publishing industry and her
father was a furniture maker.
Even in her childhood, she was
intrigued by art and the visual

world. She painted during her youth and studied under impressionist artist, Martin Brandenburg, from 1916 to 1919, but was very discouraged from continuing after a meeting with artist Oskar Kokoschka, who upon seeing a portrait of hers asked her sharply "Why do you paint?" She eventually decided to attend art school, even though the challenges for art students were often great and the living conditions harsh. Such a lifestyle sharply contrasted the affluent and comfortable living that she had been used to. Albers attended the Kunstgewerbeschule in Hamburg for only two months in 1919, then in April 1922 began her studies at the Bauhaus at Weimar.

At the Bauhaus she began her first year under Georg Muche and then Johannes Itten. Women were barred from certain disciplines taught at the school and during her second year, unable to get into a glass workshop with future husband Josef Albers, Anni Albers deferred reluctantly to weaving. With her instructor Gunta Stölzl, however, Albers soon learned to love weaving's tactile construction challenges.

In 1925 Anni and Josef Albers, the latter having rapidly become a "Junior Master" at the Bauhaus, were married. The school moved to Dessau in 1926, and a new focus on production rather than craft at the Bauhaus prompted Albers to develop many functionally unique textiles combining properties of light reflection, sound absorption, durability, and minimized wrinkling and warping tendencies. She had several of her designs published and received contracts for wall hangings. For a time Albers was a student of Paul Klee, and after Gropius left Dessau in 1928, Josef and Anni Albers moved into the teaching quarters next to both the Klees and the Kandinskys. During this time, the Albers began their lifelong habit of travelling extensively: first through Italy, Spain, and the Canary Islands.

When Gunta Stölzl left the Bauhaus in 1931, Anni Albers took over her role as Head of the Weaving Workshop, making her one of the few women to hold such a senior role at the school.

After the Bauhaus was permanently closed in 1933, Anni and Joseph Albers were invited by Philip Johnson to teach at the experimental Black Mountain College in North Carolina. Both taught at Black Mountain until 1949. During these years Anni Albers's design work, including weavings, were shown throughout the US. Albers wrote and published many articles on design. In 1949, Anni Albers became the first designer to have a one-person exhibition at the Museum of Modern Art in New York City. Albers's design exhibition at MoMA began in the fall and then toured the US from 1951 until 1953, establishing her as one of the most important designers of the day. During these years, she also made many trips to Mexico and throughout the Americas, and became an

Klee Mutations

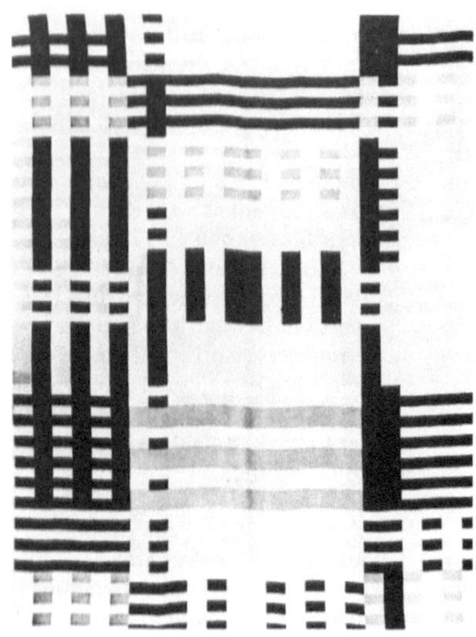

**Wall hanging
Jacquard weaving, 1925**

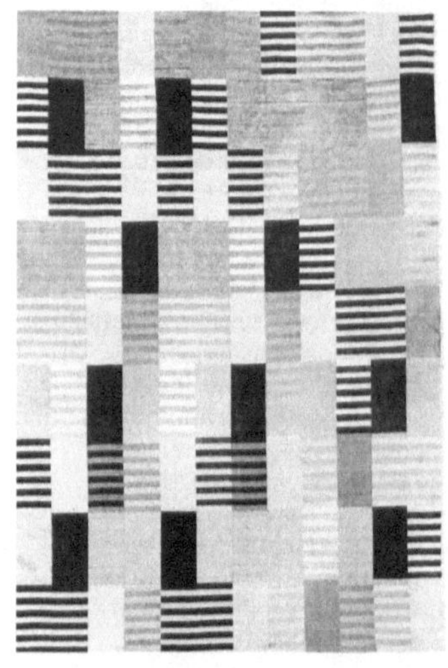

Wall hanging, three-ply weave, 1927

Generative Mistranslation as Pedagogical Design Strategy

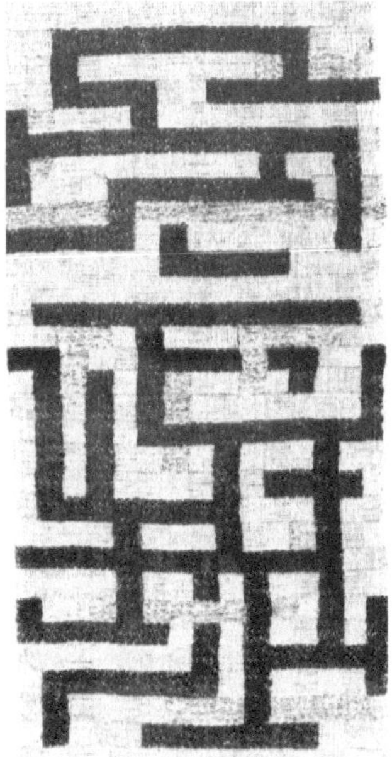

Tapestry, "Two", 1952

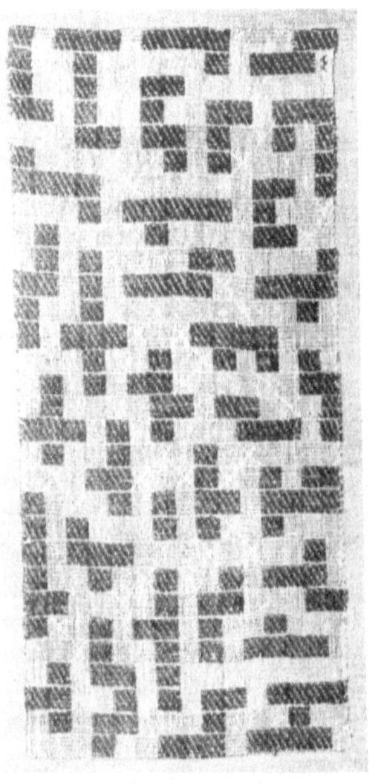

Pictorial weaving
"Pictographic", 1953

avid collector of pre-Columbian artwork.

After leaving Black Mountain in 1949, Anni moved with her husband to Connecticut, and set up a studio in her home. After being commissioned by Gropius to design a variety of bedspreads and other textiles for Harvard, and following the MoMA exhibition, Albers spent the 1950s working on mass-producible fabric patterns, creating the majority of her "pictorial" weavings, and publishing a half-dozen articles and a collection of her writings, *On Designing*. In 1963, while at the Tamarind Lithography Workshop in Los Angeles with Josef for a lecture of his, Anni Albers was invited to experiment with print media. She grew immediately fond of the technique, and thereafter gave up most of her time to lithography and screen printing. She was invited back as a fellow to Tamarind in 1964, wrote an article for *Britannica* in 1963, and then expanded on it for her second book, *On Weaving*, published in 1965. Her design work and writings on design helped establish Design History as a serious area of academic study.

In 1976, Anni Albers had two major exhibitions in Germany, and a handful of exhibitions of her design work, over the next two decades, receiving a half-dozen honorary doctorates and lifetime achievement awards during this time as well, including the second American Craft Council Gold Medal for "uncompromising excellence" in 1980. She continued to travel to Latin America and Europe, to design and to make prints, and to lecture until her death in 1994.

In 1971, the Albers founded the Josef and Anni Albers Foundation, a not-for-profit organization they hoped would further "the revelation and evocation of vision through art." Today, this organization not only serves as the office Estate of both Josef Albers and Anni Albers, but also supports exhibitions and publications focused on Albers works. The official Foundation building is located in Bethany, Connecticut, and "includes a central research and archival storage center to accommodate the Foundation's art collections, library and archives, and offices, as well as residence studios for visiting artists."

Albers was inducted into the Connecticut Women's Hall of Fame in 1994.

Research mutation: Franz Kline

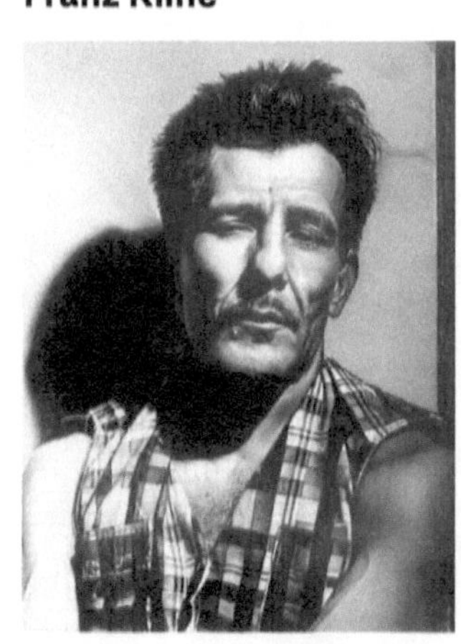

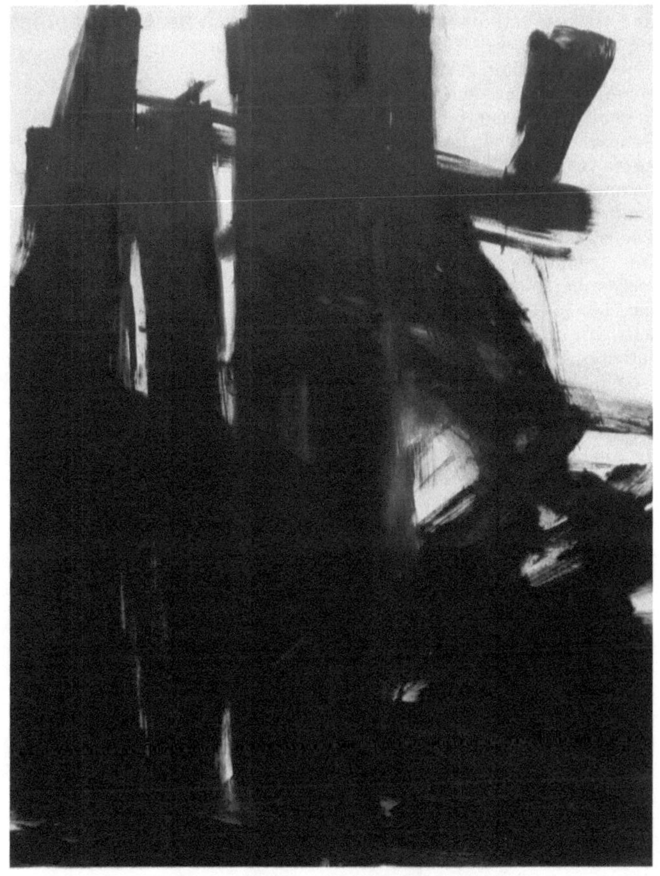

Black Iris, 1961. Oil on canvas MOCA LA

Franz Kline (1910– 1962) was an American painter. He is associated with the Abstract Expressionist movement of the 1940s and 1950s. Kline, along with other action painters like Jackson Pollock, Willem de Kooning, Robert Motherwell and Lee Krasner, as well as local poets, dancers, and musicians came to be known as the informal group, the New York School. Although he explored the same innovations to painting as the other artists in this group, Kline's work is distinct in itself

149

and has been revered since the 1950s.

Kline was born in Wilkes-Barre, a small coal-mining community in Eastern Pennsylvania. When he was seven years old, Kline's father committed suicide. During his youth he moved to Lehighton, Pennsylvania and graduated from Lehighton High School. His mother later remarried and sent him to Girard College, an academy in Philadelphia for fatherless boys. After graduation from high school, Kline studied art at Boston University from 1931 to 1935, then spent a year in England attending the Heatherley School of Fine Art in London. During this time, he met his future wife, Elizabeth V. Parsons, a British ballet dancer. She returned to the United States with Kline in 1938.

Upon his return to the country, Kline worked as a designer for a department store in New York state. He then moved to New York City in 1939 and worked for a scenic designer. It was during this time in New York that Kline developed his artistic techniques and gained recognition as a significant artist.

He later taught at a number of institutions including Black Mountain College in North Carolina and the Pratt Institute in Brooklyn. He spent summers from 1956 to 1962 painting in Provincetown, Massachusetts, and died in 1962 in New York City of a rheumatic heart disease, ten days before his 52nd birthday.

Research mutation: Max Bill

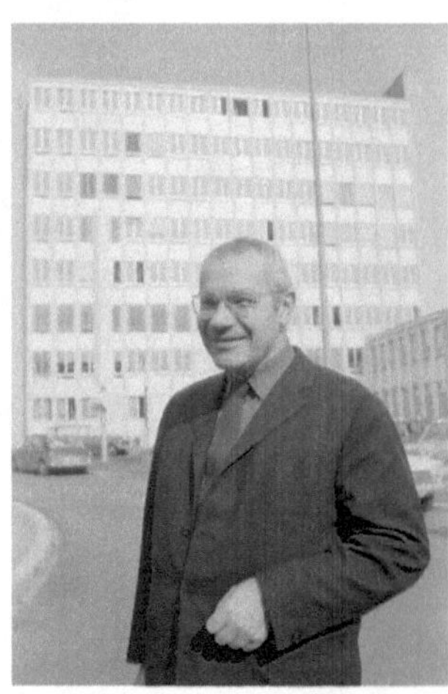

Max Bill, 1970 (Marcel Vogt, Bibliothek Zürich, Bildarchiv)

Max Bill (1908–1994) was a Swiss architect, artist, painter, typeface designer, industrial designer and graphic designer.

Bill was born in Winterthur. After an apprenticeship as a silversmith during 1924-1927, Bill took up studies at the Bauhaus in Dessau under many teachers including Wassily Kandinsky, Paul Klee and Oskar Schlemmer from 1927 to 1929, after which he moved to Zurich.

Art and design

After working on graphic designs for the few modern buildings being constructed, he built his first work, his own house and studio (1932–3) in Zurich-Höngg. From 1937 onwards he was a

Generative Mistranslation as Pedagogical Design Strategy

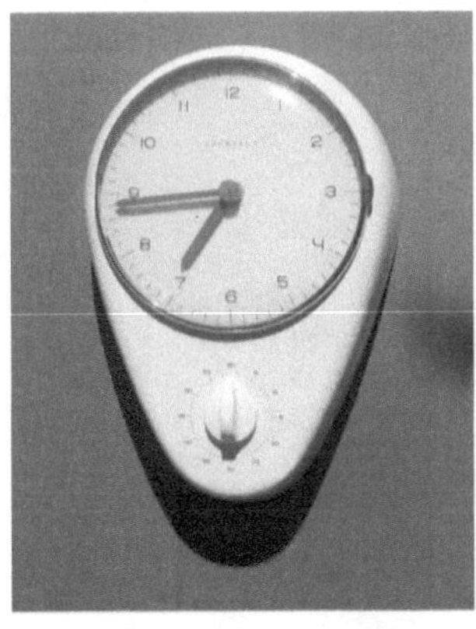

Kitchen clock designed by Max Bill for Junghans (Christos Vittoratos)

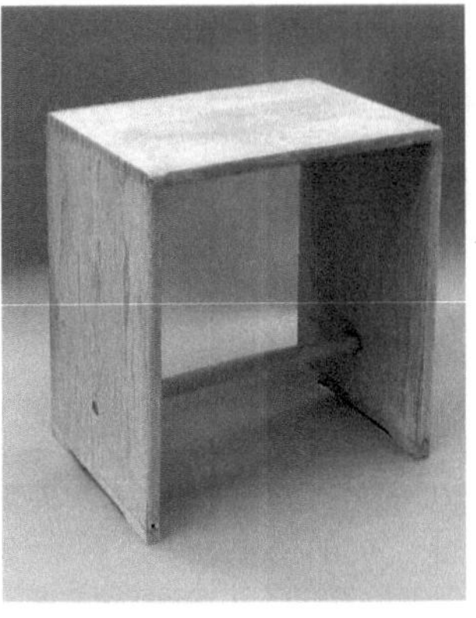

Ulmer Hocker designed by Max Bill Hans Gugelot (C.Vittoratos)

prime mover behind the Allianz group of Swiss artists.

Bill is widely considered the single most decisive influence on Swiss graphic design beginning in the 1950s with his theoretical writing and progressive work. His connection to the days of the Modern Movement gave him special authority. As an industrial designer, his work is characterized by a clarity of design and precise proportions. Examples are the elegant clocks and watches designed for Junghans, a long-term client. Among Bill's most notable product designs is the "Ulmer Hocker" of 1954, a stool that can also be used as a shelf element, a speaker's desk, a tablet or a side table. Although the stool was a creation of Bill and Ulm school designer Hans Gugelot, it is often called "Bill Hocker" because the first sketch on a cocktail napkin was Bill's work.

As a designer and artist, Bill sought to create forms which visually represent the New Physics of the early 20th century. He sought to create objects so that the new science of form could be understood by the senses: that is as a concrete art. Thus Bill is not a rationalist – as is typically thought – but rather a phenomonologist. One who understands embodiment as the ultimate expression of a concrete art. In this way he is not so much extending as re-interpreting Bauhaus theory. Yet curiously Bill's critical interpreters have not really grasped this fundamental issue. He made spare geometric paintings and spherical sculptures, some based on the Möbius strip, in stone, wood, metal and plaster. His architectural work included an office building in Germany, a radio studio in Zurich, and a bridge in eastern Switzerland.

Klee Mutations

He continued to produce architectural designs, such as those for a museum of contemporary art (1981) in Florence and for the Bauhaus Archive (1987) in Berlin. In 1982 he also entered a competition for an addition to the Neue Nationalgalerie in Berlin, built to a design by Mies van der Rohe. Pavillon-Skulptur (1979–83), a large granite sculpture, was installed adjacent to the Bahnhofstrasse, Zürich in 1983. As is often the case with modern art in public places, the installation generated some controversy. Endlose Treppe (1991), a sculpture made of North American granite, was designed for the philosopher Ernst Bloch.

In 1982 he was awarded the Sir Misha Black award and was added to the College of Medallists.

Teaching

In 1944, Bill became a professor at the school of arts in Zurich. In 1953, alongside Inge Aicher-Scholl and Otl Aicher, he founded the Ulm School of Design (German: Hochschule für Gestaltung - HfG Ulm) in Ulm, Germany, a design school initially created in the tradition of the Bauhaus and which later developed a new design education approach integrating art and science. The school was notable for its inclusion of semiotics as a field of study. The school closed in 1968. Faculty and students included Tomás Maldonado, Otl Aicher, Josef

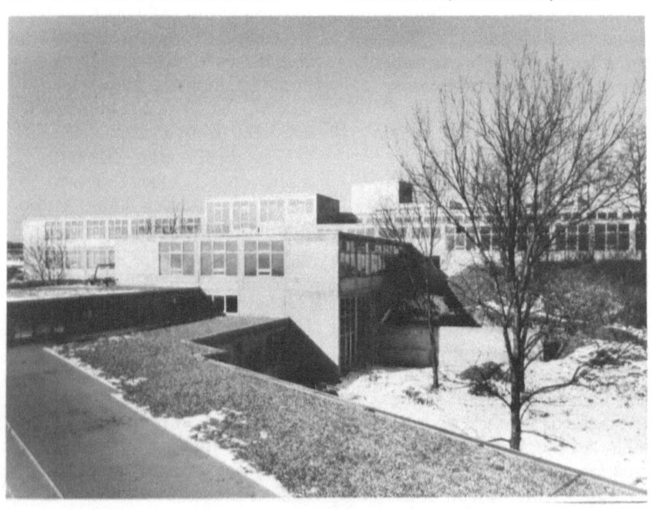

Hochschule für Gestaltung (HfG) Ulm / Ulm School of Design (1953-1968). Architekt: Max Bill. (Hans G. Conrad, René Spitz: Rechteinhaber)

Albers, Johannes Itten, John Lottes, Walter Zeischegg, and Peter Seitz.

Bill was a professor at the Hochschule für bildende Künste Hamburg and chair of Environmental Design from 1967 to 1974. In 1973 he became an associate member of the Royal Flemish Academy of Science, Literature and Fine Art in Brussels. In 1976 he became a member of the Berlin Academy of Arts. In addition to his teaching, Bill wrote and lectured extensively on art, architecture and design, appearing at symposiums and design conferences around the world. In particular, he wrote books about Le Corbusier, Kandinsky, Ludwig Mies van der Rohe, and artistic theory.

Exhibitions

Bill executed many public sculptures in Europe and exhibited extensively in galleries and museums, including a retrospective at the Kunsthaus Zürich in 1968-69. He had his first exhibition in the United States at the Staempfli Gallery in New York City in 1963 and was the subject of retrospectives at the Albright-Knox Art Gallery in Buffalo and the Los Angeles County Museum of Art in 1974, and the Solomon R. Guggenheim Museum in New York City in 1988. He participated in documentas I (1955), II (1959), and III (1964). In 1993, he received the Praemium Imperiale for sculpture, awarded by the Emperor of Japan.

Bill is credited with having been "the spark that lighted the fuse of Brazil's artistic revolution" and the country's "movement toward concrete art" with his 1951 retrospective at the São Paulo Museum of Modern Art. He strongly influenced Brazilian artists like Franz Weissmann.

Research mutation: Ulm School of Design

The Ulm School of Design (Hochschule für Gestaltung Ulm) was a college of design based in Ulm, Germany.

Founded in 1953 by Inge Aicher-Scholl, Otl Aicher and Max Bill, the latter being first rector of the school and a former student at the Bauhaus. The HfG quickly gained international recognition by emphasizing the holistic, multidisciplinary context of design beyond the Bauhaus approach of integrating art, craft and technology. The subjects of sociology, psychology, politics, economics, philosophy and systems-thinking were integrated with aesthetics and technology. During HfG operations from 1953–1968, progressive approaches to the design process were implemented within the departments of Product Design, Visual Communication, Industrialized Building, Information and Filmmaking.

The HfG building was designed by Max Bill and remains intact today as a historically important and functional building under the auspices of Foundation Ulm. The HfG was the most progressive educational institution of design in the 1950s and 1960s and a pioneer in the study of semiotics. It is viewed as one of the world's significant design schools, equal in influence to the Bauhaus.

The history of HfG evolved through innovation and change, in line with their own self-image of the school as an experimental institution. This resulted in numerous changes in the content, organization of classes and continuing internal conflicts that influenced the final decision of closing the HfG in 1968. Although the school ceased operation after fifteen years, the 'Ulm Model' continues to have a major influence on international design education.

Background and early political history

The postwar years, between 1945 and 1952 in West Germany were characterized by heavy restructuring and financing plans, such as the Marshall Plan.

The origins of HfG go back to an initiative by the brother-and-sister Scholl Foundation. The Scholl Foundation was created in 1950 by Inge Scholl in memory of their siblings Sophie and Hans Scholl, members of the resistance group "White Rose", executed in 1943 by the National Socialists (Nazis).

In 1946 Inge Scholl along with Otl Aicher and a group of young intellectuals considered creating a teaching and research institution to foster the humanistic education ideal and link creative activity to everyday life. They would seek this goal in context of the cultural reconstruction of German society morally destroyed by Nazism and World War II. The project was funded through the influx of a million marks by John McCloy of the American High Command for Germany in the post-war governing structure.

Through contacts with Max Bill and Walter Gropius, the Foundation also received financial support from the German Federal Financial Directorship and from the European Aid to Europe as well as private contributions and industry funding.

HfG began operating the new college in 1953 with Max Bill, a former student at the Bauhaus, as rector. On 3 August of that year, operations were begun in rooms at the Ulm 'Volkshochschule' (institution for adult education) with a faculty consisting of Josef Albers, Johannes Itten and Walter Peterhans (former Bauhaus instructors) and Helene Nonné-Schmidt (Bauhaus graduate). Later HfG faculty would include Hans Gugelot, Otl Aicher, Tomás Maldonado, Friedrich Vordemberge-Gildewart and Walter Zeischegg. Distinguished visiting lecturers were invited from a variety of disciplines and included: Mies van der Rohe, Walter Gropius, Charles and Ray Eames, Herbert Bayer, Josef Müller-Brockmann, Reyner Banham, Buckminister Fuller, Hugo Häring, Konrad Wachsmann, Norbert Wiener and Mia Seeger.

Generative Mistranslation as Pedagogical Design Strategy

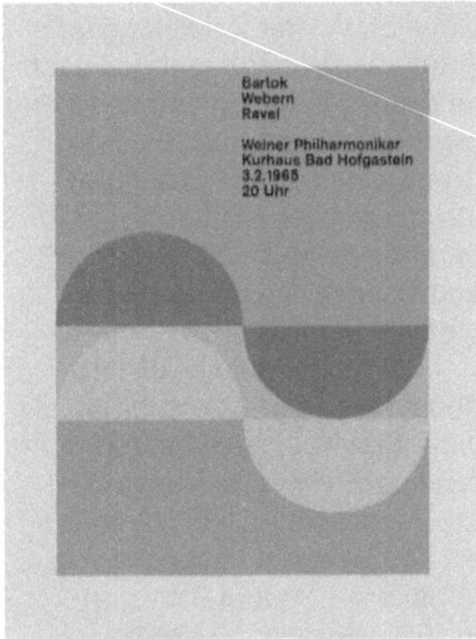

Poster designed by Margarete Kögler in the class of Otl Aicher. (Bartok, Webern, Ravel)

The teaching was based on a curriculum covering four years. The first academic year was devoted to the basic course and then students chose a specialty from Product Design, Visual Communication, Industrialized Building, Information (which lasted until 1962) and Filmmaking, which until 1961 belonged to the Visual Communications department since 1962 and became independent.

In 1953 the new building was started, designed by Max Bill, and the inauguration took place on October 2, 1955. The HfG building complex was one of the first in Germany built as reinforced concrete structures with spacious workshops, dormitories and a cafeteria. The interiors and furnishings were designed for flexible use and outdoor terraces were often used for lectures.

In 1956 Max Bill resigned as rector, due to changes in the body of academic development and differences in the approach to design school teaching. Tomás Maldonado took his place as rector. Bill continued to teach but finally left the school in 1957. Max Bill favored a teaching approach that followed the continuation of the "heroic" Bauhaus tradition, based on the Arts and Crafts model, in which the artist-designer saw their primary role in product development as form-giving. A key objective of the Bauhaus was also to ensure the form-giving artist-designer considered the technology of materials and mass production methods. However, many teachers at HfG, especially those of theoretical courses, sought to emphasize analytic methods encompassing sociological, economic, psychological and physiological considerations.

Among them was Tomás Maldonado, who saw the design process as a system embodying both scientific-based and intuitive-based thinking. Aesthetic considerations were no longer the primary conceptual basis of design. The professional designer would be an "integrator" with responsibility for integrating a large number of specialties in addition to aesthetics, mostly the diverse requirements of materials, manufacturing and context of product use, as well as considerations of usability, identity and marketing. Under the leadership of Maldonado, the school dropped the "artist" focus

Klee Mutations

of Max Bill and proposed a new philosophy of education as an "operational science", a systems-thinking approach which embodied both art and science.

Max Bill's departure also heralded a new phase: the creation of "development groups" that were created specifically to create links with industry. Many of the resulting designs went into production immediately. Among the most successful was audio equipment for the company Braun, corporate identity for the German airline Lufthansa and elevated trains for Railroad Hamburg. These industrial commissions brought a wealth of experience in teaching and decisive influence to the school and enhanced its reputation.

In the fall of 1958 a major exhibition was held in the HfG five years after its opening. The HfG was presented to the general public for the first time, showing both the results of work from student workshops and the work of teachers. That same year also came the first issue of the HfG magazine "ulm", which was published in German and English, and lasted until the school closed in 1968.

The formal education process continued to evolve during the 1960s. Teachers such as the mathematician Horst Rittel, sociologist Hanno Kesting, and industrial designer Bruce Archer were in favor of a design methodology based primarily on analytical studies, including business analysis. This approach caused internal conflicts as Otl Aicher, Hans Gugelot, Walter Zeischegg, and Tomás Maldonado resisted such an overly analytical emphasis and claimed instead that the design process had to be more than strictly a 'method of analysis'. It must be a balancing of both art and science, such as with the study of semiotics

The consequence of this debate was a great exhibition of work that had been created in the classes of HfG and showcased the successful balancing of art and science. The show was initially in Ulm and Stuttgart in 1963, later in the Neue Sammlung, Munich, and in the Stedelijk Museum Amsterdam. In addition to the fundamental debate over curriculum, changes were made in the constitution and the reintroduction of a single rector to replace the Board of Governors.

Closure of HfG

'Family' squabbles over the direction of the curriculum, led to a press attack in 1963 against HfG. The Parliament of Baden-Wuerttemberg repeatedly discussed whether the school deserved subsidies. The problems were becoming more frequent. After the unsuccessful Parliament demand that HfG join the Ulm School of Engineering, Federal subsidies were abolished and the financial situation became untenable.

With the cessation of grants, the School Foundation was in debt. In 1968 some teachers were dismissed because of the difficult financial situation and the number of classes was reduced. In November, the Regional Parliament voted to withdraw all funding, therefore, the school was closed amid protests later that same year.

Curriculum

The curriculum lasted 4 years. The first year was devoted to the basic design course (Vorkurs) that was intended to offset the deficit in primary and secondary education in terms of creative project activity.

The second and third years were for elective specialization: Product Design, Industrialized Building, Visual Communication and Information, with Filmmaking being added later.

The last year of study was intended for thesis. The plan was subject to investigations that were made in regard to new approaches to design and which were then implemented in each department of the specialties.

Basic Course

Students of all programs shared the same basic design course, which lasted a year. This course was mandatory before proceeding to one of the five specialization programs offered by the institution. The course content was:

- Visual experiments: two- and three-dimensional studies based on the perceptions and teachings of symmetry and topology.
- Workshops: wood, metal, plastics, photography, etc..
- Presentation: constructive drawing, writing, language, freehand, etc.
- Methodology: introduction to logic, mathematics, combinatorics and topology.

Department of Product Design

The product design department was the one who had more achievements and that radically changed the vision of industrial design. The development of new methods of mass production during the Second World War implored the designer to stop focusing primarily on the artistic point of view of the profession. Therefore, HfG teaching put increased emphasis on science and technology considerations, more in keeping with the times, and on industrial production processes that determine the final product quality and affect the product aesthetic form.

- Instruction in manufacturing: product design, operational organization, processes, procedures, calculations.
- Technologies: Ferrous metals, nonferrous metals, wood, plastics and forming technologies.
- Construction techniques.
- Mathematical analysis of operations: Group theory, statistics, standardization.
- Scientific theories.
- Ergonomics: Human-machine systems.
- Theories of Perception, especially social

Klee Mutations

- Mechanics: Kinematic, dynamic and static.
- Copyright and miscellaneous.

Department of Visual Communication

At first the department was called Visual Design, but it quickly became clear their goal was to solve design problems in the area of mass media, so that in the 1956/56 academic year the name changed to Visual Communication Department.

The curriculum included the development and implementation of visual reports, news systems and transmission media. Emphasis included the field of planning and analysis of modern means of communication, with a clear focus on the illustrative arts. Maldonado also introduced the study of semiotics. This department worked closely with the Department of Information. Although HfG distanced itself from an affiliation with the mass media advertising industry.

The HfG worked primarily in the area of persuasive communication in areas such as vehicular and pedestrian traffic sign systems, plans for technical equipment, visual translation of scientific content to be readily understood and unity of company communications materials.

Teaching Approach

In the early years of operation, and with the direction of Max Bill, the teaching of the school was guided by the principles of the Bauhaus, where the designer had a profile of being much more artistic than analytic. Based on the discrepancies between Bill's approach and that of other teachers, including the systems principles of Tomás Maldonado, the school shifted its ideology to a more methodological and structured field of study, but one that also strongly embraced aesthetics as a primary factor. This resulted in an academic program with a common basic course and an introduction to consolidated theoretical disciplines. The new design teaching approach became known as the "Ulm Model" which significantly influenced worldwide design education, especially industrial design, as the HfG reputation spread and many HfG graduates established Ulm-influenced education programs around the globe.

Collaboration with Braun

Midway through the 1950s, the HfG and Braun, began a phase of cooperation. Braun needed to stand out from the competition and asked Otl Aicher, Hans Gugelot, and students to work on new designs for the company. Dieter Rams, who was a newly hired Braun designer, collaborated with HfG on developing the forward-looking Braun product design approach. With this partnership the "Braun style" was developed, and according to Tomás Maldonado, "the style differed from Olivetti who sought unity in variety, while the style of Braun sought unity in the product and its coherence with other products. Because of this, the Braun-HfG collaboration was a formidable test bench for the design of "honest" form and coherent identity as an alternative to the random "styling" of individual objects.

Legacy

Until the founding of the Ulm HfG in 1953, there was no systematic approach of design education. HfG pioneered the integration of science and art, thereby creating a teaching of design based on a structured problem-solving approach: reflections on the problems of use by people, knowledge of materials and production processes, methods of analysis and synthesis, choice and founded projective alternatives, the emphasis on scientific and technical disciplines, the consideration of ergonomics, the integration of aesthetics, the understanding of semiotics and a close academic relationship with industry. In concept, the "Ulm Model" represented early foundation principles of the design management discipline.

The Ulm School of Design buildings designed by Max Bill and the surrounding green spaces are well maintained, used by various organizations and considered important heritage.

Research mutation: Friedrich Vordemberge-Gildewart

Friedrich Vordemberge-Gildewart (1899–1962) was a German Neo-plasticist (De Stijl)

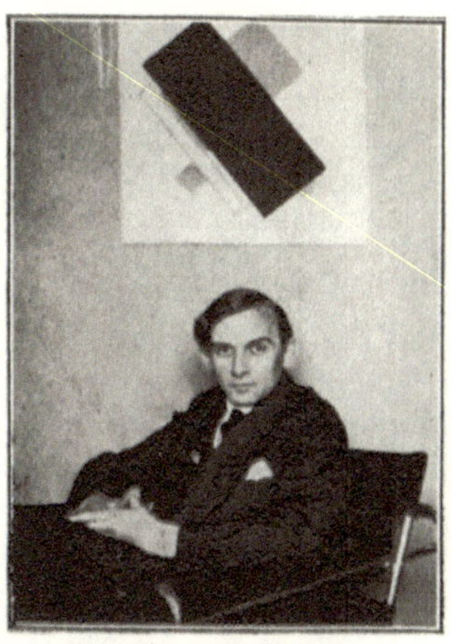

Friedrich Vordemberge-Gildewart. From *De Stijl*, vol. 7, nr. 79/84 (1927)

painter. He was one of the first painters to work for his entire career within an abstract style.

Friedrich Vordemberge-Gildewart was born in Osnabrück, Germany and studied architecture, interior design and sculpture at Hanover School of Art and the Technical College, Hanover. In 1924 he formed the abstract art group Gruppe K in Hanover with Hans Nitzschke and joined Der Sturm in Berlin. After meeting Theo van Doesburg, Kurt Schwitters and Hans Arp, he became a member of De Stijl in 1925. Together with Kurt Schwitters and Carl Buchheister he formed the 'Abstrakten Hannover' group in 1927. He was a member of a number of other artistic groups including: the Cercle et Carré, 1930, Paris and was a founding member of Abstraction-Création

Klee Mutations

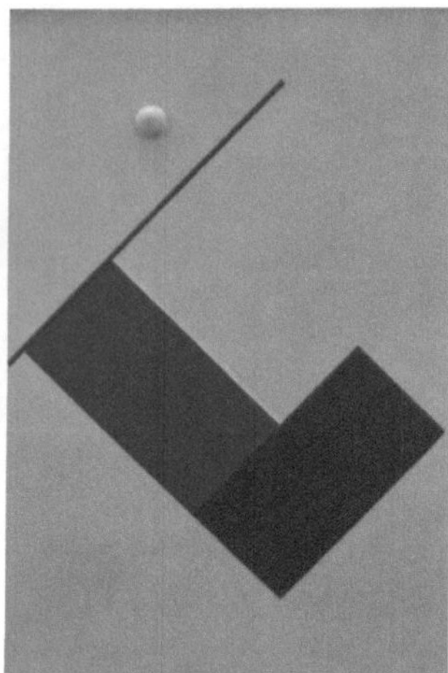

***Composition no. 24*, 1926**
Friedrich Vordemberge-Gildewart

(1931), also in Paris. In 1937, in
Munich, the Nazi regime exposed
his works in the infamous
Degenerate Art exhibition. Most
of his works were confiscated
and he was forced to leave
Germany for the Netherlands.

Research mutation: Herbert Bayer

Herbert Bayer (April 5, 1900
– September 30, 1985) was
an Austrian and American
graphic designer, painter,
photographer, sculptor, art
director, environmental and
interior designer, and architect,
who was widely recognized as
the last living member of the
Bauhaus and was instrumental in
the development of the Atlantic
Richfield Company's corporate art
collection until his death in 1985.

Training and Bauhaus years

Bayer apprenticed under the
artist Georg Schmidthammer in
Linz. Leaving the workshop to
study at the Darmstadt Artists'
Colony, he became interested
in Walter Gropius's Bauhaus
manifesto. After Bayer had
studied for four years at the
Bauhaus under such teachers as
Wassily Kandinsky, Paul Klee and
László Moholy-Nagy, Gropius
appointed Bayer director of
printing and advertising.

In the spirit of reductive
minimalism, Bayer developed a
crisp visual style and adopted
use of all-lowercase, sans serif
typefaces for most Bauhaus
publications. Bayer is one
of several typographers of
the period including Kurt
Schwitters and Jan Tschichold
who experimented with the
creation of a simplified more
phonetic-based alphabet. From
1925 to 1930 Bayer designed a
geometric sans-serif Proposal for
a Universal Typeface that existed
only as a design and was never
actually cast into real type.

Post-Bauhaus years in Germany

In 1928, Bayer left the Bauhaus
to become art director of Vogue
magazine's Berlin office. He
remained in Germany far later
than most other progressives. In
1936 he designed a brochure for
the Deutschland Ausstellung, an
exhibition for tourists in Berlin
during the 1936 Olympic Games
- the brochure celebrated life in
the Third Reich, and the authority

Bayer's *Proposal for a Universal Type (1925–1930)*

of Hitler. However, in 1937, works of Bayer's were included in the Nazi propaganda exhibition "Degenerate Art", upon which he left Germany. Upon fleeing Germany, he traveled in Italy.

Time in the United States

In 1938 Bayer settled in New York City where he had a long and distinguished career in nearly every aspect of the graphic arts.

In 1944 Bayer married Joella Syrara Haweis, the daughter of poet and Dada artist Mina Loy. The same year, he became a U.S. citizen.

In 1946 the Bayers relocated. Hired by industrialist and visionary Walter Paepcke, Bayer moved to Aspen, Colorado as Paepcke promoted skiing as a popular sport. Bayer's architectural work in the town included co-designing the Aspen Institute and restoring the Wheeler Opera House, but his production of promotional posters identified skiing with wit, excitement, and glamour.

In 1959, he designed his "fonetik alfabet", a phonetic alphabet, for English. It was sans-serif and without capital letters. He had special symbols for the endings -ed, -ory, -ing, and -ion, as well as the digraphs "ch", "sh", and "ng". An underline indicated the doubling of a consonant in traditional orthography.

While living in Aspen, Bayer had a chance meeting with the eccentric oilman, outdoorsman and visionary ecologist, Robert O. Anderson. When Anderson

Klee Mutations

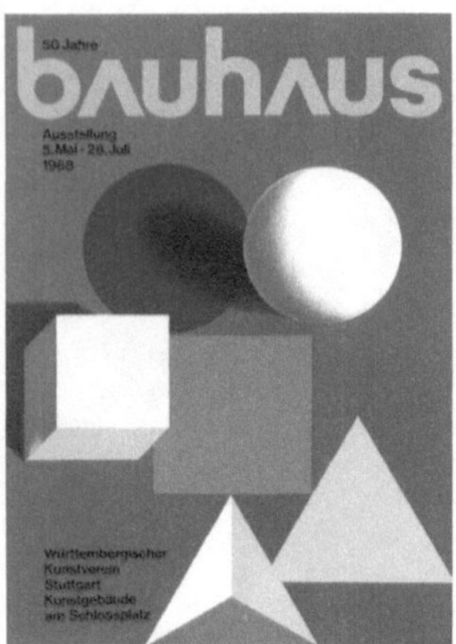

**Herbert Bayer Bauhaus
Exhibition Poster, 1968**

saw the ultra-modern, Bauhaus-inspired home that Bayer had designed & built in Aspen, he walked up to the front door and introduced himself. It was the beginning of a lifelong friendship between the two men and instigated Anderson's insatiable passion for enthusiastically collecting contemporary art.

With Anderson's eventual formation of the Atlantic Richfield Company, and as his personal art collection quickly overflowed out of his New Mexico ranch and other homes, ARCO soon held the unique distinction of possessing the world's largest corporate art collection, under the critical eye and sharp direction of Bayer as ARCO's Art and Design Consultant.

Overseeing acquisitions for ARCO Plaza, the newly built (1972) twin 51-story office towers in Los Angeles that served as the new company's corporate headquarters, Bayer was also responsible for the ARCO logo and designing all corporate branding related to the company. Prior to the completion of ARCO Plaza, Anderson commissioned Bayer to design a monumental sculpture-fountain to be installed between the dark green granite towers. Originally titled "Stairway to Nowhere" Anderson laughed, but felt the Shareholders wouldn't see the irony; thus he suggested it be named Double Ascension and it still stands between the twin skyscrapers today.

Under Bayer's direction, ARCO's art collection grew to nearly 30,000 works nationwide, managed by Atlantic Richfield Company Art Collection staff. ARCO's collection was eclectic, and consisted of an extremely wide range of media & styles; ranging from contemporary and earlier paintings, sculpture, works on paper (including drawings, watercolors and signed original lithographs, etchings and serigraphs) and signed photographs to tribal and ethnic art from many cultures, as well as historic prints and artifacts, all displayed throughout ARCO's buildings in Los Angeles and several other cities. Three years after ARCO was taken over by BP in 2000, that company's then-chairman, Lord Brown, personally ordered ARCO's art collection liquidated. It was sold through Christie's and LA Modern Auctions.

Bayer made provisions

to donate, after his death, a collection of his works which had been housed in ARCO's conference center in Santa Barbara to the Los Angeles County Museum of Art. The works are currently on loan to the Denver Art Museum. He was elected a Fellow of the American Academy of Arts and Sciences in 1979.

Research mutation: Jan Tschichold

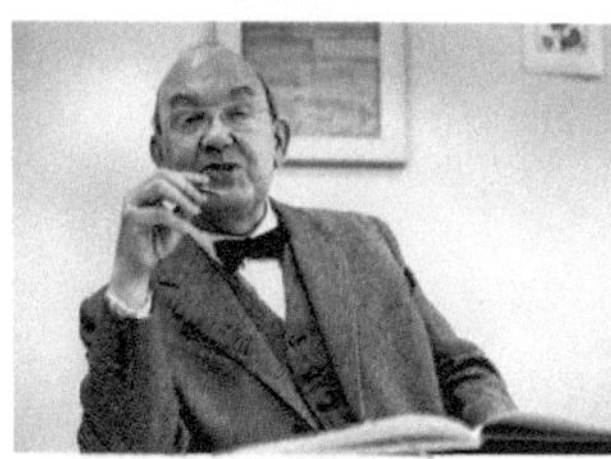

**Jan Tschichold in 1963
(Erling Mandelmann)**

Jan Tschichold (1902–1974, born as Johannes Tzschichhold, also Iwan Tschichold, Ivan Tschichold) was a calligrapher, typographer and a book designer. He designed posters, was a teacher and wrote books on typography.

He was one of the leaders of the movement *Die Neue Typographie*. His most famous type font was Sabon.

Life

Tschichold was the son of a provincial signwriter, and he was trained in calligraphy.

In 1919, he began in the class of Hermann Delitzsch a study on the "Leipzig Academy of the

arts". Due to his extraordinary achievements, he soon became a master pupil of the rector of Walter Tiemann – a type designer for the Gebr.-Klingspor foundry and was commissioned by his fellow students. At the same time, he received the first orders in the framework of the "Leipziger Messe" (The Leipzig Trade Fair, a major trade fair), and in 1923 became a typographic consultant to a independent printing companies.

This artisan background and calligraphic training set him apart from almost all other noted typographers of the time, since they had inevitably trained in architecture or the fine arts. It also may help explain why he never worked with handmade papers and custom fonts as many typographers did, preferring instead to use stock fonts on a careful choice from commercial paper stocks.

Up to this time, Tschichold was grounded in historical and traditional typography, but his attitude changed after his first visit to the Bauhaus: Tschichold met important artists such as László Moholy-Nagy, El Lissitzky, Kurt Schwitters and others whose efforts were directed into the so-called "New Typography": willingly breaking all the rules of conventional typography, to find new ways of expression and to reach a much more experimental way of working. But at the same time, they wanted to standardise, simplify and find a practical approach. Tschichold followed enthusiastically these new set

Klee Mutations

of principles and soon became one of the most important representatives of the "new typography". In contrast to others, he fell not completely out of the historic and technically reasonable frame, but made the avant-garde ideas ready for general use. In a famous special issue of 'typographic communications' by 1925 with the title of "Elemental typography", he wrote his thesis on the new approaches.

Soviet posters were found in his flat, casting him under suspicion of collaboration with communists. Copies of Tschichold's books were seized by the Gestapo "for the protection of the German people".

After six weeks a policeman somehow found him tickets for Switzerland, and he and his family managed to escape Nazi Germany in August 1933.

Apart from two longer stays in England in 1937 (at

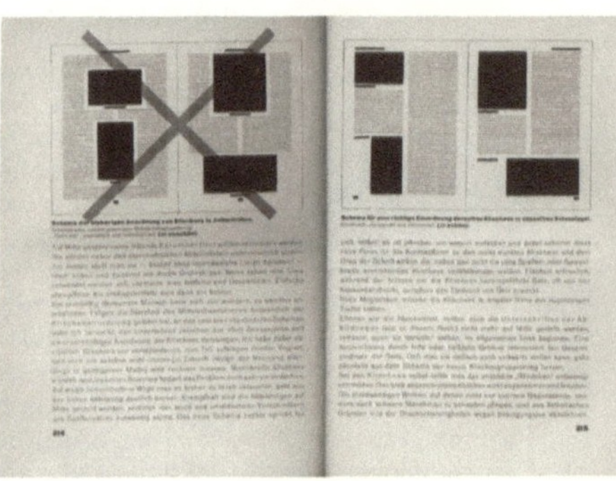

Jan Tschichold cover and pages from *Die Neue Typographie*, 1928

After the election of Hitler in Germany, all designers had to register with the Ministry of Culture, and all teaching posts were threatened for anyone who was sympathetic to communism. Soon after Tschichold had taken up a teaching post in Munich at the behest of Paul Renner, they both were denounced as "cultural Bolshevists". Ten days after the Nazis surged to power in March 1933, Tschichold and his wife were arrested. During the arrest,

the invitation of the Penrose Annual), and 1947–1949 (at the invitation of Ruari McLean, the British typographer, with whom he worked on the design of Penguin Books), Tschichold lived in Switzerland for the rest of his life. Jan Tschichold died in the hospital at Locarno in 1974.

Design

Tschichold had converted to Modernist design principles

in 1923 after visiting the first Weimar Bauhaus exhibition. He became a leading advocate of Modernist design: first with an influential 1925 magazine supplement; then a 1927 personal exhibition; then with his most noted work *Die neue Typographie*. This book was a manifesto of modern design, in which he condemned all typefaces but sans-serif (called Grotesk in Germany). He also favoured non-centered design (e.g., on title pages), and codified many other Modernist design rules. He advocated the use of standardised paper sizes for all printed matter, and made some of the first clear explanations of the effective use of different sizes and weights of type in order to quickly and easily convey information. This book was followed with a series of practical manuals on the principles of Modernist typography which had a wide influence among ordinary workers and printers in Germany. Yet, despite his visits to England just before the war, only about four articles by Tschichold had been translated into English by 1945.

Although *Die neue Typographie* remains a classic, Tschichold slowly abandoned his rigid beliefs from around 1932 onwards (e.g. his Saskia typeface of 1932, and his acceptance of classical Roman typefaces for body-type) as he moved back towards Classicism in print design. He later condemned *Die neue Typographie* as too extreme. He also went so far as to condemn Modernist design in general as being authoritarian

and inherently fascistic.

Between 1947–1949 Tschichold lived in England where he oversaw the redesign of 500 paperbacks published by Penguin Books, leaving them with a standardised set of typographic rules, the *Penguin Composition Rules*. Although he gave Penguin's books (particularly the Pelican range) a unified look and enforced many of the typographic practices that are taken for granted today, he allowed the nature of each work to dictate its look, with varied covers and title pages.

His abandonment of Modernist principles meant that, even though he was living in Switzerland after the war, he was not at the centre of the post-war Swiss International Typographic Style. Unimpressed by the use of realist or neo-grotesque typefaces, which he saw as a revival of poorly-designed models, his survey of typefaces in advertising deliberately made no mention of such designs, save for a reference to 'survivals from the nineteenth-century which have recently enjoyed a short-lived popularity.'

Research mutation: De Stijl

De Stijl, Dutch for "The Style", also known as neoplasticism, was a Dutch artistic movement founded in 1917 in Leiden. The De Stijl consisted of artists and architects. In a narrower sense, the term De Stijl is used to refer to a body of work from 1917 to 1931 founded in the Netherlands.

Klee Mutations

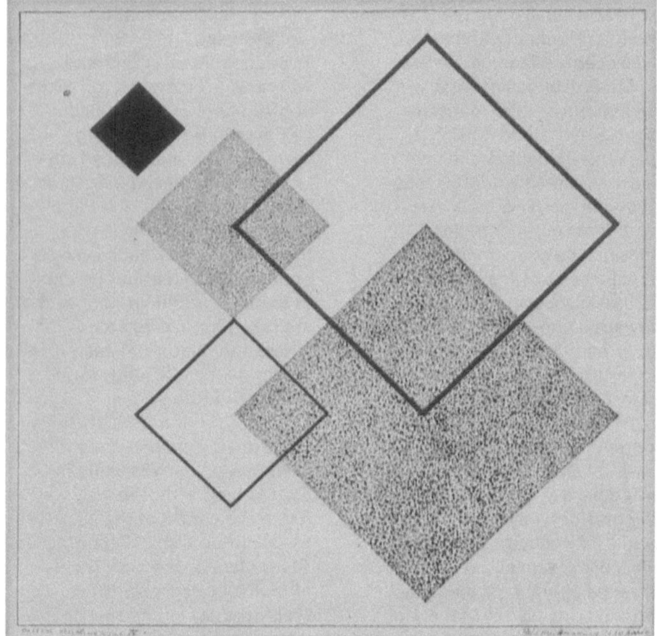

Dessin Arithmétique IV Theo van Doesburg, 1930

Proponents of De Stijl advocated pure abstraction and universality by a reduction to the essentials of form and colour; they simplified visual compositions to vertical and horizontal, using only black, white and primary colors.

De Stijl is also the name of a journal that was published by the Dutch painter, designer, writer, and critic Theo van Doesburg (1883–1931) that served to propagate the group's theories. Next to van Doesburg, the group's principal members were the painters Piet Mondrian (1872–1944), Vilmos Huszár (1884–1960), and Bart van der Leck (1876–1958), and the architects Gerrit Rietveld (1888–1964), Robert van 't Hoff (1887–1979), and J. J. P. Oud (1890–1963). The artistic philosophy that formed a basis for the group's work is known as neoplasticism – the new plastic art (or *Nieuwe Beelding* in Dutch).

Principles and influences

Mondrian sets forth the delimitations of neoplasticism in his essay "Neo-Plasticism in Pictorial Art". He writes, "this new plastic idea will ignore the particulars of appearance, that is to say, natural form and colour. On the contrary, it should find its expression in the abstraction of form and colour, that is to say, in the straight line and the clearly defined primary colour". With these constraints, his art allows only primary colours and non-colours, only squares and rectangles, only straight and horizontal or vertical lines. The De Stijl movement posited the fundamental principle of the geometry of the straight line, the square, and the rectangle, combined with a strong asymmetricality; the predominant use of pure primary colors with black and white; and the relationship between positive and negative elements in an arrangement of non-objective forms and lines".

The name De Stijl is supposedly derived from Gottfried Semper's *Der Stil in den technischen und tektonischen Künsten oder Praktische Ästhetik* (1861–3), which Curl suggests was mistakenly believed to advocate materialism and functionalism. The "plastic vision" of De Stijl artists, also called Neo-Plasticism, saw itself as reaching beyond the changing appearance of natural things to bring an audience into intimate contact with an immutable core of reality, a reality that was not so much a visible fact as an underlying spiritual vision. In general, De Stijl proposed ultimate simplicity and abstraction, both in architecture and painting, by using only straight horizontal and vertical lines and rectangular

forms. Furthermore, their formal vocabulary was limited to the primary colours, red, yellow, and blue, and the three primary values, black, white, and grey. The works avoided symmetry and attained aesthetic balance by the use of opposition. This element of the movement embodies the second meaning of stijl: "a post, jamb or support"; this is best exemplified by the construction of crossing joints, most commonly seen in carpentry.

In many of the group's three-dimensional works, vertical and horizontal lines are positioned in layers or planes that do not intersect, thereby allowing each element to exist independently and unobstructed by other elements. This feature can be found in the Rietveld Schröder House and the *Red and Blue Chair*.

De Stijl was influenced by Cubist painting as well as by the mysticism and the ideas about "ideal" geometric forms (such as the "perfect straight line") in the neoplatonic philosophy of mathematician M. H. J. Schoenmaekers. The De Stijl movement was also influenced by Neopositivism. The works of De Stijl would influence the Bauhaus style and the international style of architecture as well as clothing and interior design. However, it did not follow the general guidelines of an "-ism" (e.g., Cubism, Futurism, Surrealism), nor did it adhere to the principles of art schools like the Bauhaus; it was a collective project, a joint enterprise.

In music, De Stijl was an influence only on the work of

composer Jakob van Domselaer, a close friend of Mondrian. Between 1913 and 1916, he composed his *Proeven van Stijlkunst* (*"Experiments in Artistic Style"*), inspired mainly by Mondrian's paintings. This minimalistic – and, at the time, revolutionary – music defined "horizontal" and "vertical" musical elements and aimed at balancing those two principles.

Early history

From the flurry of new art movements that followed the Impressionist revolutionary new perception of painting, Cubism arose in the early 20th century as an important and influential new direction. In the Netherlands, too, there was interest in this "new art".

However, because the Netherlands remained neutral in World War I, Dutch artists were not able to leave the country after 1914 and were thus effectively isolated from the international art world – and in particular, from Paris, which was its centre then.

During that period, painter Theo van Doesburg started looking for other artists to set up a journal and start an art movement. Van Doesburg was also a writer, poet, and critic, who had been more successful writing about art than working as an independent artist. Quite adept at making new contacts due to his flamboyant personality and outgoing nature, he had many useful connections in the art world.

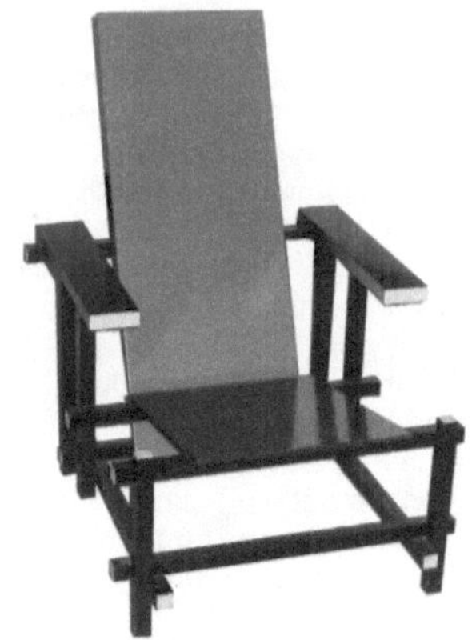

Red and Blue Chair designed by Gerrit Rietveld in 1917.

Founding of De Stijl

Around 1915, Van Doesburg started meeting the artists who would eventually become the founders of the journal. He first met Piet Mondrian at an exhibition in Stedelijk Museum Amsterdam. Mondrian, who had moved to Paris in 1912 (and there, changed his name from "Mondriaan"), had been visiting the Netherlands when war broke out. He could not return to Paris, and was staying in the artists' community of Laren, where he met Bart van der Leck and regularly saw M. H. J. Schoenmaekers. In 1915, Schoenmaekers published *Het nieuwe wereldbeeld* (*The New Image of the World*), followed in 1916 by *Beginselen der beeldende wiskunde* (*Principles of Plastic Mathematics*). These two publications would greatly influence Mondrian and other members of De Stijl.

Generative Mistranslation as Pedagogical Design Strategy

Van Doesburg also knew J. J. P. Oud and the Hungarian artist Vilmos Huszár. In 1917 the cooperation of these artists, together with the poet Anthony Kok, resulted in the founding of De Stijl. The young architect Gerrit Rietveld joined the group in 1918. At its height De Stijl had 100 members and the journal had a circulation of 300.

During those first few years, the group was still relatively homogeneous, although Van der Leck left in 1918 due to artistic differences of opinion. Manifestos were being published, signed by all members. The social and economic circumstances of the time formed an important source of inspiration for their theories, and their ideas about architecture were heavily influenced by Berlage and Frank Lloyd Wright.

The name *Nieuwe Beelding* was a term first coined in 1917 by Mondrian, who wrote a series of twelve articles called *De Nieuwe Beelding in de schilderkunst* (*Neo-Plasticism in Painting*) that were published in the journal *De Stijl*. In 1920 he published a book titled *Le Neo-Plasticisme*.

After 1920

Around 1921, the group's character started to change. From the time of van Doesburg's association with Bauhaus, other influences started playing a role. These influences were mainly Malevich and Russian Constructivism, to which not all members agreed. In 1924 Mondrian broke with the group

after van Doesburg proposed the theory of elementarism, suggesting that a diagonal line is more vital than horizontal and vertical ones. In addition, the De Stijl group acquired many new "members". Dadaist influences, such as I. K. Bonset's poetry and Aldo Camini's "antiphilosophy" generated controversy as well. Only after Van Doesburg's death was it revealed that Bonset and Camini were two of his pseudonyms.

After van Doesburg's death

Theo van Doesburg died in Davos, Switzerland, in 1931. His wife, Nelly, administered his estate.

Because of van Doesburg's pivotal role within De Stijl, the group did not survive. Individual members remained in contact, but De Stijl could not exist without a strong central character. Thus, it may be wrong to think of De Stijl as a close-knit group of artists. The members knew each other, but most communication took place by letter. For example, Mondrian and Rietveld never met in person.

Many, though not all, artists did stay true to the movement's basic ideas, even after 1931. Rietveld, for instance, continued designing furniture according to De Stijl principles, while Mondrian continued working in the style he had initiated around 1920. Van der Leck, on the other hand, went back to figurative compositions after his departure from the group.

Research mutation: Constructivism

Constructivism was an artistic and architectural philosophy that originated in Russia beginning in 1913 by Vladimir Tatlin. This was a rejection of the idea of autonomous art. He wanted 'to construct' art. The movement was in favour of art as a practice for social purposes. Constructivism had a great effect on modern art movements of the 20th century, influencing major trends such as the Bauhaus and De Stijl movements. Its influence was pervasive, with major effects upon architecture, graphic design, industrial design, theatre, film, dance, fashion and to some extent music.

appears as a positive term in Naum Gabo's *Realistic Manifesto* of 1920. Aleksei Gan used the word as the title of his book *Constructivism*, printed in 1922. Constructivism was a post-World War I development of Russian Futurism, and particularly of the 'counter reliefs' of Vladimir Tatlin, which had been exhibited in 1915. The term itself would be invented by the sculptors Antoine Pevsner and Naum Gabo, who developed an industrial, angular style of work, while its geometric abstraction owed something to the Suprematism of Kazimir Malevich.

Constructivism as theory and practice was derived largely from a series of debates at the Institute of Artistic Culture (INKhUK) in Moscow,

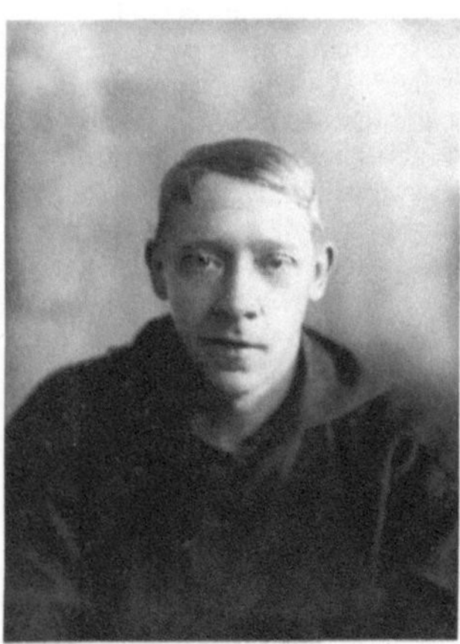

Vladimir Tatlin, circa 1916

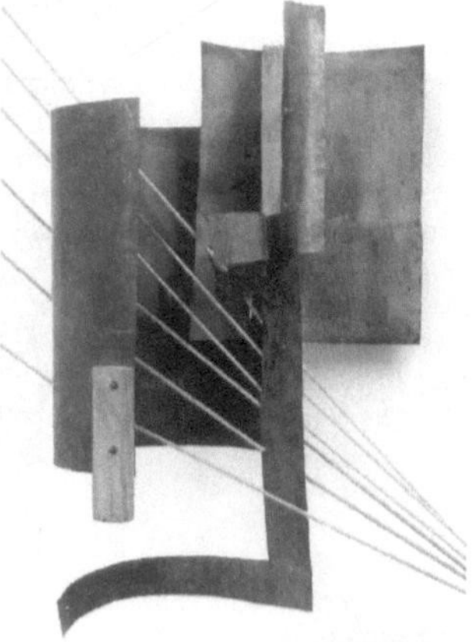

Corner Counter-Relief, detail, 1915

The term Construction Art was first used as a derisive term by Kazimir Malevich to describe the work of Alexander Rodchenko in 1917. Constructivism first

from 1920–22. After deposing its first chairman, Wassily Kandinsky, for his 'mysticism', The First Working Group of Constructivists (including

Generative Mistranslation as Pedagogical Design Strategy

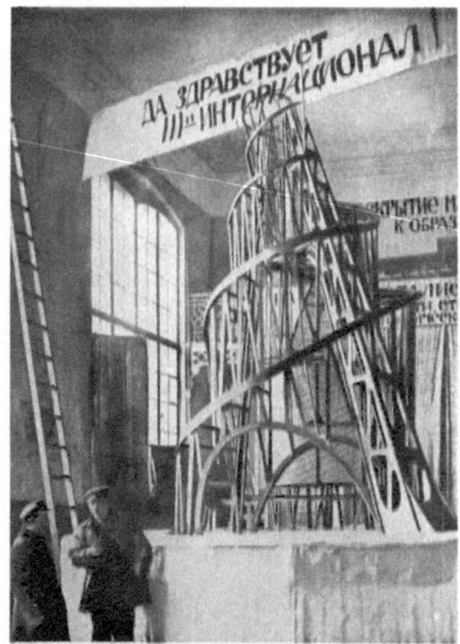

Tatlin with his assistant in front of the model for the *Monument to the Third International*, 1920

Liubov Popova, Alexander Vesnin, Rodchenko, Varvara Stepanova, and the theorists Aleksei Gan, Boris Arvatov and Osip Brik) would develop a definition of Constructivism as the combination of faktura; the particular material properties of an object, and tektonika, its spatial presence. Initially the Constructivists worked on three-dimensional constructions as a means of participating in industry: the OBMOKhU (Society of Young Artists) exhibition showed these three dimensional compositions, by Rodchenko, Stepanova, Karl Ioganson and the Stenberg brothers. Later the definition would be extended to designs for two-dimensional works such as books or posters, with montage and factography becoming important concepts.

As much as involving itself in designs for industry, the Constructivists worked on public festivals and street designs for the post-October revolution Bolshevik government. Perhaps the most famous of these was in Vitebsk, where Malevich's UNOVIS Group painted propaganda plaques and buildings (the best known being El Lissitzky's poster Beat the Whites with the Red Wedge (1919)). Inspired by Vladimir Mayakovsky's declaration 'the streets our brushes, the squares our palettes', artists and designers participated in public life during the Civil War. A striking instance was the proposed festival for the Comintern congress in 1921 by Alexander Vesnin and Liubov Popova, which resembled the constructions of the OBMOKhU exhibition as well as their work for the theatre. There was a great deal of overlap during this period between Constructivism and Proletkult, the ideas of which concerning the need to create an entirely new culture struck a chord with the Constructivists. In addition some Constructivists were heavily involved in the 'ROSTA Windows', a Bolshevik public information campaign of around 1920. Some of the most famous of these were by the poet-painter Vladimir Mayakovsky and Vladimir Lebedev.

The constructivists tried to create works that would make the viewer an active viewer of the artwork. In this it had similarities with the Russian Formalists' theory of 'making strange', and

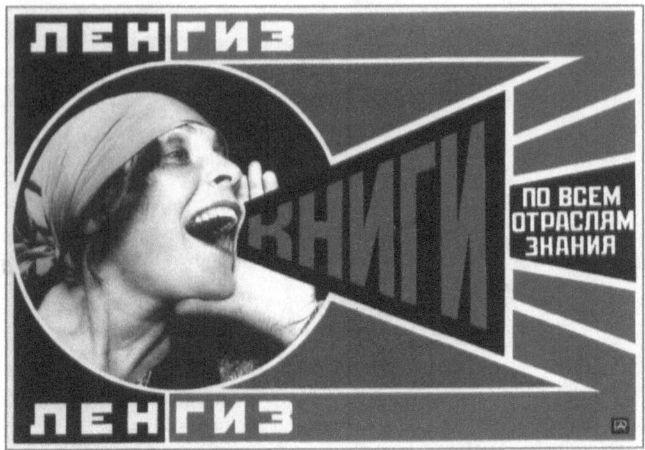

"Books (Please)! In All Branches of Knowledge" 1924 Soviet Poster featuring Lilya Brik and created by Alexander Rodchenko

accordingly their main theorist Viktor Shklovsky worked closely with the Constructivists, as did other formalists like the Arch Bishop. These theories were tested in theatre, particularly with the work of Vsevolod Meyerhold, who had established what he called 'October in the theatre'. Meyerhold developed a 'biomechanical' acting style, which was influenced both by the circus and by the 'scientific management' theories of Frederick Winslow Taylor. Meanwhile, the stage sets by the likes of Vesnin, Popova and Stepanova tested Constructivist spatial ideas in a public form. A more populist version of this was developed by Alexander Tairov, with stage sets by Aleksandra Ekster and the Stenberg brothers. These ideas would influence German directors like Bertolt Brecht and Erwin Piscator, as well as the early Soviet cinema.

Constructivist graphic design

The book designs of Rodchenko, El Lissitzky and others such as Solomon Telingater and Anton Lavinsky were a major inspiration for the work of radical designers in the West, particularly Jan Tschichold. Many Constructivists worked on the design of posters for everything from cinema to political propaganda: the former represented best by the brightly coloured, geometric posters of the Stenberg brothers (Georgii and Vladimir Stenberg), and the latter by the agitational photomontage work of Gustav Klutsis and Valentina Kulagina.

Generative Mistranslation as Pedagogical Design Strategy

In Cologne in the late 1920s Figurative Constructivism emerged from the Cologne Progressives, a group which had links with Russian Constructivists, particularly Lissitzky, since the early twenties. Through their collaboration with Otto Neurath and the Gesellschafts- und Wirtschaftsmuseum such artists as Gerd Antz, Augustin Tschinkel and Peter Alma they affected the development of the Vienna Method. This link was most clearly shown in *A bis Z* a journal published by Franz Seiwert the principal theorist of the group. They were active in Russia working with IZOSTAT and Tschinkel worked with Ladislav Sutnar before he emigrated to the USA.

The Constructivists' main early political patron was Leon Trotsky, and it began to be regarded with suspicion after the expulsion of Trotsky and the Left Opposition in 1927-8. The Communist Party would gradually favour realist art during the course of the 1920s (as early as 1918 Pravda had complained that government funds were being used to buy works by untried artists). However it was not until about 1934 that the counter-doctrine of Socialist Realism was instituted in Constructivism's place. Many Constructivists continued to produce avantgarde work in the service of the state, such as Lissitzky, Rodchenko and Stepanova's designs for the magazine USSR In Construction.

Legacy

A number of Constructivists would teach or lecture at the Bauhaus schools in Germany, and some of the Vkhutemas teaching methods were adopted and developed there. Gabo established a version of Constructivism in England during the 1930s and 1940s that was adopted by architects, designers and artists after World War I (see Victor Pasmore), and John McHale. Joaquín Torres García and Manuel Rendón were instrumental in spreading Constructivism throughout Europe and Latin America. Constructivism had an effect on the modern masters of Latin America such as: Carlos Mérida, Enrique Tábara, Aníbal Villacís, Theo Constanté, Oswaldo Viteri, Estuardo Maldonado, Luis Molinari, Carlos Catasse, João Batista Vilanova Artigas and Oscar Niemeyer, to name just a few. There have also been disciples in Australia, the painter George Johnson being the best known.

So-called Deconstructivist architecture was developed by architects Zaha Hadid, Rem Koolhaas and others during the late 20th and early 21st centuries. Zaha Hadid by her sketches and drawings of abstract triangles and rectangles evokes the aesthetic of constructivism. Though similar formally, the socialist political connotations of Russian constructivism are deemphasized by Hadid's deconstructivism.

Research mutation: Suprematism

Suprematism is an art movement, focused on basic geometric forms, such as circles, squares, lines, and rectangles, painted in a limited range of colors. It was founded by Kazimir Malevich in Russia, around 1913, and announced in Malevich's 1915 exhibition, *The Last Futurist Exhibition of Paintings 0.10*, in St. Petersburg, where he, alongside 13 other artists, exhibited 36 works in a similar style. The term *suprematism* refers to an abstract art based upon "the supremacy of pure artistic feeling" rather than on visual depiction of objects.

Birth of the movement

Kazimir Malevich developed the concept of Suprematism when he was already an established painter, having exhibited in the *Donkey's Tail* and the *Der Blaue Reiter* (*The Blue Rider*) exhibitions of 1912 with cubo-futurist works. The proliferation of new artistic forms in painting, poetry and theatre as well as a revival of interest in the traditional folk art of Russia provided a rich environment in which a Modernist culture was born.

In "Suprematism" (Part II of his book *The Non-Objective World*, which was published 1927 in Munich as Bauhaus Book No. 11), Malevich clearly stated the core concept of Suprematism:

Under Suprematism I understand the primacy of pure feeling in creative art. To the Suprematist, the visual phenomena of the objective world are, in themselves, meaningless; the significant thing is feeling, as such, quite apart from the environment in which it is called forth.

He created a suprematist "grammar" based on fundamental geometric forms; in particular, the square and the circle. In the *0.10 Exhibition* in 1915, Malevich exhibited his early experiments in suprematist painting. The centerpiece of his show was the Black Square, placed in what is called the red/beautiful corner in Russian Orthodox tradition; the place of the main icon in a house. "Black Square" was painted in 1915 and was presented as a breakthrough in his career and in art in general.

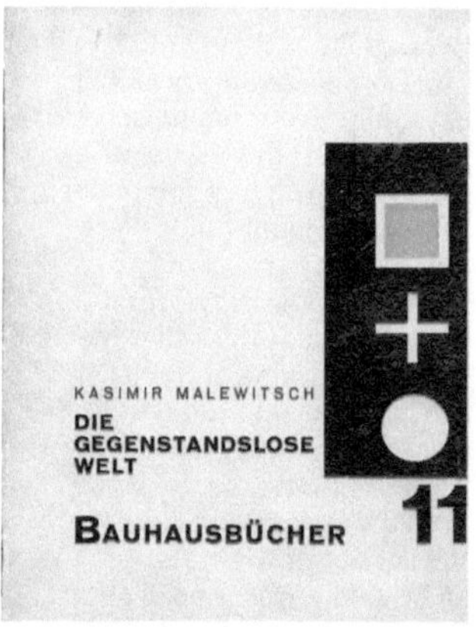

**The Non-Objective World
by Kazimir Malevich**

Black Square, 1915

Malevich also painted White on White which was also heralded as a milestone. "White on White" marked a shift from polychrome to monochrome Suprematism.

Distinct from Constructivism

Malevich's Suprematism is fundamentally opposed to the postrevolutionary positions of Constructivism and materialism. Constructivism, with its cult of the object, is concerned with utilitarian strategies of adapting art to the principles of functional organization. Under Constructivism, the traditional easel painter is transformed into the artist-as-engineer in charge of organizing life in all of its aspects.

Suprematism, in sharp contrast to Constructivism, embodies a profoundly anti-materialist, anti-utilitarian philosophy. In "Suprematism" (Part II of *The Non-Objective World*), Malevich writes:

> Art no longer cares to serve the state and religion, it no longer wishes to illustrate the history of manners, it wants to have nothing further to do with the object, as such, and

Kazimir Malevich, *White on White*, 1918

believes that it can exist, in and for itself, without "things" (that is, the "time-tested well-spring of life").

Jean-Claude Marcadé has observed that "Despite superficial similarities between Constructivism and Suprematism, the two movements are nevertheless antagonists and it is very important to distinguish between them." According to Marcadé, confusion has arisen because several artists – either directly associated with Suprematism such as El Lissitzky or working under the suprematist influence as did Rodchenko and Lyubov Popova – later abandoned Suprematism for the culture of materials. Suprematism does not embrace a humanist philosophy which places man at the center of the universe. Rather, Suprematism envisions man – the artist – as both originator and transmitter of what for Malevich is the world's only true reality – that of absolute non-objectivity.

... a blissful sense of liberating non-objectivity drew me forth into a "desert", where nothing is real except feeling ...

For Malevich, it is upon the foundations of absolute non-objectivity that the future of the universe will be built - a future in which appearances, objects, comfort, and convenience no longer dominate.

Influences on the movement

Malevich also credited the birth of suprematism to *Victory Over the Sun*, Kruchenykh's Futurist opera production for which he designed the sets and costumes in 1913. The aim of the artists involved was to break with the usual theater of the past and to use a "clear, pure, logical Russian language". Malevich put this to practice by creating costumes from simple materials and thereby took advantage of geometric shapes. Flashing headlights illuminated the figures in such a way that alternating hands, legs or heads disappeared into the darkness. The stage curtain was a black square. One of the drawings for the backcloth shows a black square divided diagonally into a black and a white triangle. Because of the simplicity of these basic forms they were able to signify a new beginning.

Another important influence on Malevich were the ideas of the Russian mystic, philosopher, and disciple of Georges Gurdjieff, P. D. Ouspensky, who wrote of "a fourth dimension or a Fourth Way beyond the three to which our ordinary senses have access".

The *Supremus* journal

The Supremus group, which in addition to Malevich included Aleksandra Ekster, Olga Rozanova, Nadezhda Udaltsova, Ivan Kliun, Lyubov Popova, Lazar Khidekel, Nikolai Suetin, Ilya Chashnik, Nina Genke-Meller, Ivan Puni and Ksenia Boguslavskaya, met from 1915 onwards to discuss the philosophy of Suprematism and its development into other areas of intellectual life. The products of these discussions were to be documented in a monthly publication called *Supremus*, titled to reflect the art movement it championed, that would include painting, music, decorative art, and literature. Malevich conceived of the journal as the contextual foundation in which he could base his art, and originally planned to call the journal *Nul*. In a letter to a colleague, he explained:

> We are planning to put out a journal and have begun to discuss the how and what of it. Since in it we intend to reduce everything to zero, we have decided to call it *Nul*. Afterward we ourselves will go beyond zero.

Malevich conceived of the journal as a space for experimentation that would test his theory of nonobjective art. The group of artists wrote several articles for the initial publication, including the essays "The Mouth of the Earth and the Artist" (Malevich), "On the

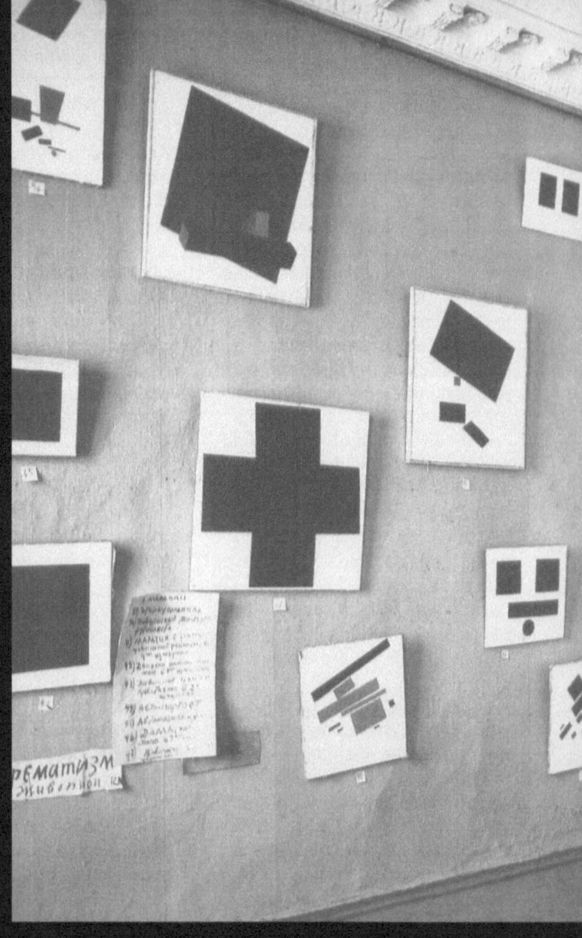

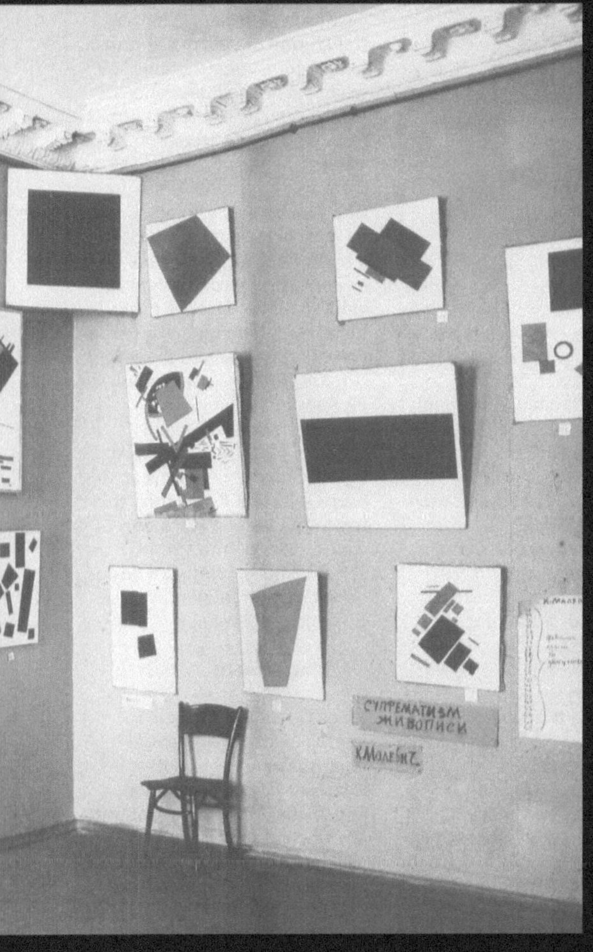

A section of Suprematist works by Kazimir Malevich
exhibited at the *0.10 Exhibition*, Petrograd, 1915

Klee Mutations

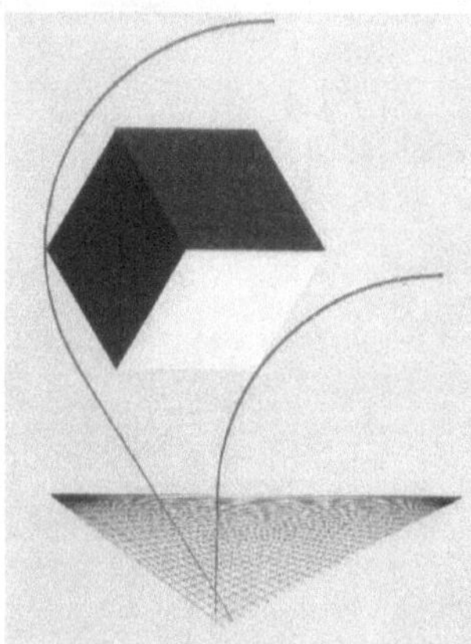

El Lissitzky, *A Proun*, c.1925

Old and the New in Music"
(Matiushin), "Cubism, Futurism,
Suprematism" (Rozanova),
"Architecture as a Slap in
the Face to Ferroconcrete"
(Malevich), and "The Declaration
of the Word as Such"
(Kruchenykh). However, despite
a year spent planning and
writing articles for the journal,
the first issue of *Supremus* was
never published.

El Lissitzky:
a bridge to the west

The most important artist
who took the art form and
ideas developed by Malevich
and popularized them abroad
was the painter El Lissitzky.
Lissitzky worked intensively
with Suprematism particularly
in the years 1919 to 1923.
He was deeply impressed by
Malevich's Suprematist works as
he saw it as the theoretical and
visual equivalent of the social
upheavals taking place in Russia
at the time. Suprematism, with
its radicalism, was to him the
creative equivalent of an entirely
new form of society. Lissitzky
transferred Malevich's approach
to his Proun constructions,
which he himself described as
"the station where one changes
from painting to architecture".
The Proun designs, however,
were also an artistic break from
Suprematism; the "Black Square"
by Malevich was the end point of
a rigorous thought process that
required new structural design
work to follow. Lissitzky saw
this new beginning in his Proun
constructions, where the term
"Proun" (Pro Unovis) symbolized
its Suprematist origins.

Lissitzky exhibited in
Berlin in 1923 at the Hanover
and Dresden showrooms of
Non-Objective Art. During this
trip to the West, El Lissitzky
was in close contact with Theo
van Doesburg, forming a bridge
between Suprematism and De
Stijl and the Bauhaus.

Black Circle

Black Circle is a 1915 oil on
canvas painting by the Kiev-
born Russian Suprematist artist
Kazimir Malevich. From the
mid-1910s, Malevich abandoned
any trace of figurature or
representation from his paintings
in favour of pure abstraction.

The work depicts a
monumental perfect black
circle floating on a flat white
background. It is, along with
his Black Square of 1915, one
of his most well known early

Kazimir Malevich, *Black circle,* **1915**

works in this field, depicting pure geometrical figures in primary colours. It was displayed in December 1915 at the '0.10' Exhibition in St. Petersburg along with 34 other of his abstract works. The exhibition coincided with the publication of his manifesto "From Cubism to Suprematism" and launched the radical Supromatism movement. Malevich described the painting, along with the similar Black Square and Black Cross (both 1915), in spiritual terms; "new icons" for the aesthetics of modern art, and believed that their clarity and simplicity reflected traditional Russian piety. In these notions, his art and ideas later chimed with those of the Bolsheviks. However, while the paintings found favour with intellectuals, they did not appeal to the general viewer and as a result Malevich lost official approval. He was later persecuted by Stalin, who had an implicit mistrust of all modern art.

In his manifesto, Malevich described the paintings as "desperate struggle to free art from the ballast of the objective world" by focusing only on pure form. He sought to paint works that could be understood by all, but at the same time would have an emotional impact comparable

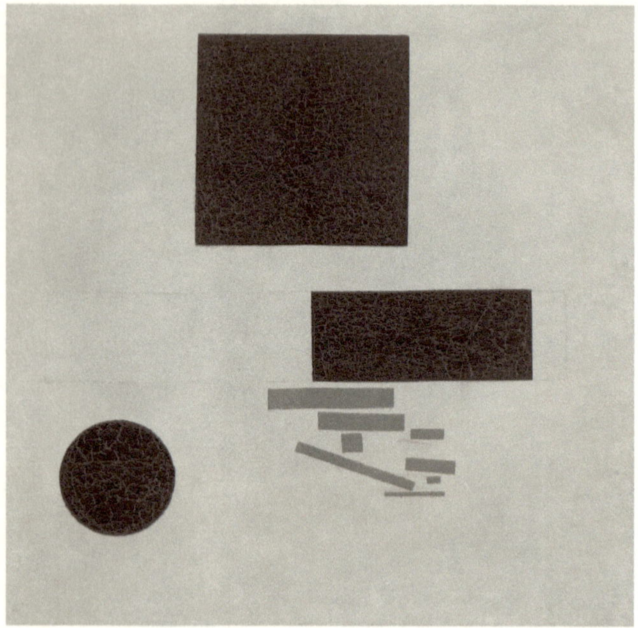

Kazimir Malevich, *Suprematist Composition*, 1915

to religious works. In 1990, the art critic Michael Brenson noted of the works, "The one constant in Malevich's Suprematism is the white ground. It is utterly selfless and anonymous yet distinct. It is a dense emptiness, or full void. It is atmospheric yet it has little air, and it does not suggest sky. It does not envelop or squeeze the rectangles, rings and lines. It is ready and available but not transparent. It is not open or closed but both at the same time. Some white shapes nestle inside it. Most shapes stick to it. Nothing is trapped. Everything seems held yet free. Shape and whiteness are different but they never struggle."In 1924, the work, along with the Square and Cross, hung at the 14th Venice Biennale. Malevich's work of this period went on to have a significant influence on 20th-century art, most especially on photography of the 1920s and 30s and on the op art movement of the 1960s.

When Malevich died in 1934, he was buried in a coffin decorated by Nikolai Suetin with a black square at the head and a black circle at the foot.

Research mutation: Kazimir Malevich

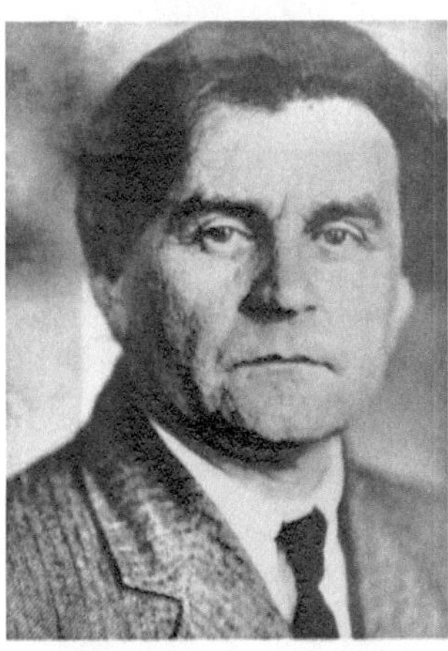

Kazimir Malevich

Kazimir Severinovich Malevich (1878–1935) was a Russian painter and art theoretician. He was a pioneer of geometric abstract art and the originator of the avant-garde Suprematist movement. He was a devout Christian mystic who believed the central task of an artist was that of rendering spiritual feeling.

Kazimir Malevich was born Kazimierz Malewicz to a Polish family, who settled near Kiev in Kiev Governorate of the Russian Empire during the partitions of Poland. His parents, Ludwika and Seweryn Malewicz, were Roman Catholic like most ethnic Poles, though his father attended Orthodox services as well. They both had fled from the former eastern territories of the Commonwealth (present-day Kopyl Region of Belarus) to Kiev in the aftermath of the failed Polish January Uprising of 1863 against the tsarist army. His native language was Polish though he spoke Ukrainian in public. Subsequently, Malevich even wrote a series of articles about art in Ukrainian.

Kazimir's father managed a sugar factory. Kazimir was the first of fourteen children, only nine of whom survived into adulthood. His family moved often and he spent most of his childhood in the villages of Ukraine, amidst sugar-beet plantations, far from centers of culture. Until age twelve he knew nothing of professional artists, although art had surrounded him in childhood. He delighted in peasant embroidery, and in decorated walls and stoves. He was able to paint in the peasant style. He studied drawing in Kiev from 1895 to 1896.

From 1896 to 1904 Kazimir Malevich lived in Kursk. In 1904, after the death of his father, he moved to Moscow. He studied at the Moscow School of Painting, Sculpture, and Architecture from 1904 to 1910 and in the studio of Fedor Rerberg in Moscow (1904 to 1910). In 1911 he participated in the second exhibition of the group, Soyuz Molodyozhi (Union of Youth) in St. Petersburg, together with Vladimir Tatlin and, in 1912, the group held its third exhibition, which included works by Aleksandra Ekster, Tatlin, and others. In the same year he participated in an exhibition by the collective, Donkey's Tail in Moscow. By that time his works were influenced by

Klee Mutations

Natalia Goncharova and Mikhail Larionov, Russian avant-garde painters, who were particularly interested in Russian folk art called lubok. Malevich described himself as painting in a "Cubo-Futuristic" style in 1912. In March 1913 a major exhibition of Aristarkh Lentulov's paintings opened in Moscow. The effect of this exhibition was comparable with that of Paul Cézanne in Paris in 1907, as all the main Russian avant-garde artists of the time (including Malevich) immediately absorbed the cubist principles and began using them in their works. Already in the same year the Cubo-Futurist opera, Victory Over the Sun, with Malevich's stage-set, became a great success. In 1914 Malevich exhibited his works in the Salon des Indépendants in Paris together with Alexander Archipenko, Sonia Delaunay, Aleksandra Ekster, and Vadim Meller, among others. Malevich also co-illustrated, with Pavel Filonov, *Selected Poems with Postscript, 1907–1914* by Velimir Khlebnikov and another work by Khlebnikov in 1914 titled *Roar! Gauntlets*, 1908–1914, with Vladimir Burliuk.

In 1915, Malevich laid down the foundations of Suprematism when he published his manifesto, From Cubism to Suprematism. In 1915–1916 he worked with other Suprematist artists in a peasant/artisan co-operative in Skoptsi and Verbovka village. In 1916–1917 he participated in exhibitions of the Jack of Diamonds group in Moscow together with Nathan Altman, David Burliuk, Aleksandra Ekster and others. Famous examples of his Suprematist works include Black Square (1915) and White On White (1918).

Malevich exhibited his first Black Square, now at the Tretyakov Gallery in Moscow, at the Last Futurist Exhibition 0,10 in Petrograd in 1915. A black square placed against the sun appeared for the first time in the 1913 scenery designs for the Futurist opera Victory over the Sun. The second Black Square was painted around 1923. Some believe that the third Black Square (also at the Tretyakov Gallery) was painted in 1929 for Malevich's solo exhibition, because of the poor condition of the 1915 square. One more Black Square, the smallest and probably the last, may have been intended as a diptych together with the Red Square (though of smaller size) for the exhibition Artists of the RSFSR: 15 Years, held in Leningrad (1932). The two squares, Black and Red, were the centerpiece of the show. This last square, despite the author's note 1913 on the reverse, is believed to have been created in the late twenties or early thirties, for there are no earlier mentions of it.

In 1918, Malevich decorated a play, Mystery Bouffe, by Vladimir Mayakovskiy produced by Vsevolod Meyerhold.

He also was interested in aerial photography and aviation, which led him to abstractions inspired by or derived from aerial landscapes.

Some Ukrainian authors claim that Malevich's

Suprematism is rooted in the traditional Ukrainian culture.

Post-revolution

After the October Revolution (1917), Malevich became a member of the Collegium on the Arts of Narkompros, the Commission for the Protection of Monuments and the Museums Commission (all from 1918–1919). He taught at the Vitebsk Practical Art School in Belarus (1919–1922), the Leningrad Academy of Arts (1922–1927), the Kiev State Art Institute (1927–1929), and the House of the Arts in Leningrad (1930). He wrote the book The World as Non-Objectivity, which was published in Munich in 1926 and translated into English in 1959. In it, he outlines his Suprematist theories.

In 1923, Malevich was appointed director of Petrograd State Institute of Artistic Culture, which was forced to close in 1926 after a Communist party newspaper called it "a government-supported monastery" rife with "counterrevolutionary sermonizing and artistic debauchery." The Soviet state was by then heavily promoting a politically sustainable style of art called Socialist Realism – a style Malevich had spent his entire career repudiating. Nevertheless, he swam with the current, and was quietly tolerated by the Communists.

International recognition and banning

In 1927, Malevich traveled to Warsaw where he was given a hero's welcome. There he met with artists and former students Władysław Strzemiński and Katarzyna Kobro, whose own movement, Unism, was highly influenced by Malevich. He held his first foreign exhibit in the Hotel Polonia Palace. From there the painter ventured on to Berlin and Munich for a retrospective which finally brought him international recognition. He arranged to leave most of the paintings behind when he returned to the Soviet Union. Malevich's assumption that a shifting in the attitudes of the Soviet authorities toward the modernist art movement would take place after the death of Vladimir Lenin and Leon Trotsky's fall from power was proven correct in a couple of years, when the Stalinist regime turned against forms of abstraction, considering them a type of "bourgeois" art, that could not express social realities. As a consequence, many of his works were confiscated and he was banned from creating and exhibiting similar art.

Critics derided Malevich's art as a negation of everything good and pure: love of life and love of nature. The Westernizer artist and art historian Alexandre Benois was one such critic. Malevich responded that art can advance and develop for art's sake alone, saying that "art does not need us, and it never did".

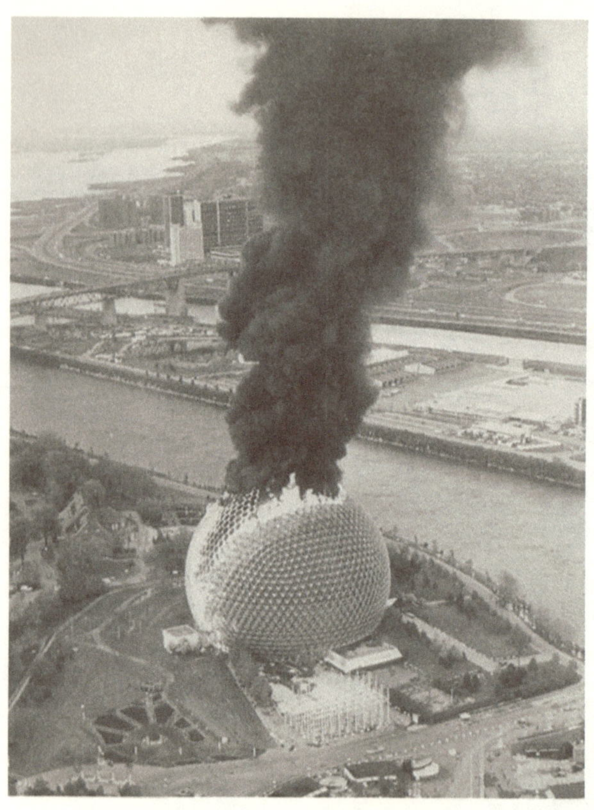

**Above: Utopian vision burns. The former US pavilion
engulfed in flames after a welder accidentally set one of
the acrylic panels on fire, Montreal, 1976.**

**Previous: Detail from Kazimir Malevich, *Hieratic
Suprematist Cross* (large cross in black over red on white),
1920-1921.**

CONCLUSION

TAPPING THE SUBCONSCIOUS: POST-DIGITAL AUTOMATISM, NEW KNOWLEDGE & THE FEAR OF A SUPERFICIAL HISTORY

André Masson began automatic drawings with no preconceived subject or composition in mind. Like a medium channeling a spirit, he let his pen travel rapidly across the paper without conscious control. He soon found hints of images – fragmented bodies and objects – emerging from the abstract, lacelike web of pen marks. At times Masson elaborated on these with conscious changes or additions, but he left the traces of the rapidly drawn ink mostly intact.

—MOMA

The SE became a mirror: our dual reflections mimicking knowledge in an all-consuming data-mine. Reckless abandon soon gave way to trenches of moral anguish.

The self-reflexive results exist now as archive: the chase of binary into warped illuminated reflective glass. With amassed ink dragged from the shallows: the SE relinquishes its role. Where we were momentarily inseparable as artificial intelligence – the onus is now squarely on post-digital flesh.

Endnotes

Unless noted, all replicated source material in the public domain and taken from [Redacted].
Books cites were accessed via (SE) Books, or PDFs obtained via the SE. No physical media used.

As part of this project, participants were required to respond to Alessandro Ludovico's 2014 essay,
Expanding books and Post-Digital Print in which Ludovico states:

> "One of the key characteristics of movable type technology is that it guarantees the
> exact reproduction of content, quickly and in multiple copies. Historically, this has had
> at least two major consequences: on one hand, print "validates" content, given that
> once it's printed it can't be changed, and this generates an aura of "legitimacy"; at the
> same time, from the perspective of preservation, the intrinsic stability of the printed
> medium has allowed the ongoing availability of content."

[Redacted] is frequently disregarded as a reliable or academically rigorous source of information:
the decision to use this material in print form is an act of questioning the legitimacy of print.
While [Redacted] advocates for contributed material to be "written from a neutral point of
view", agendas *are* inherent – sometimes by the exclusion of fact. The post-digital experience is
reminsent of Orwell's "Ministry of Truth" in Nineteen Eighty-Four, the primary difference?
Now the proles can publish too.

Prelims

1. Simon Sellars, *Journey to the Centre of Google Earth*: simonsellars.com/journey-to-the-centre-of-google-earth
2. Memory of the World Programme: [Redacted]
3. "Public Library is a recognized art project": https://gist.github.com/marcellmars/6678287
4. "Monoskop is a repository": monoskop.org
5. [Redacted]

Part 1: The fount of mutant pedagogy

1. "What follows is a post-digital": [Redacted]
2. "Karl Wilhelm Bücher was a German economist": *Wilhelm Ostwald: The Autobiography*, edited by Robert Smail Jack, Fritz Scholz, p 632
3. "Industrial Evolution is Karl Bucher's most important book": https://vernonpress.com/title?id=13#.WZKjz9OGOi4
4. "Pages from the first English": *Industrial Evolution by Karl Bücher*, 1901, Publisher H. Holt and company: https://archive.org/details/industrialevolu00bcgoog
5. "Adolph Wagner": [Redacted]
6. "Agrarianism": [Redacted]
7. "Heinrich Bernhard Oppenheim obtained a law degree": https://hoebers.wordpress.com/2016/10/13/revolutionary-politician-great-great-uncle-heinrich-bernhard-oppenheim-1819-1880/
8. "Alfred Marshall": [Redacted]
9. "Gustav von Schmoller": [Redacted]
10. "Lujo Brentano": [Redacted]
11. "an astounding document ": http://www.slate.com/blogs/the_vault/2014/10/20/british_authors_and_wwi_propaganda_manifesto_signed_by_hg_wells_arthur_conan.html
12. "Manifesto of the Ninety-Three": [Redacted]
13. The Atrocities in Belgium: [Redacted]
14. "The Verein für Socialpolitik": [Redacted]
15. The Werturteilsstreit: [Redacted]
16. Max Weber: [Redacted]
17. "Right-wing socialism in Germany ": [Redacted]
18. "The Social Question ": iroesner.files.wordpress.com/2013/02/industrial-revolution.pdf
19. "Otto von Bismarck": [Redacted]
20. "Eugen Dühring": http://www.holocaustchronicle.org/StaticPages/33.html
21. "Anti-Dühring": [Redacted]
22. "Friedrich Engels": [Redacted]
23. "Karl Marx": [Redacted]
24. "Marxism:" [Redacted]

Part 2: A return to the fount of mutant pedagogy

1. Research mutation: Bauhaus: [Redacted]
2. Gunta Stölzl: [Redacted] and https://www.bauhaus100.de/de/damals/koepfe/meister/gunta-stoelzl/index.html

Part 3: A return to the fount of mutant pedagogy

1. "Langen was also founder of the satirical publication": http://www.simplicissimus.info/index.php?id=9
2. "Early years": [Redacted]
3. In 1898 Kaiser Wilhelm's objections": [Redacted]
4. Albert Langens Verlagskatalog, 1894-1904
5. "Grétor was an outgoing adventurer": [Redacted]
6. "It concerns the dealings of a would-be entrepreneur": http://smithandkraus.com/sk/product/the-marquis-of-keith/
7. "In the Jacob Wassermann novel" *Die Pariser Bohème (1889–1895) Ein autobiographischer Bericht der Malerin Rosa Pfäffinger* Herausgegeben, kommentiert und mit einer Einführung versehen von Ulrike Wolff-Thomsen, 2017
8. "Rosa Pfäffinger's post-humously published autobiographical novel" *Die Pariser Bohème (1889–1895)* von Ulrike Wolff-Thomsen
9. "Beti Žerovc, the Slovene art historian, summarises Pfäffinger's book as follows" Radovi Instituta za povijest umjetnosti 37
10. "Willy Grétor is the subject of two biographies", Willy Grétor født Petersen by Ernst Mentze, 1965; Willy Grétor (1868-1923) by Ulrike Wolff-Thomsen, 2006.
11. "Grétor represented August Strindberg " Strindberg: Painter and Photographer By Per Hedström, August Strindberg
12. "Grétor represented August Strindberg " Strindberg: Painter and Photographer by Per Hedström, August Strindberg
13. "Research mutation: August Strindberg": [Redacted]
14. "Research mutation: Rosa Pfäffinger": [Redacted]
14. Research mutation: Bruno Paul In 1907 Paul contributed http://vsamerica.com/designpartner/
15. "At the dawn of the 20th century, Bruno Paul ": *Bruno Paul: William Owen Harrod, Bruno Paul: The Life And Work of a Pragmatic Modernist*
16. Pedagogical Sketchbook: [Redacted]
17. "Paul Klee was born on December 18, 1879" https://www.guggenheim.org/artwork/artist/paul-klee
18. "Research mutation: Color theory": [Redacted]
19. Walter Gropius: [Redacted]
20. Lazslo Moholy-Nagy: [Redacted]
16. Sibyl Moholy-Nagy: [Redacted]
21. Johannes_Itten: [Redacted]
22. Wassily_Kandinsky: [Redacted]
23. Ludwig Mies van der Rohe: [Redacted]
24. "The Deutscher Werkbund": [Redacted]
25. "The Deutscher Werkbund was a major influence on the early careers"Hermann_Muthesius [Redacted] and Marcel Breuer [Redacted]

www.ingramcontent.com/pod-product-compliance
Lightning Source LLC
Chambersburg PA
CBHW022144050726
47590CB00002B/582